# The Isaiah Effect

ALSO BY GREGG BRADEN

*Awakening to Zero Point*

*Walking Between the Worlds*

*Decoding the Lost Science of*

*Prayer and Prophecy*

# The ISAIAH Effect

## Gregg Braden

THREE RIVERS PRESS • NEW YORK

Published by Three Rivers Press,
New York, New York.
Member of the Crown Publishing Group.

Random House, Inc.
New York, Toronto, London,
Sydney, Auckland
www.randomhouse.com

Three Rivers Press is a registered trademark and the Three Rivers Press colophon is a trademark of Random House, Inc.

Originally published in hardcover by Harmony Books in 2000.

Printed in the United States of America

*Design by Jennifer Ann Daddio*

Library of Congress Cataloging-in-Publication Data

Braden, Gregg.
The Isaiah effect: decoding the lost science of prayer and prophecy / by Gregg Braden.
Includes bibliographical references.
1. Prayer.  2. Prophecy.  3. Time—Religious aspects.  I. Title.
BL560 .B63 2000
001.9—dc21                                        99-049249

ISBN 0-609-80796-X

10 9 8 7 6 5 4

The Isaiah Effect

Quantum science suggests the existence
of many possible futures
for each moment of our lives.
Each future lies in a state of rest
until it is awakened by choices made in the present.

A two-thousand-year-old scroll written by the prophet Isaiah
describes precisely such possibilities in a language
that we are just beginning to understand.
In addition to sharing his visions of our time,
Isaiah described the science of how we choose
which future we experience.

Each time we do so,
we experience the Isaiah Effect.

*Ancient traditions remind us*

*that we have come to this world for one reason*

*above all other reasons.*

*We are here to love and to find a love*

*even greater than any known*

*by the angels of the heavens.*


*This book is dedicated to our search*

*for love and the memory of our power*

*to bring heaven to earth.*

# Contents

# Beginnings

I listened carefully to what the voice on the radio was saying, to be certain I had heard correctly. On the dashboard of the new van, rented only days before, the lighted buttons felt awkward and unfamiliar. I fumbled with the volume control to drown out the roar of a relentless crosswind paving the way for a winter storm that had been visible just as the sun was setting. For as far as I could see along the interstate, there was only the hint of distant lights reflected from the low clouds above. As I reached up to adjust the rearview mirror, my eyes followed the asphalt that we had just traveled until it disappeared into the blackness surrounding us. Not even the glow of headlights announcing their arrival on the horizon was visible behind. We were alone, absolutely alone, on that county highway in northern Colorado. At the same time I wondered how many other people, in their cars or homes, were hearing what I was hearing from the man on the radio.

The moderator was interviewing a guest, inviting him to share his view of the close of the present millennium and the birth of the twenty-first century. The guest, a respected author and educator, was invited to share what he saw in store for humankind over the next two to three years. The radio crackled briefly as the man's words described a future that was immediately unsettling. Confidently, authoritatively, he spoke of his vision of an inevitable end-of-the-century collapse in global technologies, especially those based in computers. As he developed a worst-case scenario, a future emerged in which the essentials of life as we know it would become scarce, perhaps unavailable, for months or even years. He cited limited supplies of electricity, water, natural gas, food, and the loss of communications as the first signs of a breakdown in national and local governments. The guest continued, speculating about a time in our foreseeable future when national law would be suspended, and martial law imposed to maintain order. In addition to such frightening conditions, he cited the growing threat of uncontrollable diseases and the potential of a third world war with weapons of mass destruction, all leading to the loss of nearly two-thirds of the world's population, *approximately 4 billion people,* within a span of three years.

I had certainly heard such terrifying forecasts before. From the visions of biblical prophets to the prophecies of Nostradamus and Edgar Cayce, in the sixteenth and twentieth centuries respectively, rising oceans, great inland seas, and catastrophic earthquakes have been a consistent theme in predictions for the close of the second millennium. Something was different about that night. Perhaps it was because I felt alone on the highway. Maybe it was because I knew that so many others were hearing the same message, an authoritative voice of an invisible guest carried into their homes, offices, and automobiles. I found myself immersed

in a range of experiences that ran from powerful feelings of hopelessness and tears of deep sadness to equally powerful surges of
anger and rage.

"No!" I found myself screaming out loud. "No, it does not have
to be the way you have described! Our future has not happened yet.
It is still forming and we are still choosing the outcome."

Topping the crest of a hill, I descended into a valley and the
reception faded. The last portion of the interview that I heard was
the guest advising people to "head for the hills" and be prepared for
the long haul. For those whose lives were immersed in poverty, living on the fringes of society or oblivious to the events unfolding as
our future, the guest offered three words of advice: "God help
them." As the voices from the radio crackled and faded, the impact
of their words remained.

I share this story now because the perspective that echoed
through the airwaves that night was precisely that—*one perspective,*
rather than a certainty that awaits as our future. In addition to
describing scenes of tragedy and despair, ancient prophets foresaw
equally viable futures of peace, cooperation, and great healing for
the peoples of the earth. In rare manuscripts over two millennia old,
they left the secrets of a lost science that allows us to transcend catastrophic prophecies and predictions and the great challenges of life
with grace. At first glance, the science encoded within these rare
documents may sound more like fiction, or at least the subject of a
futuristic film. Viewed through the eyes of twentieth-century
physics, however, the principles contained within these ancient texts
shed new light, and new possibilities, upon our role of directing the
outcome of our moment in history. Tattered fragments of these texts
describe a lost science with the power to bring a lasting end to all
war, disease, and suffering; initiate an unprecedented era of peace
and cooperation between governments and nations; render destruc-

tive patterns of weather harmless; bring lasting healing to our bodies; and redefine ancient prophecies of devastation and catastrophic loss of life.

Recent developments in quantum physics support precisely such principles, bringing new credibility to the role of mass prayer and ancient prophecy. I first saw hints of this empowering wisdom in translations of Aramaic texts written over five hundred years before the time of Christ. The same texts stated that records of secret traditions were taken from the homeland of their authors in the Middle East into the mountains of Asia during the first century A.D. for safekeeping. In the spring of 1998 I had the opportunity to organize a group of twenty-two people on a pilgrimage into the highlands of central Tibet, to witness and confirm the traditions referred to in these two-thousand-year-old texts. Coupled with large-scale research carried out in Western cities, our journey adds new credibility to these ancient reminders of our power to end the suffering of countless numbers of people, avert a third world war, and feed every child, woman, and man living today, as well as those of future generations. It is only after climbing to the monasteries, locating the libraries, and witnessing ancient practices carried into modern times that I can confidently share the subtleties of such traditions.

As modern science continues to validate a relationship between our outer and inner worlds, it becomes more and more likely that a forgotten bridge links the world of our prayers with that of our experience. Perhaps this link represents the best of all that science, religion, and the mystics have to offer, taken to new levels that may have never seemed possible before. The beauty of such an inner technology is that it is based upon human qualities we already possess. In the comfort of our own homes, with no outward expression of science or philosophy, we are simply invited to *remember*. In doing so we empower our families, communities, and those whom we hold dear with a lifegiving message of hope from beyond the veils of time. From prophets who saw us in their dreams, we are reminded that in honoring all life we accomplish nothing less than the survival of our species and the future of the only home we know.

Gregg Braden
Northern New Mexico
January 1999

# The Isaiah Effect

# Introduction

Could there be a lost science that allows us to transcend the themes of war, destruction, and suffering long predicted for our time in history? Is it possible that somewhere in the mists of our ancient memory an event occurred that has left a gap in our understanding of how we relate to our world and one another? If so, could the filling of that gap avert the greatest tragedies ever to face humankind? Twenty-five-hundred-year-old texts, as well as modern science, suggest that the answer to these and similar questions is a resounding "Yes!" Additionally, in the languages of their times, those who have come before us remind us of two empowering technologies with direct relevance to our lives today. The first is the science of prophecy, which allows us to witness the future consequences of choices that we make in the present. The second is the sophisticated technology of prayer that allows us to choose which future prophecy we live.

The secrets to our lost sciences appear to have been shared openly by societies and traditions of our past. The last vestiges of this empowering wisdom were lost to Western tradition with the disappearance of rare texts in the fourth century. It was in A.D. 325 that key elements of our already ancient heritage were taken from the general population and relegated to the esoteric traditions of mystery schools, elite priesthoods, and sacred orders. Through the eyes of modern science, recent translations of such texts as the Dead Sea Scrolls and the Gnostic libraries of Egypt have shed new light and opened the doors to possibilities hinted at in ancient folklore and fairy tales. Only now, nearly two millennia after they were written, are we able to authenticate the power of a force that lives within us, a very real power with the ability to end suffering and bring a lasting peace to our world.

Ancient authors left us their empowering message of hope described in the words of their time. The visions of the prophet Isaiah, for example, were recorded over five hundred years before the time of Christ. The only manuscript discovered intact among the Dead Sea Scrolls in 1946, the entire Isaiah Scroll is unrolled and mounted upon a vertical cylinder displayed at the Shrine of the Book Museum in Jerusalem. Considered irreplaceable, the exhibit is designed to retract into a vault covered by steel doors to preserve the scroll for future generations in the event of nuclear attack. The age, completeness, and written nature of the Isaiah Scroll provides a unique opportunity to consider it as representative of many prophecies regarding our time in history. Beyond the specifics of precise events, a generalized view of ancient predictions reveals threads of a common theme. In each glimpse into our future, the prophecies follow a clear pattern: descriptions of catastrophe are immediately followed by a vision of life, joy, and possibility.

In the oldest known manuscript of its kind, Isaiah begins his vision of possible futures by detailing a time of global destruction on an unparalleled scale. He describes this ominous moment as a time when "the earth is utterly laid waste, utterly stripped."[1] His glimpse into a time yet to come closely mirrors the descriptions of many other prophecies from various traditions, including those of the Native American Hopi and Navajo, as well as the Maya of Mexico and Guatemala.

In the verses that follow Isaiah's description of devastation, however, his vision shifts dramatically to a theme of peace and healing: "Streams will burst forth in the desert, and rivers in the steppe. The burning sands will become pools and the thirsty ground, springs of water."[2] Additionally, Isaiah suggests that "the deaf shall hear the words of a book; and out of gloom and darkness the eyes of the blind shall see."[3]

For nearly twenty-five centuries, scholars have largely interpreted such visions as a description of events expected to occur in precisely the order in which they are described in Isaiah's scroll: first the tribulation of destruction, followed by a time of peace and healing. Is it possible that these visions from another time were saying something else? Could the insights of the prophets reflect the skills of adept masters slipping between the worlds of possible futures and recording their experiences for future generations? If so, the details of their journeys may offer powerful clues to a time still to come.

Echoing the beliefs of twentieth-century physicists, ancient prophets viewed time and the course of our history as a path that may be traveled in two directions, reverse as well as forward. They recognized that their visions merely portrayed possibilities for a given moment in time, rather than events that would occur with certainty, and each possibility was based upon conditions at the time of prophecy. As conditions changed, the outcome of each prophecy would reflect that change. A prophet's vision of war, for example, could be viewed as a future to be expected only if the social, political, and military circumstances at the time of the prophecy were to continue unimpeded.

The same line of reasoning reminds us that by changing our course of action in the moment, sometimes in a very small way, we may redirect our entire future. This principle applies to individual circumstances such as health and relationship, as well as to the general well-being of our world. In the case of war, the science of prophecy could allow a visionary to project his sight into a future time and alert the people of his day to the consequences of their actions. Many prophecies, in fact, are accompanied by emphatic pleas for change in an effort to avoid what the prophets have seen.

Prophetic insight into distant possibilities often reminds us of an analogy to parallel roads, paths of possibility that run into our future as well as our past. Once in a while the courses of the roads appear to bend, bringing each path very close to its neighbor. It is at these points that ancient prophets believed the veils between the worlds became very thin. The thinner the veils, the easier it became to choose new courses for the future, by jumping from one path to another.

Modern scientists give careful consideration to such possibilities, creating names for the events themselves, as well as the places where the worlds are connected. Through the language of time waves, quantum outcomes, and choice points, prophecies such as those of Isaiah take on powerful new meanings. Rather than being forecasts of events expected one day in our future, they are glimpses into the consequences of choices made in the present. Such descriptions often bring to mind the image of a great cosmic simulator, allowing us to witness the long-term effects of our actions.

Surprisingly similar to quantum principles which suggest that time is a collection of malleable and diverse outcomes, Isaiah goes one step further, reminding us that the possibilities of our future are actually determined by collective choices in the present. By sharing a common choice, many individuals amplify the effect and accelerate the outcome. Some of the clearest examples of this quantum principle are found in mass prayers for miracles; sudden jumps from one future outcome into the experience of another. In the early

1980s, the effects of focused prayer were documented through controlled experiments in urban high-crime areas.[4, 5] Through such studies, the localized effect of prayer has been well documented in the open literature. Do the same principles apply over larger areas, perhaps on a global scale?

On Friday, November 13, 1998, a mass prayer was implemented on a worldwide basis, as a choice of peace during a time of escalating political tension in many parts of the world. Of specific interest that day was the expiration of a timeline imposed on Iraq to comply with the United Nations' demands for weapons inspections. Following months of unsuccessful negotiations for access into sensitive sites, the nations of the West had made it clear that Iraq's failure to comply would result in a massive and extended bombing campaign designed to destroy suspected weapons sites. Such a campaign would certainly have resulted in great loss of life, civilian as well as military.

Linked through a global community accessing the World Wide Web, several hundred thousand people chose peace in a mass prayer carefully synchronized to precise moments that evening. During the time of the prayer, an event occurred that many consider to be a miracle. Thirty minutes into the aerial attack, the President of the United States, having received a letter from Iraqi officials stating that they would now cooperate with the requested weapons inspections, issued a rare order to U.S. forces to "stand down," the military term for aborting a mission.[6]

The chances of such an event happening by coincidence in the same time window as the global prayer are small. Skeptics have viewed the synchronicity in this example as "chance." However, given that similar results had been seen previously in events occurring in Iraq, the United States, and Northern Ireland, a growing body of evidence suggests that the effect of mass prayer is more than coincidence. Confirming a tenet discovered in centuries-old texts, the evidence simply states that the choice of many people, *focused in a specific manner,* has a direct and measurable effect on our quality of life.

Though such changes appear unexplainable by ordinary means, quantum principles allow for them as a result of the inner force of collective or group choice. Perhaps encrypted in ancient traditions until the thinking of our day could recognize it, the lost science of prayer offers a course of action now to avoid the sickness, destruction, war, and death predicted for our future. Our *individual* choices merge into our *collective* response to the present, with implications that range from a matter of days to many generations into our future. Now we have the language to bring this powerful message of hope and possibility into each moment of our lives.

Though the full extent of Isaiah's darkest visions has yet to pass, a growing number of scientists, philosophers, and researchers believe that we are witnessing the precursors to many of the events he predicted for our lifetime. Could ancient keys such as the Isaiah Scroll have survived for over two millennia with a message so empowering that they could not be recognized until the very nature of our world was understood? Our willingness to allow for such a possibility may become our road map to avoiding the suffering predicted by an entire class of visions for our future.

And I saw a new heaven and a new earth. . . .

I heard a voice saying

there shall be no more death,

neither sorrow, nor crying,

for the former things are passed away.

—*THE ESSENE BOOK OF REVELATIONS*

# LIVING THE DAYS
# OF PROPHECY

## *History Points to Now*

For some reason the man caught my eye as I strolled down the hallway past the rest rooms and telephones. It could have been his artwork displayed on the walls. Perhaps it was his jewelry, modestly peeking from the handcrafted box lined with felt. More likely than not, however, it was the three children that surrounded him. Having no children of my own, over the years I've gotten better at estimating the ages of those that belong to other people. The oldest with the man was nearly eight years old. Working toward the youngest, there was perhaps two years' difference between one and the next. *What beautiful children,* I thought to myself as I passed their display in the lobby of the restaurant.

I had just finished a long-overdue meal with friends near a small seaside town north of San Francisco. Preparing to offer a workshop that would continue over the next three days, I knew that I had been a little distant at dinner. From my vantage point at one end of the table, the conversations seemed to be happening all around me. I had felt like an observer as the rest of the group quickly paired off in catch-up conversation regarding careers, romance, and future plans. I remember wondering if my choice of seating was intentional, my way of avoiding direct participation while still enjoying the presence of old friendships in intimate conversation. More than once I had found myself looking out of the tall plate-glass windows that stood between me and the tide rising under the pier. My mind was focused on the presentation that I would make the following evening. What words would I share in the opening? How would I invite an audience of mixed backgrounds and varied beliefs to follow me into an ancient message of life-affirming hope regarding our time in history?

"Hey, how is it going?" the man with the children and jewelry said as I walked toward him. The unexpected greeting of a stranger jolted me into the present. I smiled and nodded.

"Great," I replied, without even thinking. "It looks like you have some good helpers," I said, gesturing toward his three children. The man laughed, and as I stopped we quickly found ourselves in conversation about his jewelry, his wife's artwork, and their four children.

"I was the midwife for each of my children," he said. "I was the first eyes that they saw when they came into this world. My hands were the first hands that touched their bodies." His eyes sparkled as he described how his family had grown. Within a matter of moments, this man whom I had never met before began describing the miracle of birth that he and his wife had experienced four times together. I was quickly moved by his trust and the sincerity of his voice as he shared intimate details of each birth.

"It's easy to bring a baby into this world," he said.

*Easy for you to say,* I thought to myself. *What would your wife say if I were to ask her about having babies?* Just as I had the thought, a woman appeared from down the hallway. Immediately I knew that she and the man were together. They were one of those couples that just look as though they are part of one another. She walked up to us and smiled warmly as she slipped her arm around her husband. I would have passed her display down the hallway if I had not stopped to speak with her husband first. Knowing the answer to the question that I was about to ask, I spoke first.

"Are you the mother of these beautiful children?"

The pride in her eyes gave away her answer, even before the words left her mouth. "Yes, I am," she replied. "I'm the mother *to all five* of them." With the wide grin that comes from the privilege of sharing years with another person, she laughed and poked her husband in the arm. I caught on immediately. She was referring to him as the fifth child. She held in her arms the fourth and youngest, a small boy perhaps two years old. As he squirmed, his mother placed him feet-first on the tiled floor of the restaurant entryway. He stepped to his father, who picked him up in a single motion and cradled him in the crook of one arm. The young boy seated himself upright so he could look directly into his father's eyes, and he remained that way for the rest of our conversation. It was obviously something that they had done many times before.

"So, it is easy to have a child?" I said, as a reminder of where we had left our conversation before the man's wife had appeared.

"Usually," he replied. "When they are ready, there is not much stopping them. They just shoot right out!" With his youngest son still in his arms, the man stooped a little to mimic an athlete catching a ball, or a baby in his arms.

We all laughed as he and his wife looked at each other. Then an air of stillness came over the couple as well as their children. Now and then someone crosses our path in precisely the right moment, with precisely the right words to jolt our memories and awaken possibilities that lie sleeping within each of us. I believe that, on unspoken levels, we work together in this way. In the innocence of the unexpected, a magical moment unfolds. I knew that this was one of those moments. The man looked directly at me. The expression on his face and the feeling in my heart told me that whatever was about to happen was the reason we were together in that moment.

"Usually there are no problems," the man continued. "Once in a while, though, something happens. Something goes wrong."

Looking at the young boy in his arms, the man drew the child even closer as he reached up and brushed the hair off the boy's forehead with his hand. For an instant the two gazed into each other's eyes. I was honored by their ability to share their love without making me feel like an observer. They were allowing me to participate in their moment.

"It happened with this one," the man continued. "We had some problems with Josh." I listened carefully as he continued. "Everything was going fine, just the way it should. My wife's water had broken and her labor had progressed to the point where we found ourselves having our fourth home birth. Josh was in the birth canal when suddenly everything stopped. He just stopped coming. I knew that something was wrong. For some reason I thought back to a police operations manual that I had read years earlier. There was a chapter on emergency births, with one section dedicated to possible complications. My mind raced to that section. Isn't it funny how just the right things seem to come to our minds at just the right moment?" He laughed a nervous laugh as his wife stepped closer. Placing her arm around her husband and her youngest child, I knew that they were sharing an experience that had brought the three of them together through a rare bond of intimacy and wonder.

"The manual said that every once in a while during birth, the baby may become lodged against the mother's tailbone. Sometimes it's the head, sometimes the shoulder, that gets wedged. It's a relatively simple procedure to reach inside and free the child. This is just what I believed was happening to Josh.

"I reached inside my wife, and the most amazing thing happened. I found her tailbone, moved my hand upward a little bit, and sure enough, I felt Josh's shoulder blade, lodged up against the bone. Just as I was about to shift him myself, I felt a movement. It took a moment for me to realize what was happening. It was Josh's hand. He was reaching up toward his mother's tailbone *to free himself!* As his arm brushed my hand, I was given an experience that I believe very few fathers have ever had." By this time, we were all in tears.

"The story isn't over yet," the man's wife said softly. "Go ahead, tell the rest," she whispered encouragingly to her husband.

"I'm getting to that part." He grinned as he wiped his eyes with his hands. "As his arm brushed my hand, Josh stopped moving, just for a couple of seconds. I believe he was trying to understand what he had found. Then I felt him again. This time he was not reaching up to free himself from his mother's tailbone. This time he was reaching for me! I felt his tiny hand move across my fingers. His touch was uncertain at first, as if he were exploring. In just a matter of seconds there was a strength in his grip. I felt my unborn son reach out and wrap his fingers around mine confidently, as if he knew me! In that moment I knew that Josh would be okay. Together, the three of us worked to bring Josh into this world, and here he is today." We all looked at the little boy in his father's arms. Noticing all eyes on him, Josh nestled his face into his father's shoulder.

"He's still a little shy," the man said with a laugh.

"I can see why he's so drawn to you," I said. "You two have quite a history together."

We looked at one another through the tears that had welled up in each of our eyes. I remember the feeling of awe and wonder, and perhaps a little surprise, at the intensity of what we had just shared. We all laughed, easing the awkwardness of the moment without detracting from the power of what had been shared. After a few more words and many warm hugs, we said good night.

I never saw the family again. Now, nearly three years later, I don't even know their names. What remains is their story, their openness and willingness to share an intimate moment of their lives. Their honesty had touched something very ancient, deep within me. Though we had known one another less than twenty minutes, the three of us had created a powerful memory that I would share many times over the next months. It was one of those moments when there is no need for explanation. We did not even try.

## The Shift of the Ages

A well-known phrase in the teachings of Hermes Trismegistus, considered the father of alchemy, suggests that the experiences of our daily lives, such as the birth of a new life, are reflections of events occurring on a much larger scale in the cosmos. With eloquent simplicity, the tenet simply states, "As above, so below." Chaos theory, a specialized study of mathematics, carries the explanation one step further, suggesting that our experiences are holographic as well. In a holographic world, the experience of one element is mirrored by every other element throughout the rest of the system. To the degree that our cosmos works this way, the tenet may also be applied to an experience much closer to home: the relationship between our bodies and our earth. As the family standing with me shared the memories of birthing their youngest member, I found myself thinking back to the tenet of Hermes. Suddenly the story of Josh making his way into our world became a powerful analogy to our planet giving birth to a new world. The similarities are compelling.

For just one moment, if we could imagine ourselves coming to earth from a world where the miracle of birth was an unfamiliar experience, the story of Josh offers a new perspective to the events of our time. Witnessing a life emerging into this world by any account is a magical experience. Knowing what the outcome of the labor will be, however, in some way must change our feelings regarding the experience. How would our perspective be different if we did not know the outcome? What if we viewed the process of labor without the privilege of understanding that a new life was being invited into our midst?

We would begin by seeing a woman in obvious pain. Her face would grimace, synchronized with the screams of labor. Blood and fluids would flow from her body. For all intents and purposes, as witnesses to the labor of new life, we would see precisely the same symptoms that often accompany the loss of life in our world. How would we ever know that from the outward symptoms of pain a birth would emerge? Is it possible that we are making the same assumptions regarding the labor of a new earth that someone unfamiliar with labor might make watching a human birth? This is precisely the scenario that ancient traditions suggest is unfolding; we are witnesses to the cyclic birth of a new world. In the prophetic visions of the Gospel of Matthew, the author actually uses birth as a metaphor to describe the events that the people of our time may expect to see: "There will be famines and earthquakes from place to place. All these things are the beginnings of the labor pains."[1]

During the last quarter of the twentieth century, scientists in fact have documented unprecedented events for which there appear to be no points of comparison. From the innermost regions of earth's cores to the very edges of our known universe, instruments are recording events that exceed previous measurements in strength and duration, sometimes by several orders of magnitude. In the autumn of 1997, reports of catastrophic earth and social changes began to flood the World Wide Web, magazines, and other media relating to such topics. The articles described a variety of events ranging from mega-earthquakes, rises in sea level, and near collisions with asteroids, to powerful new viruses and the breakdown of a fragile peace in the Middle East, each with the potential to wreak havoc and destruction. Many of the articles describe phenomena that follow predictions envisioned thousands of years ago for this time in history. Ancient as well as modern prophecies suggest that the events of 1997 marked the beginning of a rare period in which we may expect to see some dramatic changes.

## The Language of Change

It was the second week of July 1998. My wife and I had just returned from an extended journey comprising three weeks in Tibet and five weeks in southern Peru. Together we had led sacred journeys into some of the most pristine and isolated places remaining on Earth today. The purpose of each journey was to document clear and relevant examples of an ancient wisdom lost to the West 1,700 years ago. In journeying to remote locations where customs have been preserved for hundreds of generations, we had the opportunity to speak with those living the practices today. Rather than speculating about the validity of faded texts, or translating lost languages from temple walls, we spoke to the monks, shamans, and nuns of those regions directly. Through guides, interpreters, and our own language skills, we asked specific questions regarding the practices that we were privileged to witness.

Though we had watched news broadcasts whenever possible in the larger cities, Melissa and I had been largely out of touch with the "outside world" for much of our time away. I walked into my office just as the fax machine beeped, signaling an incoming message. Already there was a crumpled roll of fax paper cascading onto the floor. I wondered what message could be so urgent as to greet us in this way on our first day back.

Allowing the first few pages to tumble off the machine, I picked them up and began to skim the papers. They were pages and pages of information gathered from a variety of scientific institutions ranging from the National Aeronautics and Space Administration and the United States Geological Survey to major universities and news services. Each page was covered with tables, graphs, and statistics documenting unusual events that had occurred over the last few months. Apparently researchers had been keeping me informed of these events, and I happened to walk into my office just as another update was arriving.

The first sheets detailed a cosmic event of unprecedented proportions. On December 14, 1997, astronomers detected an explosion on the edge of our known universe, second in magnitude only to the primordial Big Bang. As reported in the scientific journals nearly seven months later, researchers at the California Institute of Technology had documented the explosion as lasting from one to two seconds, with a luminosity equal to the rest of the entire universe.[2] Since the original blast, additional explosions of similar magnitude had been detailed.

Following were reports from June of 1998, when scientists had witnessed two comets slamming into our sun, an event never seen or documented before. The impacts were followed within hours by a "dramatic ejection of hot gas and magnetic energy known as coronal mass ejection (CME)."[3] Flares of this nature are triggers for major disturbances in the earth's magnetic field, often knocking out communications and power over large areas. Still fresh in the minds of many scientists are the effects of similar disturbances in March of 1989, caused by flares that broke previous records of occurrence by 50 percent.[4, 5]

The next papers detailed studies released in April of 1998 documenting what many had suspected regarding weather and temperature extremes in recent years. For the first time an international team confirmed that temperatures in the northern hemisphere have climbed higher in the last decade than during any other period in the last six hundred years.[6] Furthermore, studies had disclosed that an error in satellite data had confused the reading of weather trends in the past by masking the signs of increasing air temperatures.[7] Assuming a similar increase in the southern hemisphere, scientists from the National Snow and Ice Data Center were still in awe at how quickly a 200-square-kilometer (approximately 124 square miles) mass of the Larsen-B ice shelf had broken off from Antarctica and disappeared from satellite photographs. Appearing intact on February 15, it was gone eleven days later, submerged under the water. The report stated a concern that the entire Larsen-B shelf, covering more than 10,000 square kilometers (approximately 6,200 square miles) could "crumble in as little as one to two years."[8] Additional studies went on to explain the significance of such events, calculating that "a collapse of Antarctic ice could raise sea levels by 6 meters (nearly nineteen and one-half feet)."[9]

Beginning in early 1997, an anomalous weather pattern known as El Niño had wreaked havoc on crops, industry, and the lives of hundreds of thousands of people on a global scale. The summaries noted that more than 16,000 people had died worldwide and that damage estimates were running as high as $50 billion. Conventional climate models completely missed predicting this pattern, which resulted from a breakdown and reversal of ocean currents, until it had already begun.

Additional papers noted the 1991 discovery of mysterious new signals originating from the center of our galaxy,[10] and confirmed that Earth's magnetic North Pole has now wandered over five degrees since 1949–50.[11, 12] Accompanying the articles were commentaries from leading researchers regarding both the acceleration and rising intensity of the phenomena. Events from years past that many had viewed as isolated and anomalous, such as the solar flares in the late 1980s, were now viewed as stepping-stones paving the way to these recent displays of even greater extremes. All had occurred within a nine-year window of time! Though not surprised, I was in awe of the number and timing of the events. Many researchers suspect that the rare physical shifts may represent the beginning of the catastrophic cycle of change predicted in so many traditions and prophecies.

At first glance, without a framework within which to view such reports, they may appear frightening at best. The variety of events occurring so closely in time seems more than merely chance or coincidence. Any one of these events in itself warrants the attention of leading scientists and governments. The fact that many occurred within a few short weeks suggests that another scenario may be unfolding that is not accounted for by our models of society and nature.

Many scholars, modern-day prophets, and laypeople believe that such powerful examples of natural and social extremes are in fact the precursors of events fulfilling long-standing prophecies of war and destruction. *The same prophecies considered in their entirety, however, offer a message of very different kind.* Far from terrifying, ancient predictions viewed through the eyes of new research offer an empowering perspective of hope and possibility.

## History Points to Now

I had been on hold only moments when I heard the technician's voice come onto the telephone.

"We'll begin the program in three minutes, with a station ID at twenty and half past the hour," he said.

Radio has always been a good medium for me. Still, there was a familiar wave of emotion that rolled through my body as I heard the man's voice. I knew that over the next three hours, each word that I spoke would be heard on syndicated stations across the country. For months, sometimes years, I would be quoted with regard to specific statements that I would make on this night. At the same time, I knew that the message of possibility within the interview would offer a perspective of hope for those listening. I took a deep breath to focus and prepare myself. The program was live and unrehearsed. My immediate thought was, *What will the first question be?*

As if he had heard my thought, the technician suddenly came back on the line. "We would like to begin by addressing your optimism. In the face of so many predictions of catastrophic destruction for the end of the millennium, why are you so positive about the future of our world?"

"Good," I replied. "I see we will begin with the easy questions first."

Together we laughed, easing any last-minute tensions. Moments later the voice of our program's host began a live interview. Quickly our conversation led to questions from random callers regarding challenges that could be expected as we transition through the turn of the millennium into the twenty-first century. Though the words varied, there was a common theme underlying each question: concern about destructive changes for the peoples of the earth. Some of the callers' voices quivered as they shared cultural insights and personal visions for the end of the century. One Native American elder from an unspecified tribe described specific earth changes that his ancestors said would mark the last of three "great shakings" upon the earth. They included earthquakes, alterations in weather patterns, and the collapse of certain forms of government. From his people's perspective, the changes prophesied had already begun.

I listened carefully. To the best of my knowledge, each caller was accurate with regard to the predictions, detailing prophecies precisely the way I had heard them as well. At the same time the stories were incomplete. In the visions of those who have come before us, an outcome of catastrophic destruction was only one of the possibilities they saw for our future. Many prophecies also indicate another outcome. Additional futures of joy and hope, however, appear to be the visions that have become clouded, or lost altogether, as the prophecies have passed from generation to generation.

Our program continued into the early hours of the next morning. The moderator and I carefully pieced together a framework within which the extremes of natural and social phenomena began to make sense. I described a lost series of revelations recently discovered in pre-Christian texts. Supported through new research validating such traditions, the source of my optimism soon became clear. While our challenges may appear more formidable with each passing day, my faith in our collective ability to become more than the events that challenge us has only become stronger.

## Window to the Inner Worlds

To many researchers, recent extremes documented in our solar system, weather patterns, geophysical shifts, and social patterns have no frame of reference in Western models of understanding. Their training asks them to view the anomalous events witnessed by science as discrete, nonrelated phenomena—mysteries without context. Ancient and indigenous traditions such as those of the native North and South Americans, the Tibetans, and the Qumran communities of the Dead Sea, however, offer a framework that allows us to make sense of the apparent chaos in our world. These teachings provide a unified view of creation, reminding us that our bodies are made of the same materials as our earth—nothing more and nothing less.

Perhaps the ancient Essenes, the mysterious authors of the Dead Sea Scrolls, provide some of the clearest insights into our relationship with our world and the sciences of time and prophecy. Supported by modern research, those 2,500-year-old texts suggest that events observed in the world around us mirror the development of beliefs within us. Fourth-century documents preserved in the private Vatican libraries, for example, offer details of this relationship, reminding us that "the spirit of the Son of Man was created from the spirit of the Heavenly Father, and *his body from the body of the Earthly Mother. Man is the Son of the Earthly Mother,* and from her did the Son of Man receive his whole body. You are one with the earthly mother; she is in you and you in her . . ." (my emphasis).[13]

In the only words that they knew, the Essenes remind us of a relationship that modern sciences have now confirmed. The air in our lungs is the same air that glides over the greatest oceans and rushes through the highest mountain passes. The water that makes up 98 percent of the blood in our veins is the same water that was once the great oceans and the mountain streams. Through the writings of another time, the Essenes invite us to view ourselves as one with the earth, rather than separate from it. From such an ancient worldview, we are offered two key precepts to guide us through the greatest challenges of our modern time.

First, we are reminded that imbalances imposed upon the earth are mirrored as conditions within our bodies. Such traditions view the breakdown of our immune systems and cancerous growths in our bodies, for example, as the inner expression of a collective breakdown that prevents our outer world from giving us life.

Second, this line of thinking invites us to consider earthquakes, volcanic eruptions, and weather patterns as mirrors of great change occurring within human consciousness. Clearly, from such a worldview, life becomes much more than a group of daily experiences occurring on a random basis. The events of our world are living barometers showing us our progress on a journey that began long ago. As we look to our relationships within the patterns of societies and nature, we are actually witnessing changes within ourselves.

These holistic perspectives suggest that world changes offer a rare opportunity to gauge the consequences of our choices, beliefs, and values in a dramatic fashion, as a feedback mechanism of sorts. Once the mechanism is recognized, we awaken to new possibilities of even greater choices in our lives.

Such possibilities of healing have been silently held in tribal traditions and pre-Christian prophecy for hundreds of generations. Through the eyes of those who have come before us, our timetable appears to be intact; the time of the great change is now. If our outer world does in fact mirror our beliefs and values, is it possible to end the pain and suffering of earth through choices of compassion and peace made in our lives? At present, the scenarios of melting ice caps, dangerously rising sea levels, a worldwide increase in earthquake activity, and a third world war are just beginning. Carried to its fullest expression, each of these scenarios may be regarded as a serious threat to the very survival of humankind. Our message of hope is that they have not yet come to completion. The key to addressing such events is in the timing: the sooner we recognize our relationship with the world around us, the sooner we will recognize our inner choices of peace mirrored as gentle weather patterns, the healing of our societies, and peace between nations.

We already have the evidence of a powerful technology, forgotten long ago, hidden deep within our collective memories. We see the evidence of our feeling-based technology each day in the joy of new life and lasting love, as well as the conditions that take our joy away from us. It is this inner science that empowers us to transcend with grace the destructive prophecies of future time and the challenges of life. In our collective wisdom lies the opportunity for a new era of peace, unity, and global cooperation unprecedented in human history.

## Quantum Prophecy in the Days of Hope

Developed in the early twentieth century, the science of quantum physics offers principles that allow for time, prayer, and our future to be closely related in ways that we are just beginning to understand. Among the intriguing properties of quantum theory we find the existence of many outcomes for a given moment in time. Reminiscent of the biblical passage that "in my father's house are many mansions," the "house" of our world is the home of many possible outcomes for the conditions that we create in our lives. Rather than *creating* our reality, it may be more accurate to say that we create the conditions into which we *attract future outcomes,* already established, into the focus of the present.

The choices that we make as individuals determine which mansion, or *quantum possibility,* we experience in our personal lives. As our individual choices fall into broad categories that either affirm or deny life in our world, our many choices merge into a single, collective response to the challenges of the moment. For example, choosing forgiveness, compassion, and peace attracts futures that reflect such qualities. The beauty of our earlier analogy to Hermes Trismegistus's "as above, so below" is that we are shown the significance of every choice made by each man and woman, from all walks of life, in each moment. In the absence of money or privilege, all choices carry equal strength and value. Clearly, navigating our course through the possibilities of life is a group process. In a quantum world there are no hidden deeds, and each action by every individual counts. We are here in the world that we create together.

Neither ancient nor current prophecies can predict our future; we are refining our choices in every moment! While we may appear to be on one path destined for a specific outcome, our path can change radically to produce another outcome that is quite unexpected (within the space of only thirty minutes in our example of the bombings in Iraq). Predictions offer possibilities only. The physicist Richard Feynman, considered by many to be one of the greatest innovators of new thought since Albert Einstein, spoke to precisely this key of prophecy when he stated, "We do not know how to predict what will happen in a given circumstance. The only thing that can be predicted is the probability of different events."[14]

Perhaps the most empowering passages of our lost pre-Christian texts refer to an ancient science known today as *prayer*. Regarded by many to be the root of all technology, prayer, which is the union of thought, feeling, and emotion, represents our opportunity to speak the language of change in our world as well as in our bodies. Through the words of another time we are reminded of the potential that prayer may bring into our lives. Now modern research, in the language of our own science, offers the same insights.

In the late 1980s, the effect of mass prayer and meditation was documented through studies in major cities where the occurrence of violent crime decreased measurably in the presence of continuous peace vigils held by those trained for the purpose.[15] The studies eliminated the possibility of "coincidence" stemming from natural cycles, changes in social policy, or law enforcement. While a state of calm and peace was created *within* the study groups, the effects of their efforts were felt beyond the boundaries of the walls and buildings that they occupied. Through an invisible network that appeared to penetrate the belief systems, organizations, and social strata of the inner cities, the choice of peace within a few individuals touched the lives of many. Clearly there was a direct, observable, and measurable effect of human behavior correlating with groups focused through prayer and meditation.

Was the change actually *created* by those holding the continuous focus of peace, or did the prayer vigils demonstrate yet another possibility, carrying great implications, only documented thus far under laboratory conditions? If the quantum theories cited earlier are correct, then for each incident of crime observed in a city, another outcome already existed in that very moment: one with an absence of crime. Researchers call such possibilities "overlays," as they appear to blanket one reality with the outcome of a new possibility.

Are there certain kinds of prayer that call such overlays into the focus of the present? For this to be possible in the experiments above, for example, the outcome of peace and the outcome of crime had to exist *in the same moment,* as one gave way to the focus of another. For two somethings to share the same place at the same time is an impossibility from our way of thinking—or is it?

In his recent book, *Cracking the Bible Code,* Jeffrey Satinover, M.D., relates extraordinary new research offering insight into precisely such possibilities. In one of these studies, reports Satinover, two atoms of very different properties were documented in an act that defies the laws of nature as we understand them today. Under the right conditions, *the two atoms were occupying exactly the same place at precisely the same time!*[16] Until these studies were verified, such a phenomenon had been believed to be impossible. Now we know that it is not. The outcome of our world at any given moment in time is made of people, machines, earth, and nature. At their most fundamental level, our outcomes are made of atoms. If two of the basic building blocks of our world may coexist at the same instant, then the doorway has been opened for many atoms, resulting in many outcomes, to do the same. The difference may simply be one of scale.

Through our refined language of quantum science, we now have the vocabulary to describe precisely how we participate in determining the outcome of our future. Recognizing that the experiences of our lives exist as events situated along the course of time, the ancients remind us that to change the nature of our experience, we must only choose a new course. The difference between this line of thinking and the suggestion that we create our reality by manipulating the fabric of creation is vast and, at the same time, extremely subtle.

Rather than creating or imposing change upon our world, perhaps it is our ability to change our focus that was the ancient key suggested by the masters of passive change in history. Buddha, Gandhi, Jesus of Nazareth, and those who participated in the mass prayer of November 1998 each experienced the effect of such change. Quantum physics suggests that by redirecting our focus—where we place our attention—*we bring a new course of events into focus* while at the same time releasing an existing course of events that may no longer serve us.

Perhaps this is precisely what happened on that November evening with the campaign against Iraq. Although achieving our political goals through military force may have served us in the past, we may have reached a time when we have outgrown such tactics. As odd as it may sound, the past threat of mutual destruction between powers of comparable strength has actually created one of the longest eras of relative peace that our world has known in recent years. Nonetheless, something changed that night in November. With a unified voice, our global family chose to direct its attention toward the overlay of peace, rather than achieving peace through a military solution. While the thirty or so countries participating in prayer that night represent only a small fraction of our world, the effects were powerful. On that night, no lives were lost to warplanes in Iraq. Could bringing peace into our lives be as simple as a concerted, unified effort to focus upon peace as if it were already here? Ancient traditions ask us why we would make it any more difficult.

## Rewriting Our Future

The membrane between future possibilities may be so thin that we fail to recognize when we have crossed into a new outcome. The "sudden urge," for example, to exercise more often, eat differently, or recommit to a floundering relationship represents a new choice that breaks the structure of a present pattern and promises a new outcome. Though we may feel that the choice has been *spontaneous* or *natural,* the change now allows us to experience a possibility of health or relationship that was only a dream in the past. Prayer is the language that allows us to express our dreams, making them real in our lives. What if our choices were made intentionally?

Now, perhaps more than any other time in human history, the choice of outcome is ours. Once we have read the words, recognized the possibilities, and exposed ourselves to new ideas, we cannot return to the innocence of the moment before. In the presence of what we have seen, we must make sense of our experience. We may disregard what we have been shown, citing lack of proof or too little data, or we may allow ourselves to embrace the opportunity of a new way. The moment that we reconcile each new possibility is the moment where the magic begins; it is the moment of choice.

As our world gives birth to a new earth, landmasses, weather patterns, ice caps, and magnetic shifts bear witness to the changes. In light of recent research, what is the potential of applying the wisdom of two-thousand-year-old texts on a global scale, to answer the challenges of the new millennium with an outcome of healing, peace, and graceful transition? The labor has already begun as history points to *now,* the last days of prophecy.

Thou hast made known unto me

thy deep, mysterious things.

—THE BOOK OF HYMNS,
DEAD SEA SCROLLS

# LOST WORDS
# OF A FORGOTTEN
# PEOPLE

## *Beyond Science, Religion, and Miracles*

It had happened so quickly. Sometimes the feeling of an event lasts longer than the event itself. This was one of those times. I played the scene over in my mind, again and again. In slow motion I could freeze-frame each act. Poised safely as an observer, I studied the details, searching for an answer—something in my knowing world to make sense of what I had just witnessed.

Only moments before, I had noticed the elderly gentleman as I strolled across the parking lot toward the seaside restaurant. I had seen him, and a woman I assumed to be his wife, threading their way through a small crowd of people onto the sidewalk in front of the reception area. Together they had just passed through the swinging doors into the hot, thick air of a summer night in coastal Georgia. His stainless-steel walker preceded each step, securing a stable position from which he could shuffle through his next movement.

Suddenly the rhythm changed. Unexpectedly, he had reached a curb that dropped six inches or so, to the surface at street level. In slow motion, I watched as his walker rocked with uncertainty, tipped, then crashed onto the asphalt, still hot from the relentless daytime sun. The man, confidently gripping the handles of his companion device, crumpled into a heap on top of it. He lay there motionless. Like a surrealistic voyeur, I stood motionless, in the street. Silent. Witnessing.

The wind seemed to tease my ears, carrying away fragments of terrified screams from the man's wife. "Help us! Please, someone help us!" The power of her voice betrayed her thin, frail body.

Within seconds I was there beside them in the street. As quickly as I had moved, however, I was not the first. In my silent witnessing, I had not noticed anyone nearby, nor had I seen anyone approach. Already kneeling at the fallen man's side, however, cradling his head in her lap, was another woman. A zigzag trail of red glistened along the base of the man's head, just below his ear. Gently she tilted his body in the overhead light, searching for the source of blood. In the faint glow of lobby lights from the restaurant, I could see the folds of his skin, overlapping one another, hiding whatever injury was at the source of the bleeding.

Carefully the woman separated each fold until she found the wound. The blood took on an odd color in the glare of the mercury vapor street lamp overhead. At first it looked like another layer of skin. Then I could see a darker place, a deep shimmer, as she parted the fold. Without saying a word, the woman touched the broken tissue, then began to stroke the wound as if she were petting a tiny animal. I looked into her face. Her eyes were closed as she tilted her head upward toward the sky. Seeing the incident from inside the restaurant, a group of people had gathered around us. Except for an occasional whisper from someone just arriving, not one word was spoken. The entire crowd stood motionless and quiet, as if a silent cue had been given. Later that evening, some of the onlookers said that they had sensed a kind of sacredness in that moment. Some went so far as to suspect that a holy act was occurring.

Together, we were entranced by what we saw. At first we were uncertain what was happening. While our senses suggested one thing, our logic dictated something else. There, in the poorly lit parking lot of this little restaurant, I witnessed what modern science would consider a miracle. In full view of a dozen or so witnesses, as the woman silently stroked the tear in the man's flesh, it began to disappear. Within moments his wound had healed without any trace of the injury from his fall just moments earlier.

Someone in the restaurant had called 911, and the paramedics arrived within moments. As their flashing lights signaled their arrival, the crowd separated, allowing the attendants into the small circle where the man was still lying in the woman's lap. Still cradling the man's head and shoulders, the woman made room for the EMT. We watched as he examined the bloodstains on the man's shirt. Expertly the technician traced them to the back of the fallen man's head, then to the place just below his ear. Just as the woman had done moments earlier, the paramedic carefully separated the folds of skin where blood had pooled. To the amazement of the paramedics and the awe of the onlookers, there was no wound. The blood seemed to have *just appeared* at a point on the elderly man's neck, run its course, and spilled onto the collar of his shirt. There was no trace of wound, opening, or scar. Still wet on the man's skin, the blood appeared to have no source! The questions flashed into my mind as I watched: How was this possible? In the presence of a science so advanced that it can peer into the world of an atom and build machines that travel to the edge of our galaxy, why does the same science consider the healing that I had just witnessed a miracle?

## Lost Words

Though in Western science we have no frame of reference for such an event, it falls well within the scope of indigenous traditions and ancient texts. Additionally, the same traditions remind us that it is now, during the convergence of many cycles of time, that we will recognize the importance of such miracles. As we witness events that are beyond the scope of accepted science, we rekindle the memory of a power that has lived within each of us for hundreds of generations. For nearly two millennia, our power has slept while we have tested ourselves through the challenges of human history. The same traditions suggest that now we will awaken our gifts to meet even greater challenges within our lifetime. In doing so, we open the door to an unprecedented era of peace and cooperation, while insuring a future for generations still to come.

Why, then, are the extremes of nature and social unrest in our world today such a mystery to Western understandings? As well as our explanations of natural processes have worked thus far, could our understandings be incomplete? Is there something missing? Is it possible that in the recesses of our collective wisdom, we lost the knowledge that allows us to make sense out of the seemingly senseless?

The last half of the twentieth century has uncovered documents that shed light on this frequently asked question. Centuries-old manuscripts of Aramaic, Ethiopian, Coptic Egyptian, Greek, and Latin origin support indigenous traditions and confidently suggest that the answer to this question is "Yes!"

## Forgotten Technology

Seventeen hundred years ago, key elements of our ancient heritage were lost, relegated to the elite priesthoods and esoteric traditions of the day. In an effort to simplify the loosely organized religious and historic traditions of his time, early in the fourth century A.D. the Roman emperor Constantine formed a council of historians and scholars. What would later be known as the Council of Nice fulfilled the directive of its charter and recommended that at least twenty-five documents be modified or removed from the collection of texts.[1] The committee found many of the works under consideration to be redundant, with overlapping stories and repeated parables. Other manuscripts were so abstract and in some cases so mystical that they were believed to be beyond any practical value. Additionally, another twenty supporting documents were removed, held in reserve for privileged researchers and select scholars. The remaining books were condensed and rearranged, to give them greater meaning and make them more accessible to the common reader.

Each of these decisions contributed to further confusing the mystery of our purpose, possibilities, and relationship to one another. Following the accomplishment of their task, the council produced a single document in A.D. 325. The result of their labor remains with us as perhaps one of the most controversial texts of sacred history. It is known today as the Holy Bible.

Seventeen hundred years later, the implications of the Nicean Council's actions continue to mold the politics, social structure, religious understandings, and technology of our lives. Although we live in a sophisticated world based in science, the assumptions that led to our technical achievements are firmly rooted in our beliefs of how we relate to our world. Such understandings, developed over thousands of years, have become the very foundation of our science. For example, how would the petroleum technology that drives our economy today differ if we had instead recognized the laws of harmony and powered our machines by simply tuning them to the seven-centimeter bandwidth of energy that permeates our world? Such technology is only possible in the presence of a belief system that understands the holistic laws of nature, the very tenets that disappeared from our sacred traditions nearly two millennia ago. Perhaps our failure to recognize these relationships is mirrored in a technology that believes we must *harness* burning or exploding forms of energy to power our world. Such outward expressions of technology may mirror our inner sense of separateness.

Clearly, these implications could not have been seen by the council members of Nice nearly two thousand years ago, or even by the translators of such texts hundreds of years later. For example, a statement attributed to the Archbishop of Canterbury Wake suggests an innocence with respect to the Nicean edits when, asked why he chose the drudgery of translating texts rather than the creative freedom of publishing his documents, the Archbishop replied, "Because I hoped that such writings as these would find a more general and unprejudiced acceptance with all sorts of men than anything that could be written by anyone now living."[2] How could the council members of the fourth century know that the book they produced would eventually become the basis for one of the great religions of the world?

In recent years, individual documents and entire libraries lost after the death of Christ have been recovered, translated, and made available to the general public. To the best of my knowledge, there is no single compilation containing all of the information, as the translations are products of different authors working in different languages over the centuries. There have, however, been groups of translations from time to time. It is through the work of modern scholars that one such compilation of lost biblical books was published earlier in the twentieth century.[3] Among the documents identified as being edited out of our modern Bible are these books:

| | |
|---|---|
| Barnabas | Mary |
| I Clement | Magnesians |
| II Clement | Nicodemus |
| Christ and Abgarus | Paul and Seneca |
| The Apostles' Creed | Paul and Thecla |
| I Hermas-Visions | Philippians |
| II Hermas-Commands | Philadelphians |
| III Hermas-Similitudes | Polycarp |
| Ephesians | Romans |
| I Infancy | Trallians |
| II Infancy | Letters of Herod and Pilate |

Below is a partial summary of supporting texts removed during the fourth-century edits. These texts have typically been reserved for scholars.[4]

| | |
|---|---|
| The First Book of Adam and Eve | Simeon |
| The Second Book of Adam and Eve | Levi |
| The Secrets of Enoch | Judah |
| The Psalms of Solomon | Issachar |
| The Odes of Solomon | Zebulum |
| The Fourth Book of Maccabees | Dan |
| The Story of Ahikar | Naphtali |
| The Testament of Reuben | Gad |
| Asher | Benjamin |
| Joseph | |

The consequences of removing, or in some cases altering, these forty-one books, and possibly others detailing our heritage and relationship to the cosmos, remain with us today. The absence of such key texts may explain the sense many individuals have expressed that our biblical records are scattered and incomplete. For serious researchers and casual historians alike, knowing the existence of these documents offers a sense of resolution. Much like a modern mystery, it is only now, nearly two thousand years after they disappeared from our open literature, that we may at last complete our history.

While each of the lost books contributes to understanding our past, there are some that are certainly of greater consequence than others. Among the most significant are those describing the lives of the people that time has come to view as more than human in their accomplishments. The biblical Book of Mary, the mother of Jesus, offers just one example. For centuries, scholars have speculated that Mary played a much greater role in the life of Jesus than we can see in the abbreviated descriptions of her life in our modern Bible. Through the book created in her name, we are given insight into her heritage and the family values that led Mary to her role as the mother of Jesus. In the texts that follow the Book of Mary, we are shown how she guided her son, instilling in him the values that would allow his gifts of healing and prophecy to better serve the people of his world and beyond.

Mary's parents, for example, were descendants of the lineage of David, one of the original tribes of Israel. Her father and mother, Joachim and Anna, had been married approximately twenty years before they conceived their first and only daughter. Mary's spirit came into Anna's womb following a dream that both she and Joachim shared from different locations, on the same evening. In the presence of an "angel of the Lord," they agreed to a vow that their daughter would "be devoted to the Lord from her infancy, and be filled with the Holy Ghost from her mother's womb."[5] Their daughter's name would be Mary, and it would be through her purity that she would agree to a rare conception in her fourteenth year. Additional books go on to describe the time leading up to and immediately following the birth of Jesus, as well as previously unreported miracles performed throughout his childhood.

Perhaps the Books of Adam and Eve offer some of the greatest insights into our role in history and our present-day beliefs. The First Book of Adam and Eve begins after the time of Creation, with a description of the location of "the garden," implied to be the Garden of Eden. Planted "in the east of the earth," the garden was located "on the border of the world eastward, beyond which, toward the sun-rising, one finds nothing but water, that encompasses the whole world, and reaches unto the borders of heaven. And to the north of the garden there is a sea of water, clear and pure to the taste, like unto nothing else."[6]

Following the time when Adam and Eve were driven from the garden, a rare timetable was given to them, describing the duration of their exile, extended to all of their descendants, until a specific moment in time. In what may be the first of the great prophecies, Adam and Eve are told by their Creator that he has "ordained on this earth days and years, and thou and thy seed shall dwell and walk in it until the days and years are fulfilled." This time of the fulfillment is envisioned following the "great five days and a half," further defined as "five thousand and five hundred years." It would be then, at the close of a great cycle of time, that "One would then come and save" Adam and his descendants.

For nearly two thousand years we have speculated about the missing time and obvious gaps in the biblical records. Now the recovery of the Bible's lost books has shed new light, and possibly opened the door to even greater questions regarding our understanding of the world. What we know is that, at best, our view and interpretation of history, as well as our role in creation, are incomplete. Is it possible that the very foundation of our society and culture, our language, religion, science, technology, and even the way we love one another is built upon an incomplete understanding of our most sacred and ancient history? What have we forgotten about our relationship with the forces of our world that prevents us from understanding the healing that occurred in the parking lot of the restaurant that evening in Georgia? Perhaps the gap in our understanding may be filled at last, in light of new revelations from a wisdom that forms the basis for the world's major religions: the teachings of the ancient Essenes.

## The Mysterious Essenes

Five hundred years before the birth of Christ, a mysterious group of scholars formed communities to honor an ancient teaching that began before history as we know it. Collectively known as the Essenes, these were various sects that included the Nazirenes and the Ebionites. Roman and Jewish scholars referred to the Essenes as "a race by themselves, more remarkable than any other in the world."[7] Portions of their traditions are found in ancient writings such as the Sumerian glyphs, dating to 4000 B.C. Elements of nearly every major world belief system existing today may be traced back to this original lineage of wisdom, including those of China, Tibet, Egypt, India, Palestine, Greece, and the American Southwest. Additionally, many of the great traditions of the Western world have roots in the same body of information, including the Freemasons, Gnostics, Christians, and Kabalists.[8]

Also known as "the Elect" and "the Chosen Ones," the Essenes were the first people openly to condemn slavery, the use of servants, and the killing of animals for food. Viewing physical labor as a healing communion with the Earth, they were agriculturists, living close to the land that gave them life. The Essenes viewed prayer as the language through which to honor nature and the creative intelligence of the cosmos; they made no distinction between the two. They practiced prayer on a regular basis. The first prayer of the day was offered upon arising in the predawn darkness to work in the fields. This was followed by prayers before and after each meal and again upon retiring at the end of the day. They viewed their practice of prayer as an opportunity to participate in the creative process of their lives, rather than as a structured ritual required throughout the day.

Strict vegetarians by today's standards, members of the Essene communities abstained from animal flesh, blood foods, and fermented liquids. Perhaps one of the clearest explanations of their diet may be found in the following passage from the Dead Sea Scrolls: "Kill not the food which goes into your mouth. For if you eat living food, the same will quicken you, but if you kill your food, the dead food will kill you also. For life comes only from life, and death comes always from death. For everything which kills your foods, kills your bodies also."[9] Their lifestyle permitted them to reach advanced ages, attaining 120 years or more with vitality and great endurance.

The Essenes were meticulous scholars, recording and documenting their traditions for future generations that they could only imagine. Perhaps the best example of their work may be seen in the hidden libraries that they left throughout the world. Like methodically placed time capsules, their manuscripts provide snapshots into the thinking of an ancient people and a forgotten wisdom. What was their message to us today?

## Scrolls from the Dead Sea

One of the most accessible and controversial of the Essene libraries was discovered hidden among forgotten caves in the Qumran area, above the Dead Sea. Known collectively as the Dead Sea Scrolls, the documents hidden for safekeeping are believed to have numbered nearly one thousand. Following the initial discovery of the scrolls by Bedouin tribesmen in 1946–47, the great antiquity of the texts was not validated until the spring of 1948. It was during this time that specialists at the American Schools of Oriental Research confirmed the ages of the first seven manuscripts. The Manual of Discipline, Tales of the Patriarchs, Thanksgiving Psalms, Commentary on Habakkuk, War Scroll, and Book of Isaiah (two copies), were determined to have been written *hundreds of years earlier* than any other texts discovered to date in the Holy Land. By 1956, a total of eleven caves had been discovered. Together, they contained the remains of approximately eight hundred and seventy scrolls, composed of over 22,000 fragments of papyrus, animal hide, and metallic rolls. One site alone, Cave Number Four, contained approximately 15,000 fragments, the largest cache of Dead Sea texts unearthed so far.

The translation and publication of the scrolls has been the subject of tremendous controversy for over forty years. Until recently, access to the Dead Sea library was the sole responsibility of a team consisting of eight scholars. It was not until the 1990s, as a result of political and academic pressure, that the contents of the scroll library from the Qumran caves were released to the public. In 1991, southern California's Huntington Library announced that it was in possession of a complete set of photographs of the Dead Sea Scrolls, and that they would be made available to the public. Following suit, in November of the same year, Emanuel Tov, chief of the official scroll team, announced "free and unconditional access to all the photographs of the Dead Sea Scrolls, including previously unreleased scrolls."[10]

The ongoing controversy over the scrolls invites us to ask the same question, again and again. What message could possibly be held in a two-thousand-year-old text, that would warrant keeping it from the public for nearly a half-century after its discovery? What could these 22,000 fragments of copper, animal hide, and papyrus possibly say that would have any impact upon our lives today?

One of the reasons for the delay in publishing the scroll translations is that the cave scrolls appear to be the earliest versions of our modern Bible. As exciting as such a discovery may sound initially, the problem lies in the discrepancies between the original texts transcribed by the Essenes and the biblical versions accepted today. The documents found in the Dead Sea caves have not undergone the edits of the fourth-century Council of Nice, the translations into the languages of the West, or the interpretation of scholars over the last two thousand years.

Contained within the scrolls are stories, parables, and a history that has not been seen since they were removed from the canonized version of our Bible early in the fourth century. Written in Hebrew and Aramaic, the scrolls include writings said to have come, in some cases, from the angels themselves. Additionally, the library contains rare insights into the lives of prophets such as Enoch and Noah, and at least twelve previously unknown texts written by Moses. None of these documents is included in our Bible today. Clearly, the scrolls from the Qumran caves are just beginning to open the door to new possibilities in our relationships to our collective past and with one another.

## Secrets of the Essenes

An excerpt from the Dead Sea Scrolls offers insight into why the ancient Essenes separated themselves from the urban areas of their time, forming their own communities in the desert: "Always have the children of light lived where rejoice the angels of the earthly mother: near rivers, near trees, near flowers, near the music of the birds, where sun and rain may embrace the body which is the temple of the spirit."[11] Nature and natural laws were key to the Essene way of life. The path to understanding their worldview may be found in their beliefs regarding the relationship between the human body and the elements of the earth.

For the Essenes of Qumran, the word *angel* described the elements of our world that today we see as electrical and magnetic forces. Some forces were visible and tangible, while others were etheric, though nonetheless present. For example, a reference to "the angel of the earth" may include the angel of the air and angels of water and light. Forces of emotion and consciousness were also referred to as angels, such as the angels of joy, work, and love. Such insights into the thinking of the Essenes allow us to view their words 2,500 years later with new hope and understanding.

In the language of their time, the authors of the Dead Sea Scrolls offered a worldview that considers a holistic and unified relationship between the earth and our bodies. Through eloquent words and poetic reminders, the Qumran texts remind us that we are the product of a very special union, a *sacred marriage* between the soul of the heavens and the tissue of our world. The principle states, without exception, that we are a part of, and intimately enmeshed within, all that we see as our world. Through unseen threads and immeasurable cords, we are a part of each expression of life. All rock, each tree and mountain, every river and ocean is a part of each of us. Perhaps most important, you and I are reminded that we are a part of one another.

Essene traditions refer to this union as that of "our Mother Earth" and "our Father in Heaven": "For the spirit of the Son of Man was created from the spirit of the Heavenly Father, and his body from the body of the Earthly Mother. Your Mother is in you, and you in her. She bore you: she gives you life. It was she who gave to you your body . . . even as the body of the newborn babe is born of the womb of his mother."[12] We are the genderless union of these forces, the masculine of "our Father in Heaven" merged with the feminine of "our Mother Earth."

This unified view invites us to consider that through the common thread that binds our bodies to the earth, the experiences of one are mirrored in the other. As long as the marriage is honored, the union between the earth and the spirit continues and the soft temples of our bodies live. When the agreement is dishonored, the union ends, our temple dies, and the forces of earth and spirit return to their respective places of origin.

Essene wisdom containing such subtle concepts was among the loose collection of texts that would become our biblical traditions of today. Those very texts, among other documents, were removed by the Nicean Council during the fourth-century edits. The elegant simplicity that weaves the great teachings of the Essenes into meaningful elements of our lives today was rediscovered, preserved in very good condition, in the great libraries of the royal German Hapsburgs and the Catholic Church during the early part of the twentieth century. The Vatican manuscripts, held for over 1,500 years, were key in the documents that led Edmond Bordeaux Szekely to publish revised translations of the rare Essene texts. In 1928 he offered the first in a series of works that would become known as *The Essene Gospel of Peace,* offering new insights, and a renewed respect, for this lineage of wisdom that predates nearly every major religion of today.

## The Library of Nag Hammadi

Two years before the discovery of the Dead Sea Scrolls, another library of ancient wisdom had already been discovered, one that would forever change the way we think of early Christianity. In the Nag Hammadi region of Upper Egypt, a collection of scrolls was found by two brothers in December of 1945. Buried in a sealed jar, the texts consisted of twelve complete manuscripts and eight pages from a thirteenth, each written on an ancient paper made of papyrus strips. The entire collection of documents become known as the Nag Hammadi Library, and is now kept in the Coptic Museum in Cairo, Egypt. The library of Nag Hammadi passed through an amazing number of hands before its volumes were recognized, authenticated, and entered into the museum register on October 4, 1946. Although some of the scrolls were destroyed in their use as fuel for local ovens, the remainder survive today in a remarkable state of preservation, offering fresh and, in some cases, unexpected insights into the traditions of ancient Gnostic and early Christian traditions.

Dating to the fourth century A.D., the Nag Hammadi Library begins at the approximate time that the Dead Sea Scrolls leave off. Never before have we seen such continuity in the spiritual and religious teachings of early Christians, including their view of our time through future prophecy. The Gnostic traditions originated during a time when early Christian doctrines were being reshaped and were taking on a new identity. Gnostics identified with the central teachings of Christianity, *in their original form,* and chose to separate, rather than follow the tide of change that was leading Christian traditions from the original basis of their belief. As the Roman Empire converted to conventional Christianity, Gnostic followers were first relegated to the status of a radical sect and eventually eradicated from the consideration of Christianity entirely. Books such as the Gospel of Mary, the Apocalypses of Paul, James, and Adam, and the Book of Melchizedek survive today as a testament to the Gnostic wisdom of preserving rare teachings for future generations.

## THE APOCALYPSE OF ADAM

Because Gnosticism is generally acknowledged to have originated within the traditions of early Christianity, many of the Gnostic texts have counterparts in the stories, myths, and parables of early

Christian texts. Of special note among the Nag Hammadi documents is a rare text known as the Apocalypse of Adam. A collection of teachings that were divinely inspired and transmitted, this book is the account of the Adam that we read of in the Book of Genesis. What makes the Apocalypse of Adam so unique is the apparent absence of any relationship to earlier material. It appears that this particular text was already complete and well established as an earlier form of Gnosticism long before the time of Christian literature.

Adam began his account by describing the presence of three visitors from heaven, guides that led him through his visions into the futures of humankind. Shortly before his death, he dictated his revelations to his son, Seth. Similar to the teachings of the prophet Enoch, who dictated the secrets of Creation to his son, Methuselah, at an advanced age, the texts begins with Adam teaching his son "in the seven hundredth year. . . ."[13] Establishing a brief history of his life with Eve, Seth's mother, Adam shares his visions of events that are yet to occur. "Now then, my son Seth, I will reveal to you the things which those men whom I saw before me at first revealed to me. . . ."[14] Adam tells of the time of the great flood of Noah, still to come in his future, complete with accurate references to Noah's family and the ark that saves them.

Perhaps the most significant in the revelations of Adam is his description of a savior whom he calls the "illuminator." Adam tells of an earth continuously ravaged by floods and fires until the illuminator appears for the third time. After his appearance, the great powers of the world question his power, authority, and abilities in disbelief. Through a series of thirteen scenarios, Adam describes thirteen kingdoms that falsely identify the illuminator as originating from sources as varied as "two illuminators," "a great prophet," and from another time, "the aeon which is below. . . ." It is the generation in Adam's future "without a king over it" that correctly identifies the origins of the illuminator as being divinely chosen from all time, past and future, and brought into the present: "God chose him from all the aeons. He caused knowledge of the undefiled one of great truth to come to be. . . ."[15] Clearly, such texts offer new perspectives and fresh insights into the fragmented details that commonly remain in "authorized" versions of our ancient heritage.

## THE THUNDER: PERFECT MIND

Perhaps the most powerful among the Nag Hammadi works is a rare text written by a woman of the Gnostic traditions, titled *The Thunder: Perfect Mind.* In the words of one of the text's translators, George W. MacRae, this work is "virtually unique in the Nag Hammadi Library and very unusual."[16] Written in the first person, the manuscript is in the form of a dialogue in which the unnamed author proclaims herself to have experienced many dichotomies of human experience. "For I am the first and the last. I am the honored one and the scorned one. I am the whore and the holy one. I am the wife and the virgin. I am the barren one and many are her sons."[17]

Through collections of words that are reminiscent of the poetry found in the Dead Sea Scrolls, she reminds us that within every person lives all possibilities of all experience, from the lightest of the light to the darkest of the dark. The text continues with a final verse admonishing readers to remember that as men go to their resting place, "There they will find me, and they will live, and they will never die again."[18]

## THE GOSPEL OF THOMAS

One of the most controversial of the Nag Hammadi texts is the document known as the Gospel of Thomas. At least a portion of this manuscript is identified as being translated from Greek into Coptic Egyptian, the language used in Christian monasteries of Egypt early in the first millennium. The Gospel of Thomas is a rare collection of sayings, parables, stories, and direct quotes from Jesus, believed to have been recorded by the brother of Jesus, Didymos Judas Thomas. This is the same Thomas who later founded Christian churches in the East.

Portions of the gospel are very similar to the manuscript of the Gospel Q,[19] a source manuscript, believed to date to the first century. The "Q" texts, so called from the German word *Quelle,* meaning "source," are known to have been used as a reference by New Testament authors. There are, however, many portions of the Gospel of Thomas that are not found in the Gospel Q, suggesting that it is an independent resource that may confirm and validate other texts dating from the same time.

The words of Thomas's gospel are some of the most mystical of the Gnostic texts. At the same time, in light of the rich context provided by the Dead Sea Scrolls, the same words take on new meaning, and offer new understandings. For example, in response to a question from his disciples regarding their eventual fate in this world, the Gospel of Thomas records Jesus as answering with a parable: "For there are five trees for you in Paradise which remain undisturbed summer and winter and whose leaves do not fall. Whosoever becomes acquainted with them will not experience death."[20] In the absence of a frame of reference for the "five trees," these words offer little more than a mystical proverb to ponder. Within the context offered by the Essene angels of life, however, these words become a source of confirmation for the ancient science of eternal life: the five keys of thought, feeling, body, breath, and nutrient. Texts confirming that Jesus was a master of the Essene traditions lend additional credibility to the interpretation of this mystical reference to eternal life.

# Beyond Science, Religion, and Miracles

The same texts that preserved the prophecies suggest that it is possible to transmute such predictions of catastrophic change, even those that appear to be imminent. Texts such as the Essene Gospels and the Nag Hammadi Library detail a wisdom that allows us to pool our individual life-affirming visions into a collective will to reshape our future. In doing so, we redefine ancient visions of rising sea levels, devastating earthquakes, life-threatening solar flares, and the threat of global war.

As different in some respects as the details of our lost heritage may appear to be, there are common themes that bind the same texts into a meaningful source of knowledge for today. Throughout the wisdom that predates history, we are reminded that choices affirming life in the world of our thoughts, feelings, and emotions are mirrored as times of peace and forgiveness in the larger world of our families and communities. In the same manner, choices that deny the gift of life in our bodies are mirrored as unrest, oppression, and warfare in our cities, governments, and nations. Once again we are invited to remember that our inner and outer worlds are mirrors of each other. It is the simplicity of this single memory that allows the miracles, such as the healing recounted at the beginning of this chapter, to be expected rather than hoped for.

Perhaps the most empowering of the elements lost in the fourth-century edits of the Nicean Council are the sciences of prophecy and prayer. Regarded by many as the most ancient of all sciences, these inner technologies represent our opportunity to first identify the future consequences of present-day choices, then to choose our future with confidence and trust.

I read therein what had always been, what was

now, and what would come to pass.

—*THE ESSENE GOSPEL OF PEACE*

# THE PROPHECIES

## *Silent Visions of a Forgotten Future*

Almost universally, centuries-old traditions remind us that our lifetime is no ordinary time in the history of humanity or the earth. Those who have come before us left their prophetic messages encoded in sacred texts, oral traditions, and systems of timekeeping. Written to a people that they could only imagine in dreams, their messages keep alive the memory of visions that in some instances predate the earliest moments of our recorded history. Over time, the themes of their visions have been incorporated into a variety of religious traditions and spiritual practices. As diverse as they appear, hints of similarity in such traditions offer clues to the meaning of these sacred words today. Only recently, with the aid of computers and other twentieth-century science, have references of ancient visions into future time been confirmed and validated.

## Keepers of Time: The Mysterious Maya

As we near the dawn of the twenty-first century, among the unsolved mysteries of our past are those of the ancient Maya. Almost as sudden as their appearance in the remote areas of the Yucatán peninsula, nearly a millennium and a half ago, these architects of massive temples and celestial observatories suddenly vanished around A.D. 830. In addition to their sprawling plazas and stone towers, they left clues to their past, and perhaps our future, in their unsurpassed calculations of time.

The calendar of the Mayan people may be one of the oldest and most sophisticated systems of timekeeping known to mankind. Until the advent of our atomic clocks, based on the vibration of the cesium atom, the Mayan calendar rivaled the accuracy of any records of time known before the twentieth century. To the present day, descendants of the ancient Maya track time and ascertain the correct date through a system that, according to experts, has "not slipped one day in over twenty-five centuries."[1] Recognizing nature as recurring cycles of events, the Mayan calendar mirrors that people's understanding of time as a system of intermeshing periods.

Key to the Mayan timekeepers was a 260-day count called the *tzolkin* or "Sacred Calendar." Common among other Mesoamerican traditions as well, the *tzolkin* is created as the interface between twenty named days and a counter based on the number thirteen. The Maya, however, carried their timekeeping a step further. Intermeshed with a 365-day count called the "Vague Year," the two cycles of time progressed like the cogs of two wheels until the rare moment when one day on the Sacred Calendar matched the same day of the Vague Year. Marking the end of a fifty-two-year cycle, this much-celebrated day defined an even longer expanse of time. The "Great Cycle" of the previous 5,200 years was measured as one hundred of the fifty-two-year cycles. Based on these calculations and the traditions of the Maya calendar priests themselves, their records of our last Great Cycle begin in the biblical time of Moses, 3114 B.C., and end in our near future, in 2012.

Mayan visions of our future and their system of timekeeping are closely related. These ancient prophets suggested that cycles of time have unique characteristics based upon a "great wave" that travels periodically through the cosmos. As the wave ripples through creation, its movement synchronizes life and the forces of nature on a cyclic basis. The completion of our course in the present cycle is viewed as particularly significant to earth as well as humankind.

Recognized as an expert in Mayan cosmology, Dr. Jose Arguelles suggests that the present twenty-year subcycle, which began in 1992, marks "the emergence of nonmaterialistic, ecologically harmonic technologies . . . to compliment the new decentralized mediarchy information society. . . ."[2] The Mayan elders of today believe that the close of this great millennial cycle will occur within our lifetime, in 2012, and has been anticipated for over three thousand years. They view this rare moment as both the culmination and the birth of a time of rare change. Referring to specific attributes assigned to the cycles, Dr. Arguelles echoes the Mayan belief, suggesting that with the convergence of the Mayan cycles, our purpose to "gather whole the mind of earth . . . and seal it with the star-seed harmony"[3] is fulfilled.

In a similar fashion, the Aztec traditions of central Mexico track the great expanses of earth's history as cycles called "Suns." Their history tells of a time of the First Sun, named *Nahui Ocelotl,* when our world was inhabited by giants living within the earth. Reminiscent of biblical references to a similar world, the pre-Nicean Book of Enoch describes the days when "the women conceiving brought forth giants, whose stature was each three hundred cubits.*

---

*In ancient times, the cubit was a measure of length taken from the tip of the longest finger to the elbow of the person in power at the time. Obviously the measurement varied. The average length of such a measurement on an adult male today is 17–22 inches.

These devoured all which the labor of men produced until it became impossible to feed them. . . ."[4] This period ended when the animal kingdom overcame the human kingdom. There are no indications of survivors from this unusual time in earth's history.

The Second Sun, or next great cycle, named *Nahui Ehecatl,* was noted as the time when new humans began to cultivate and cross-breed plants. The completion of this period was marked by a great wind that swept across the surface of the earth, clearing everything in its path.

During the Third Sun, *Nahui Quiauhuitl,* earth's populations constructed great temples and cities. Tremendous openings within the earth and a "rain of fire" are said to have marked the end of this cycle. We can see in the geological record that there was, in fact, a time when portions of the earth appeared to be covered with fire. It is generally believed that the scorching was the result of a direct hit by an object, possibly an asteroid, nearly 65 million years ago. The ending of the Fourth Sun, in ice and a great flood, is confirmed geologically as well as in oral and written tradition common the world over. The Aztec calendar indicates that today we are living the last days of the Fifth Sun. The close of that fifth world is predicted to occur in our lifetime, coinciding with the last Mayan cycle and making way for the next great cycle, the birth of the Sixth Sun.

With the past as a template, many ancient traditions describe the days of change as times of tribulation and purification. During these times we are invited to consider the rare and, in some instances, destructive displays of nature as an opportunity to strengthen and prepare us for even greater changes yet to come in our world. Themes common to the prophecies for this time in history include unusual weather phenomena and the loss of coastlines due to sea level increases, famines, droughts, earthquakes, and the breakdown of global infrastructures.

Twentieth-century prophets, such as Edgar Cayce, have foreseen massive earth changes predicted to redefine the geography of North America throughout the late 1990s and into the twenty-first century. These include visions of a great inland sea connecting the Gulf of Mexico with the Great Lakes, for example, and the submerging of much of the eastern and western seaboards. Graphic descriptions of our future, sometimes created hundreds or thousands of years in our past, have set a new standard for the possibilities of inner technology and prophecy. How could our ancestors have glimpsed events still to come in our time? Perhaps more important, how accurate are their visions of our future?

## Remote Viewing: Twentieth-Century Prophets

The word *prophet* conjures up images of ancient seers draped in hooded robes, embarking upon open-eyed dream quests into a time yet to come. In the traditions of biblical prophets, this may well be the case. The science of prophecy, however, has continued into the present as a respected profession clad in the mystery of a new name.

Based on research conducted at the prestigious Stanford Research Institute (SRI) during the early 1970s,[5] the ability to witness events from a distance has been called *remote viewing*. Though the specifics for remote viewing may vary from person to person, the general procedure is similar for each viewer. Often beginning in a mild, closed-eye state of relaxation, the receiver works with sensory impressions regarding events that may be occurring anywhere on the planet—in the next room or at a desert outpost halfway around the world. Trained to distinguish among the many kinds of sensations, the viewer then assigns identifiers to the experience, refining the impressions to greater levels of detail. Sounds, smells, tastes, and sensations, as well as images, may accompany such a journey. The training that teaches remote viewers to accept and record such impressions without bias is the expertise that sets them apart from the casual dreamer. With obvious implications for secrecy and intelligence, such capabilities suggest an entire new realm of intelligence gathering with fewer risks.

Remote viewing now plays a viable role in the security and defense of nations in the free world. In 1991, for example, remote viewers working under the auspices of Science Applications International Corporation (SAIC) were asked to narrow the search area for a particular kind of missile in western Iraq.[6] Confining the search to specific portions of the Iraqi desert held the potential to save time, fuel, and lives, as well as money. Clearly, remote viewing, the ability to project the awareness of an individual from one location to another, had become the subject of serious study. Ironically, it is only now, in the last years of the second millennium, that modern science has confirmed the principles of such inner technology, understood by prophets 2,500 years ago.

For many people, their first exposure to the science of viewing real-time events from a distance has come about through guests on late-night radio talk shows. Sparked by the approaching millennium, a variety of experts in the field of future and remote vision claim to have ventured into the world of a postmillennial earth, sometimes with disturbing, yet not surprising, results. Similar to the descriptions of other millennial prophecies, remote journeys into our future have generally fallen into one of two categories of experience. Some viewers found that they could see no further than the year A.D. 2012, the familiar year of the Mayan calendar and the close of our great cycle. In 2012, the time travelers reported seeing a very different earth. From their present-day vantage point, the world appeared to have experienced some form of cataclysm. They reported no buildings, no sign of commerce or normalcy by today's standards. The viewers of A.D. 2012 may well have found themselves in the presence of an outcome that has been described by seers and prophets alike, the postwar destruction of much of our world as we know it today.

Other viewers peering into our future in recent times report a similar scenario, with the addition of a great wave of fire and heat. This scenario is reminiscent of theories anticipating cyclic waves of proton flux and plasma that travel through the cosmos over tremendous cycles of time, occasionally finding earth in their path. With either scenario, the reports of the remote viewers describe a future that appears to be something less than inviting. Following a common theme of many millennial prophecies, there may be an alternative to such outcomes.

## Nostradamus

For over four hundred years, the word *prophecy* has been nearly synonymous with the name of a great seer whose visions extended hundreds of years into the future. Born on December 14, 1503, Michel de Nostredame became known as Nostradamus, perhaps the most illustrious prophet of recent memory. His gift of second sight allowed him to peer into the future of his time, witnessing events with extraordinary detail and accuracy. As he studied ancient oracles, he developed his own techniques for navigating the waves of time as an observer, often bringing future technologies seen in his visions back into his time. Eventually, Nostradamus became a physician, incorporating many of the ideas from his prophecies into his practice. His techniques, appearing as common sense today, were revolutionary for sixteenth-century Europe during the time of the Black Plague, and included the use of herbs, fresh air, and clean water. Additionally, he prescribed mixtures of aloe and rose petals, rich in vitamins unknown in his time.

One of the best-known reports of Nostradamus's ability to peer into the future began unexpectedly as he met a group of friars walking along a road. Immediately kneeling at the feet of one man, Nostradamus kissed the robe of the friar. When asked why, he simply replied, "I must bend a knee before His Holiness." It was not until forty years later, *nineteen years after the death of Nostradamus,* that the mysterious event on the lonely road made sense. In 1585, the friar whose robes the prophet had kissed became Pope Sixtus V.

In what is perhaps his best-known work, *The Centuries,* Nostradamus recorded his visions of our future. By the time of his death he had recorded visions for ten centuries, each with one hundred verses of four lines each, called quatrains. Remaining in print consistently since the time of his death, the prophecies of Nostradamus extend into the year 3797 and, depending upon interpretation, perhaps beyond.

Foreseeing social, political, and scientific events of global magnitude, many of his visions appear to be exceedingly accurate. Without specific dates, others are nebulous at best and subject to interpretation. Nostradamus noted two world wars, complete with the name of Hitler and a description of the swastika symbol, the discoveries of penicillin and nuclear energy, the assassination of John F. Kennedy, the AIDS virus, and the failure of Communism. Though dates and events may be subject to interpretation, there is a thread of agreement among scholars of Nostradamus that the prophet foresaw cataclysmic change, on a global scale, for the close of our millennium.

Although the precise timing of an event could certainly be calculated by his readers from key phrases, it was only when he felt that a particular event was critical that Nostradamus offered the actual date. It is of particular interest, then, that one of these dates occurs within our lifetime. Centuries X, quatrain 72, reads, "In the year 1999, and seven months from the sky will come the great King of Terror. He will bring to life the great King of the Mongols. Before and after, war reigns happily."[7] Additional insight into this ominous quatrain may be found in *The Epistle to Henry II,* verse 87, where Nostradamus writes that, "This will be preceded by an eclipse of the sun, more obscure and tenebrous than has ever been since the creation of the world, except that after the death and passion of Jesus Christ." A solar eclipse, visible from much of the European continent, did occur on August 11, 1999.

Nostradamus's visions also foresaw cataclysmic earth changes reminiscent of those found in Native American and biblical traditions. Continuing in verse 88 of the epistle to Henry II, specifics are offered down to the actual month. "There will be omens in the spring, and extraordinary changes thereafter, reversals of nations and mighty earthquakes. . . . And there shall be in the month of October a great movement of the globe, and it will be such that one will think the earth has lost its natural gravitational movement and that it will be plunged into the abyss of perpetual darkness."

Looking farther into our future, Nostradamus saw a much happier time following the days of earth's darkness. In a passage from Centuries II, quatrain 12, scholars interpret Nostradamus's vision as depicting a time of spiritual renewal: "The body without a soul is no longer at the sacrifice. At the day of death it comes to rebirth." Centuries III further describes this time in our future in quatrain 2: "The divine word will give the sustance containing heaven and earth. . . . Body, soul, and spirit are all powerful. Everything is beneath his feet, as at the seat of heaven." Certainly less than scientific and open to much interpretation, nevertheless these sixteenth-century visions of our future share common threads with those of other prophets, both older and more recent.

# Edgar Cayce

Edgar Cayce is the man who came to be known as the "sleeping prophet" of the twentieth century. Born in March 1877, Cayce's formal education ended when he completed the ninth grade. Though he reported paranormal experiences as a child, he did not develop his gifts of clairvoyance and healing on a large scale until adulthood.

Limiting his healing sessions to two per day, Cayce often journeyed into the past experiences of his clients in an effort to understand their present conditions. Though he did not remember the contents of his readings when he awakened from the trancelike state in which he conducted them, Cayce's secretary, Gladys Davis, was always present to record the sessions. Through hundreds of such records, systematically catalogued for study at the Association for Research and Enlightenment (ARE), Cayce offered brief glimpses into the recesses of our forgotten past, as well as our millennial future.

Edgar Cayce's first healing, reported to have occurred at the age of twenty-four, was one that he performed upon himself. With the aid of a hypnotist, Cayce was asked to address a persistent throat condition while in a relaxed state of altered consciousness. To the surprise of others in the room, in his "sleeping state" Cayce began to speak, directing the hypnotist to offer suggestions to his unconscious body. Responding almost immediately to instructions redirecting the flow of blood in his upper body, the throat condition disappeared and Edgar Cayce began what would become a lifelong service of performing similar readings for others.

The accuracy of Cayce's readings is well documented. He foresaw the crash of the stock market in October of 1929 through reading #137-117: "There must surely come a break where it would be panic in the money centers—not only of Wall Street's activity but a closing of the boards in many centers. . . ."[8] Cayce witnessed what would later be called the Second World War, years before it occurred. In his future vision of the conflict (reading #416-7), he stated that countries would begin to take sides as "indicated by the Austrians, Germans and later the Japanese joining in their influence. . . ."[9] His description continues, stating that unless there was intervention by a force that he described as supernatural, "the affairs of nations and peoples, the whole world, as it were, will be set on fire by the militaristic groups and those that are for power and expansion. . . ."[10]

In what were to become some of his best-known yet confusing prophecies, Cayce suggested that the final years of the twentieth century and the early years of the twenty-first would be a time of unprecedented earth changes. As with past seers, he envisioned global changes falling into two broad categories: a future brought about by gradual change, and a time of tumultuous shifts that may be described as nothing short of catastrophic. *Interestingly, both kinds of prophecy occur for the same period in time.*

In reading #826-8, dated August 1936, Cayce is asked specifically about changes that he sees for the actual years of the millennium, 2000 to 2001. Far from the vagueness of many such prophecies, his response is a direct statement regarding a tangible shift of measurable change on the earth. "There is the shifting of the pole. Or a new cycle begins. . . ."[11] Fluctuations of the earth's magnetic poles of over five degrees in the last forty years, considered with the rapid decrease of magnetic intensity preceding such polar reversals in earth's history, have brought a renewed respect to such visions.

In a series of readings that culminated in January of 1934, Cayce described geographic and geophysical changes that he saw beginning within a forty-year period between 1958 and 1998.[12] One key to interpreting these indicators is that they were prophesied to *begin,* rather than *happen,* by 1998. Such changes could conceivably extend well into the next century. Mark Thurston, a leading expert in the teachings and philosophies of Edgar Cayce, summarizes Cayce's descriptions as follows:

1. There will be a breaking up of the landmass of the western portion of America.
2. The larger part of Japan will go into the sea.
3. There will be certain changes to the northern parts of Europe that will happen so quickly that it might be called "in the twinkling of an eye."
4. Lands will rise up out of the Atlantic Ocean off the coast of America.
5. Major upheavals will hit the Arctic and Antarctic.
6. Volcanoes will erupt, especially in the tropics.
7. A shifting of the poles will alter climatic conditions. For example, certain frigid and semitropical areas will become tropical.

As Thurston points out, several of these changes appear to be connected directly to a magnetic pole shift. Although a complete shift has yet to occur, a growing body of scientists and researchers believe that recent shifts of earth's magnetic fields are the precursors to precisely such an event.[13]

Although a number of Cayce's earlier predictions regarding millennial prophecies appear to be catastrophic in nature, later readings note an interesting though subtle change. In a reading dated 1939, Cayce's view into the close of the century describes *gradual changes* rather than the sudden shifts described earlier. Cayce states that "in 1998 we will find a great deal of activity that has been created by the gradual changes that are coming about."[14] He continues speaking about the millennial shift by stating that "as to the changes, the change between the Piscean and the Aquarian Age is gradual, not a cataclysmic one."[15]

In offering two different views of the change of centuries, Cayce may additionally have offered a new insight into the value of prophecy in our lives today. Recognizing that his readings of catastrophic as well as gradual changes were made within a matter of years from one another rather than centuries, what change in our future could the difference in his readings suggest?

Regardless of whose visions into our future we consider, for the most part each appears to escape exact measurements of time. They appear to represent moments of possibility, rather than a concrete appointment with a precise outcome. In his own words, the "sleeping prophet" offers a key to the science of prophecy, reminding us that we influence the outcome of history through the course of our lives in the present. In reading #311-10,[16] Cayce suggests that our response to the challenges of our lives may determine, at least in part, the degree to which we experience the changes he foresaw. "[It] may depend upon much that deals with the metaphysical. . . . There are those conditions that in the activity of individuals, in line of thought and endeavor, keep oft many a city and many a land intact through their application of spiritual laws."

## Native American Prophecies

Native North and South American peoples believe firmly that present-day events echo details of their ancestors' prophecy. For many, visions of a world to come have been held secretly in tribal traditions to preserve the integrity of their ancestors' insight. Sensing that the shift of the millennium represents the day of tribal prophecies, their guidelines for this time in history are now shared openly. The belief is that people of all walks of life, in all nations, may benefit from the insights left long ago. Allowing for specific differences in family and tribal traditions, there are common threads that link many of the tribal prophecies of the Americas in a unified vision of our future.

The Hopi of the American Southwest offer some of the most concise visions of our future in their prophecies of the birth of a new sun. Similar to the traditions of the Maya, the Aztecs, and earlier indigenous traditions found throughout the Americas, the Hopi believe that there have been great cycles of human experience before our time. Each ended in a period of destruction, the most recent of which was the Great Flood. We are living near the close of one such cycle, they say, preparing to move into the days of the Fifth Sun. Prior to the close of our cycle, Hopi prophecies describe a period of decline followed by a transition period into the next cycle. From their perspective, the time of decline is a time of great challenge, often called the "time of purification." Understanding that the earth and our bodies are one, the Hopi view the conditions of the earth as a "feedback mechanism," a barometer of sorts, reminding us of when we have made choices that affirm or deny life in our world.

One of the first Hopi visions to be disclosed were three signs denoting a timetable for the Great Shift. The first sign was the appearance of the moon "on the earth as well as in the heavens." The fulfillment of this portion of the prophecy remained a mystery until 1993, when lunar images began to appear as crop circles in the grain fields of the English countryside. The unmistakable images of the crescent moon were interpreted by Hopi elders as the fulfillment of the first portion of their prophecy.

The second sign was the appearance of the "blue star," a symbol that is common in the folklore and myths of many Hopi traditions. Some Hopi elders saw the 1994 impact of the Comet Shoemaker-Levy into Jupiter as the fulfillment of this prophecy. Researchers were mystified as to how the impact of a broken comet could be seen as the fulfillment of the prophecy. Their answer was revealed when spectrographic images of the giant planet were viewed following the collisions; Jupiter was glowing with a curious blue hue that could be seen only with sophisticated imaging devices!

Perhaps the most mystical sign of the Hopi prophecies is the third and last. Prominent in the dance, weavings, and sand paintings of the Hopi are curious, humanoid images that often adorn their homes and ceremonial sites. With strange costumes and very otherworldly faces, these representations of Hopi ancestry, the sky people, are called *kachinas*. The third portion of the Hopi prophecy states that the time of the great change has occurred when the kachinas return from the stars and dance once again in the plazas of their villages on the mesas. To the best of my knowledge at the time of this writing, this third sign has yet to happen.

## Biblical Prophecies

As documented in chapter 2 of this book, a number of books related to the modern Bible were deemed inappropriate for official acceptance by the Catholic Church in the fourth century. Relegated to the obscurity of Church vaults and private libraries, one of the most fascinating, and perhaps most mystical, is the ancient book of the prophet Enoch. Containing eloquent descriptions of the Creation, human lineage, and astronomical information so detailed that it could only be verified with twentieth-century technology, this ancient text came to be known as the Book of the Secrets of Enoch. We find direct references to this now-rare text in the work of the second-century theologian Tertullian. In recently recovered letters he explains that the "Scripture of Enoch" is not treated in the same way as other scriptures because it is not included in the Hebrew Canon.[17] Such references confirm that the Book of Enoch was regarded as a viable work by scholars before the fourth-century edits of the Nicean Council.

The prophecies of Enoch bear a remarkable resemblance to those of subsequent biblical prophets such as Isaiah and, later, John in the Book of Revelation. In tremendous detail, Enoch describes his journey of prophecy into our future to his son, Methuselah, who records his father's experience for the generations that will follow. From an Ethiopian manuscript discovered in the Bodleian Library in 1773, Enoch shares his vision of weather and celestial changes that he foresaw during the close of our century. Identified as the "seventh son after Adam," Methuselah characterizes his father's prophetic experiences very differently from those of the sleeping Cayce, for example, when he says that Enoch "spoke while his eyes were open, and while he saw a holy vision in the heavens."[18]

Following his great visions of our future, Enoch stated that he had "heard all things, and understood what he saw; that which will not take place in his generation, but in a generation which is to succeed at a distant period, on account of the elect. . . . In those days . . . the rain shall be restrained . . . the fruits of the earth shall be late, and not flourish in their season; and in their season the fruits of the trees shall be withholden . . . heaven shall stand still. The moon shall change its laws, and not be seen at its proper period. . . ."[19]

Immediately following the tribulation that he describes for the earth, Enoch describes an additional sequence of events embodying a time of beauty, hope, and possibility. In this sequence, appearing as if it originates from a different vision describing a different time, Enoch sees the former heaven "depart and pass away," and declares that "a new heaven shall appear." This odd pattern of tribulation, appearing to be followed by redemption, is common throughout the visions of Enoch, as well as other prophecies that we will examine.

Perhaps the most emotionally charged insights into future times may be found as a collection of prophetic visions in the modern biblical texts. Ranging from the fate of specific leaders and heads of state to global visions of the end of time, prophecies of the Bible continue to elicit powerful responses from those who read them, thousands of years after the visions themselves occurred. Ranging from ceaseless curiosity to adamant fervor, clues into the power, as well as confusion surrounding such visions may be found in tracing their modern interpretations to the roots of the original visions themselves.

It is not uncommon to discover, for example, that many of the prophecies referenced today were not even recorded until years, *sometimes hundreds of years,* after an original prophecy was received. Because they were handed from mouth to mouth, from generation to generation, it is uncertain whether some prophetic books were written by the prophets themselves or by others using the name of a prophet as a metaphor in the stories.

The Book of Daniel offers such an example. In the Saint Joseph Edition of the New American Bible, the preface to the Book of Daniel states that "this book takes its name, not from the author, who is actually unknown, but from its hero, a young Jew taken early to Babylon, where he lived at least until 538 B.C."[20] The introduction goes on to say, "The Book contains stories originating in and transmitted by popular traditions which tell of the trials and triumphs of the wise Daniel and his three companions."

This interpretation directly contradicts that of other biblical scholars, such as John Walvoord, who states that "it is clear that the book itself claims to be a product of Daniel as he is referred to in the first person in numerous passages in the second half of the book. . . . Daniel is also mentioned in Ezekiel, which would be quite natural as Ezekiel was a contemporary of Daniel. . . ."[21] Even today, nearly two millennia after the texts were compiled, experts have yet to reach a consensus regarding even the basics of some of our most sacred texts. Adding to the confusion of deciphering biblical prophecies is the question of the precision with which the wording has, or has not, been translated through the centuries. Unlike portions of the Hebrew Bible, known to be translated letter for letter with exacting precision for at least the last thousand years,* the Western Bible has undergone many changes. Even since the time of our country's founding, less than three hundred years ago, adaptations, translations from one language to another, and various interpretations of the Bible have introduced a certain margin of error. As accurate as our biblical collection of history, genealogy, and wisdom may be in some respects, it cannot be taken word for word; the text changes with each translation. Often there are simply no words in one language that represent exactly the same concept, in the same way, as it is expressed in another language. In these instances, the translators must do the best that they can. This is where an *approximation* of themes and concepts may be introduced into such translations.

The Western Bible, as we know it today, has undergone many such processes, including a translation from the highly symbolic language of Egyptian, following its origins in the Aramaic and Hebrew languages. An example of how approximation may subtly alter a well-intended translation is illustrated in the Aramaic words for the first line of the Lord's Prayer. In English, this phrase reads as the familiar "Our Father which art in heaven." In the original Aramaic, however, the same phrase reads simply as two words: *Abwoon d'bwashmaya.* There are no exact words in English for these two Aramaic words. Translators are left to skillfully create collections of English words that approximate the original meaning. A

---

*The Leningrad codex dates to A.D. 1008. Since that time, scholars agree that the first five books of the Hebrew Old Testament have remained unchanged.

sampling of such approximations is illustrated by the following possible translations of this example from the Lord's Prayer: "O Birther! Father-Mother of the Cosmos," "O Thou! The Breathing Life of all," "Name of names, our small identity unravels within you," and "Radiant One: You shine within us."[22] Each of these is a valid translation of the original words, and each expresses a very different feeling for the intent of the original text.

From this example alone, we may see that the theme remains constant, although the specifics of language may vary. As in photocopying the original of a text today, many copies down the line the final outcome may bear a resemblance to the original, though it has lost clarity. In the last century of biblical history, there have been many such opportunities to introduce error into the original intent of the ancient prophets. Today we may choose from a variety of interpretations and translations, each meeting a special need and serving a particular application for its reader. A student of biblical studies may choose from the King James Version of the biblical texts or a host of others, such as the New International Standard Version, The New Living Bible, and the Saint Joseph Edition. Each version originates from the same collection of scrolls, books, documents, and manuscripts accepted by the Church in the fourth century A.D.

## The Lost Prophecy

In modern renditions of biblical prophecies, we find a particular class of visionary texts identified by such names as "the End of Time," "the End Days," or "in those days." Collectively these works are known as the *apocalyptic prophecies*. Often believed to identify a frightening time of darkness and cataclysm in earth's future, these works may, in fact, have been showing future generations something of a vastly different nature.

In modern times the word *apocalypse* conjures up deep feelings of gloom, hopelessness, and judgment in our collective psyche. Taken from the Greek word *apokalypsis,* the word has a brief and seemingly innocent definition. It simply means to disclose or reveal. This is precisely what the ancient prophets offered through their masterful insights into our future. They *revealed* possible outcomes based on the conditions of their time, and *disclosed* their discoveries to future generations.

*The Essene Book of Revelation* is an example of one such book. Recovered and translated from the native Aramaic language that it was written in, this version of Revelation is so similar to later canonized versions known as the Revelation to John that researchers and scholars suspect the Dead Sea manuscript may be the original rendition of this ancient view into our future.

Regarded by many as the most mystical of the biblical prophecies, the visions of John the Apostle also portray some of the most graphic descriptions of tribulation in any prophecy, ancient or modern. Contributing to what is already a deeply symbolic and esoteric text is the fragmented nature of John's vision. During the canonization of the Bible in 325, it appears almost as if a compromise were reached regarding some of the key texts. Rather than discarding the manuscripts completely, they were retained as edited versions, thus condensing them into a format that was believed to be more accessible to the readers of the time.

The journey that becomes John's revelation to future generations begins as he asks to be taken from his time, ahead of our time, and allowed to see our probable future and one possible end to the close of our millennium. Through graphic detail, John describes his vision of chaos, death, terror, and destruction, the magnitude of which had never been seen before. He asks his angelic guide why these things are happening, and the angel replies, "Man has created these powers of destruction. He has wrought them from his own mind. He has turned his face away from the Angels [forces] of the Heavenly Father and the Earthly Mother, and he has fashioned his own destruction."[23]

Upon witnessing this outcome, John's heart is "heavy with compassion." He asks, "Is there no hope?" The voice replies to John, echoing a memory of the greatest possibilities for today and future generations: "There is always hope, O thou for whom heaven and earth were created. . . ."[24]

Suddenly the vision of death and destruction fades from view and he is shown another scenario, *a second possibility.* Rather than the end of all that humanity has grown to know and love, this new possibility illustrates an outcome of a very different nature. "But I saw not what befell them, my vision changed, and I saw a new heaven and a new Earth: for the first heaven and the first earth were passed away. . . . And I heard a great voice . . . saying, there shall be no more death, neither sorrow, nor crying, neither shall there be any more pain."[25]

As John's vision continues, he sees a time when peace and cooperation envelop the nations of the world. During this time there is no longer a need for war. He hears his guide describe the end of warfare: "Nation shall not lift up sword against nation, neither shall they learn war anymore, for the former things are passed away."[26] Through these and similar passages, we are offered a message of hope.

Following a theme now familiar from other prophecies, John was shown two possibilities for the future of humankind. Both outcomes were real, and either could be chosen by the peoples of the earth. The key, reminiscent of our mass prayer of peace, was that the collective outcome would be determined through individual choices. The ability of the people in John's time to honor the laws of life were the experiences that would bring about new outcomes, diverting the possibility of destruction.

With each vision, John is reminded that people living "in those days" will determine how they experience the great change of humankind's future. He asks what must occur so that the second outcome of peace may come to pass? Again, the voice guiding his vision replies, "Behold, I make all things new. . . . I am the beginning and the end. . . . I will give unto him that is athirst of the fountain of the water of life freely. He that [remembers] shall inherit all things. . . ."27

The final passages record John acknowledging his understanding of what he has seen, and the effect that his vision has had upon him: "I have reached the inner vision. . . . I have heard thy wondrous secret. . . . Through thy mystic insight thou hast caused a spring of knowledge to well up within me, a fountain of power, pouring forth living waters; a flood of all-embracing wisdom."28

Additional passages from the Essene scrolls continue to detail the possibility of a time in our future when we have outgrown the need for catastrophic shifts to bring about change. During this time, the conditions that have taken life from the inhabitants of the earth are no longer present: "In the reign of peace, there is neither hunger nor thirst, neither cold wind nor hot wind, neither old age nor death. In the reign of peace, both animals and men shall be undying."29

Clearly the biblical prophets often found themselves describing very different—at times conflicting—outcomes for our future. The question is why? Why are there different visions of prophecy for the same time in our future? How can a prophet see two very different possibilities for the same period of time?

In the mid-1990s a new tool of prophecy was discovered in a very ancient format. It may be that the time lock of technology has allowed us to peer through the eyes of this prophetic instrument only as we have matured to recognize its possibilities.

## The 3,000-Year-Old Time Map

In 1995, an ancient instrument of prophecy was abruptly thrust into public view in a graphic and dramatic fashion. On November 4 of that year, an event occurred that the instrument had predicted with a precision far exceeding the possibility of chance or coincidence. The event was the assassination of Yitzhak Rabin, the prime minister of Israel, in the city of Tel Aviv. The assassination had been prophesied with such accuracy that the prime minister's name, the date of the assassination, the name of the city, and even the assassin's name, Amir, were no secret; each had been encoded into a document over three thousand years ago!

The irony was that the document was not a rare manuscript held by a secret organization or privileged individual. The coded map of our future was the same map that has provided comfort and guidance for at least seventy-five generations and is held sacred today by several hundred million people worldwide. The map of time was discovered as a hidden code encrypted into the Bible at the time of its origin! Specifically, the code was found in the first five books of the Hebrew Bible, known as the Torah, the one version that is said to have been unaltered since it was given to man over three thousand years ago.

Discovered by an Israeli mathematician, Dr. Eliyahu Rips, the key, known as the Bible Code, has been reviewed and validated by mathematicians in leading universities worldwide, as well as agencies specializing in encryption, such as the U.S. Department of Defense. For over two hundred years, scholars have suspected that biblical texts were more than an assemblage of words to be read in a strictly linear fashion. An eighteenth-century scholar, known as the Genius of Vilna, stated that "the rule is that all that was, is, and will be unto the end of time is included in the Torah, from the first word to the last word. And not merely in a general sense, but as to the details of everything that happened to him from the day of his birth until his end."[30]

The encrypted messages of our past and future may be studied by creating a matrix from the letters of the first five books of the Hebrew Bible. Beginning with the first letter of the first word, all spaces and punctuation are removed until the last letter of the last word is reached, leaving a single sentence hundreds of characters in length. Using sophisticated search programs, the remaining matrix is examined for patterns and intersections of words. For example, in the book of Genesis, the word *Torah* is spelled out with sequences of fifty Hebrew characters between each of the letters of the word. The same sequence is found in the books that follow: Exodus, Leviticus, Numbers, and Deuteronomy. The observation of this sequence by Rabbi H. M. D. Weissmandel in the 1940s became the key to unraveling the patterns of words encoded in the text.

In his book of the same name, Michael Drosnin describes the precision and accuracy of the Bible Code in predicting past events. Circumstances as varied as the Kennedy assassinations, the impact of Comet Shoemaker-Levy into Jupiter, the election of Israeli Prime Minister Netanyahu, even the dates and location of the SCUD missile attack that the Iraqis launched against Israel during the 1990 Gulf War, are described with a level of detail that defies mathematical and statistical odds. The Bible Code offers specifics rather than broad generalities that may be open to interpretation. Drosnin details many such references. In the prediction of World War II, for example, the code spells out words such as "world war" and "final solution," accompanied by the names of leaders during the time: "Roosevelt," "Churchill," "Stalin," and "Hitler." Clearly stated are the countries involved in the conflict: "Germany," "England," "France," "Russia," "Japan," and "United States." Even the words "atomic holocaust" and "1945," the year that the nuclear device was detonated over Hiroshima are disclosed, the only time those words appear in the Bible.

It was with the development of high-speed computers that the code embedded within the Hebrew Bible was finally decrypted. The new computers replaced tedious manual decoding with sophisticated search programs. Running against control groups of other texts and ten million test cases created by the computer, only the Bible was found to have the puzzlelike encryptions. Vertically, horizontally, and diagonally, names of countries, events, dates, times, and persons intersect with one another, providing a snapshot into the events of our past and the possibilities of our future. While the actual mechanism of such an extraordinary predictor is discussed in chapter seven, perhaps more relevant to the question of prophecy is how this seemingly miraculous book of time relates to our future.

In light of the Bible Code's accuracy for detailing our past, how accurate could the same matrix be in peering into a time yet to come? In his discussions with Drosnin, Dr. Rips suggests that the entire Bible Code had to be written all at once as a single act, rather than in a series of writings that took place over time. Such a statement infers that all possibilities of all futures are already in place. "We experience it like we experience a hologram—it looks different when we look at it from a new angle—but the image, of course, is prerecorded."[31] The key to applying this ancient time code to the events of our future may be in viewing it through the eyes of a quantum physicist.

In modern physics there is a tenet stating that it is impossible to know the "when" of something and the "where" of the same thing, at the same time. If you measure *where* something is, you lose information about how fast it is moving. If you measure how fast it is moving, then you cannot know with certainty *where* the something is. This key to the quantum world was developed by the physicist Werner Heisenburg, and is known as the Heisenberg uncertainty principle.[32]

Demonstrating the unpredictable behavior of nature in the quantum world, it may be that our sense of time follows precisely this kind of behavior. If so, the possibilities portrayed in the Bible Code may exist as just that, *possibilities*. The events stated, both past and future, are the end result of a sequence of conditions that may have begun days, or even hundreds of years, before the actual event plays out. Stated as we would a modern equation, *if* we choose a particular course of events, *then* we may expect to see such-and-such an outcome.

Viewing any prediction tool as a lens into possibilities sheds new light on the role of prophecy in our lives. Coinciding with many biblical, Native American, and other prophecies for our future, the Bible Code alerts us to a series of apocalyptic scenarios. Beginning in our near future, such occurrences as a third world war originating in the Middle East, catastrophic earthquakes, and the devastation of major population centers all appear as possibilities. The threat of a direct collision with a comet at the end of the twentieth century or early in the twenty-first appears to be one of the most immediate concerns.

In 1992, astronomer Brian Marsden of the Harvard-Smithsonian Center for Astrophysics announced the return of the Swift-Tuttle comet, originally discovered in 1858. The precise day of the comet's rediscovery was encrypted in the Bible Code, along with its predicted return 134 years later. The actual words "comet," "Swift-Tuttle," and the year of the comet's return, 2126, are clearly encoded in the text. Initially thought to be on a collision course with the earth at the time of its return, revised calculations now suggest that the comet will pass a safe distance away. Astronomers do, however, warn of a series of "near misses" leading up to the time of Swift-Tuttle in 2126, the first occurring in 2006. Intersecting the 2006 dateline in the Hebrew text are the words, "Its path struck their dwelling," accompanied with the phrase in an associated line, "Year predicted for the world."

Following this warning are similar words leading up to the year 2010. The words "days of horror" cross this date with additional descriptions of "darkness," "gloom," and "comet." Perhaps the most unsettling sequence of words regarding our future is found above the year 2012. It is here, coincidentally in the same year that the Mayan calendar ends, that we see the words "Earth annihilated." This glimpse into an ancient possibility for our future provides an intriguing example of an element found throughout the Bible Code. Drosnin states that in the location where the date is encoded, a second passage, describing a very different outcome, is described. The words simply say, "It will be crumbled, driven out, I will tear it to pieces, 5772" (the Hebrew year for 2012).[33]

Similar to the theme of other prophecies, on one hand the Code appears to be saying to us that the year 2012 brings an end to life as we know it, while at the same time, in another location, the threat to the earth is destroyed. How can both outcomes be possible at the same time? Similar paradoxes show up from time to time throughout the Bible Code, particularly regarding outcomes of elections, political events, and warfare. In addition to the opportunity to model specific outcomes for our future based on choices of the present, perhaps the Bible Code is reminding us of something even more significant.

In close proximity to specific outcomes, such as assassinations and the seeds of global warfare, four words appear again and again. Accompanying many of the gravest outcomes, the words pose a simple question: *"Will you change it?"* Reminiscent of the beliefs preserved for us by the ancient Essenes, the Bible Code also appears to suggest that we play a significant role in the outcome of events, even those already set into motion as possibilities. Apparently our role is so important that we may actually change the course of events! "Will you change it?" appears to be a direct question asked of those who would be certain to read the codemaker's message three thousand years after it was written. It is as if the writers knew that it would take a technology with a high degree of sophistication to understand their code; as if we are being reminded that now, as we unravel the message of the codemakers, we are ready to participate in the unfolding of time and change the darkest possibilities of our future. How could the appearance of these and other specifics appear today, in a manuscript that was encoded over three millennia ago? The Bible Code brings us back to the same questions that the prophecies of others have led us to.

## A New Prophecy

Of the many calculations and indigenous prophecies regarding our current time in history, 1998 appeared to mark the beginning of a window in time where we may expect to witness some of the greatest changes upon the earth. Precisely where within that window our lifetime places us is questionable, even to the prophets themselves. Edgar Cayce, for example, viewed 1998 as the *last year* of a cycle four decades long, in which we may expect "extraordinary planetary transformation" to begin. Nostradamus, on the other hand, placed 1998 at the *beginning* of a cycle of cataclysmic changes that he foresaw from that point to over three hundred years into our future. Beyond the discrepancies of exact dates, prophecies for our time almost universally reveal a common theme; they point to the birth of the new millennium as a time when we may expect to see great change upon the earth and within our bodies.

Along with insights into our possible future, ancient seers reminded us of a great mystery. This mystery is particularly fascinating in light of the sophistication of calendars and the precision of systems tracking time. As accurate as the oral, written, and prophetic traditions appear to be, *each stops short of detailing precisely how this great cycle of time will end and the next great cycle will begin.* In addition to outlining possibilities for our future, those who have come before us acknowledged a potent force with the power to choose which possibility we experience. Largely overlooked in recent times, that force is the power of mass choice expressed as the science of mass prayer.

In the language of their time, ancient prophets suggested that we have the ability to avert their visions of destruction in our future by consciously shifting the course of time in the present. It would appear as though many of the traditions of those before us had insight into a relationship between the actions of the people in this world and the outcome of the prophecies that they foresaw. That connection between our day-to-day routines and the outcome of prophecy has remained a mystery until the twentieth century. It is during this time, with the formulation of a new physics, that the possibilities of time, prophecy, miracles, and our role in the future of humankind have became clearer. We now know that predictions offer isolated possibilities only. We also know that we choose our possibilities with each breath that we take in each moment of each day.

Time is not at all what it seems.

It does not flow in only one direction,

and the future exists simultaneously

with the past.

—ALBERT EINSTEIN

4

# WAVES, RIVERS, AND ROADS

### The Physics of Time and Prophecy

On the threshold of a new millennium, two lines of thinking have surfaced regarding the significance of this rare moment in history. There are those who believe we are in danger, living in a dangerous time of perilous uncertainty. They have become preoccupied with preparations for physical survival in the days that they believe begin the "end times." Referencing ancient prophecies, the ills of society, and the looming potential of world disasters to support their beliefs, for them each news item of global conflict, new diseases, or the pending collapse of the world economy becomes further evidence to support their beliefs. At the same time others, *citing identical evidence,* see change of a very different kind unfolding.

Witnessing the same diseases, military conflicts, and extremes of nature, and referencing the same prophecies, those who subscribe to this second viewpoint sense that a rare birth is occurring, an integral element of which is an equally rare shift within humankind. Ultimately, this view suggests that we are entering a time of joy, peace, and unprecedented cooperation among the peoples and nations of the world. How can interpretations of the same evidence produce such varied and diverse viewpoints? Perhaps of more significance, is our future already sealed as the product of an ancient plan, or is there a science that allows us to choose which future we experience?

## Time and Group Will

Quickly I reached under the seat for my belt pack and personal belongings. I could smell the unmistakable odor of hot brake pads as the driver brought our German-built touring coach to a stop. For the last two hours or so, we had negotiated a winding mountain road that became little more than a jeep trail in places. Because of rockslides, blowing sand, and infrequent maintenance, several times the road had narrowed to just a fraction of a single lane. Each time our driver had masterfully eased us through the tight spots, sometimes choosing circuitous detours that always brought us back to the safety of the main roadway. Descending from the village of St. Catherine, 4,300 feet above the Egyptian desert, I knew that the checkpoint on the road ahead was near sea level.

The engine, a rest room, and bulging luggage compartments replaced the windows normally located in the rear of a touring bus. Moving to a side window, I glanced to the large mirrors on one side of the bus to see behind us. The military truck that had escorted us through the mountains was still there, perhaps two car lengths back. Looking over the head of our driver, I could see that an escort vehicle similar to the one behind us had pulled off the road, near a concrete guardhouse. The camouflaged truck was a troop carrier, its back covered by dull, sand-colored fabric, stretched over a series of wire hoops and fastened to the bed of the vehicle. I remember thinking of the similarities between the military trucks in the deserts of Egypt and the covered wagons of the American West that I had seen in museums as a child.

The morning light peeking from behind the mountains suddenly brought the reality of these trucks to life. In the first rays of the desert sun, I could see the faces of soldiers, young Egyptian men peering back at us from their benches beneath the tarp. With perhaps five men seated on either side of the truck bed, their job was to escort us safely across the Sinai Desert, into the massive city of Cairo. Nearly as fast as the local weather changes, the political situation had unexpectedly shifted during our time in the mountains. Now, for our overland route back to the hotel, a checkpoint system had been set up for our safety and to establish our whereabouts at all times. I knew that it would only be a matter of moments before a guard stepped onto our bus and approved our travel papers, and we would be on our way.

Clearing the first of a series of checkpoints, we soon found ourselves winding our way along the brilliant white beaches of the Red Sea toward the Suez Canal. I closed my eyes and imagined the same scene over three thousand years ago, as the people of Egypt traveled a similar route to the mountain from which we were now returning. Except for the transportation and roads, how much had really changed? In the warmth of the late-morning sun, I soon found myself in conversation with members of our group, anticipating our entrance into the ancient chambers of the Great Pyramid that evening.

Suddenly I looked up as our bus came to a halt along a busy boulevard. From my seat near the front, I glanced through the windows at landmarks to orient myself. To our left was a familiar sight, one that I had seen many times in magazines, as well as in person. To confirm our location, I looked to our right. We were stopped in front of a monument that is one of the most powerful symbols to all Egyptians, perhaps of even greater significance than the pyramids themselves: the tomb of former Egyptian president Anwar Sadat.

As I moved toward the front of the bus, I could see the escorts in front of us. The soldiers had jumped out from under the canopies and were milling around in front of our bus with our driver. Hopping from the last step of our bus onto the street, I noticed something very unusual. The escorts, our driver, and our Egyptian guide, Mohammed, all had puzzled expressions on their faces. Some were tapping their wristwatches. Others were anxiously speaking to one another in short bursts of Egyptian.

"What's happening?" I asked our guide. "Why have we stopped here rather than at our hotel, still an hour or so away?"

Mohammed looked at me in awe. "Something is not right," he said, with a rare intensity to his normally playful voice. "We should not be here yet!"

"What are you saying?" I asked. "This is precisely where we should be, on the way to our hotel in Giza."

"No," he said. "You do not understand. We *cannot* be here yet. It has not been long enough since our departure from St. Catherine's for us to be in Cairo! It takes at least seven hours for us to make the drive under the Suez Canal, across the desert, and into the mountains. *At least seven hours.* With the checkpoint stops, *we should be even later.* Look at the guards. They do not believe their eyes! It has been only four hours. Our being here is a miracle."

Watching the men in front of me, an odd feeling swept over my body. Though I had had experiences similar to this one when I was alone, it had never happened to me in a group. Observing the speed limits, with the extra stops of checkpoints, how could we have cut our driving time nearly by half?

Though the distance between Mount Sinai and Cairo had not changed, our experience of time while we traveled the distance had.

It was recorded on the wristwatches of every military man, armed guard, and passenger on the bus! It was as if our memories of the day, in the presence of one another, had somehow been squeezed into an experience a fraction of the time expected. Where was the rest of our time? Clearly we were not aware of the phenomenon when it was occurring. The questions are, how did it happen and why?

Perhaps herein we find the clue. In our innocence of anticipating the experiences within the pyramids and speaking of the experiences as if we were already there inside of the ancient chambers, our awareness had shifted from how long the trip was taking to what it felt like to *be there*.

## Medicineless Miracle

The lights dimmed as we neared the chairs in the back of the room. Arriving later than expected, my wife and I found few choices remaining for two seats together. Facing generally toward a table at the opposite end of the ballroom, the stainless-steel chairs appeared to have been arranged rather haphazardly by the hotel staff. Within moments of finding our seats, the class began with the usual formalities and introductions.

While studying at a specialized clinic outside of Beijing, our instructor had documented on video the effects of an ancient healing art based on techniques of movement, breath, thought, and feeling. He began by preparing us for what we were about to see. The video would show a phenomenon from Asian traditions that Western science could not explain. Anomalous experiences of this kind are often classified as miracles. For people who had turned to this clinic as a last resort, the choice of love, specialized movement, and the development of life force (*ch'i*) over medicine and surgery was the answer to their prayers.

Just as the light in our room disappeared, a television near our instructor came alive. My wife and I gripped the steel legs underneath our seats and scooted forward, vying for a better view of the screen. The videotape that we were seeing had been recorded at the Huaxia Zhineng Qigong Clinic and Training Center, the "medicineless hospital" in the city of Qinhuangdao, China. The footage began by showing a female patient lying on her back in a clinical setting. She appeared to be fully awake and conscious, not anesthetized, and there were no indications that an anesthetic would be used. The woman was loosely clothed, and her shirt had been modestly drawn up to expose her lower abdomen. In the lights of the video and the hospital room, her stomach glistened with a preparatory gel that appeared shiny and wet. Seated to the patient's right, a nurse practitioner moved an ultrasound wand across the taut, smooth surface of the woman's stomach.

Directly behind the patient were three male practitioners. Dressed in white medical jackets, they were standing only inches from her side. The men appeared to be very focused, standing quietly near her upper body. One of the men began a motion with his hands, silently moving them through the air above the woman's face and chest.

The video next showed the ultrasound image, allowing us to peer into the woman's bladder during the procedure. The lining and curvature were clearly present. In this image, something else began to appear, something that should not have been there.

"You are looking at a bladder cancer," our instructor explained, "a tumor approximately three inches in diameter inside the woman's bladder."

We were seeing the tumor as it actually appeared in that moment, captured by the ultrasound wand. The camera zoomed in on the screen as we witnessed an event for which Western science has no explanation. Anticipating what was about to happen, our room became very still. Even the old folding chairs stopped squeaking while our group watched, in awe, as the miracle unfolded before our eyes.

While the nurse continued to monitor the event through ultrasound, the three men standing behind the patient worked together. In unison, they participated in a mode of healing that has been known for centuries. The only sound that betrayed the process was coming from the men themselves. They repeated a single word again and again, a word that became louder and more intense as the healing progressed. Loosely translated into English, they were saying "already gone," "already accomplished."

The shift began slowly, almost indiscernibly. The cancerous form began to quiver, as if responding to some unseen force. As the movement continued, with the rest of the image in perfect focus, the entire mass began to fade from view. Within seconds, the tumor appeared to melt before our eyes. In only two minutes and forty seconds, the tumor was gone. It had simply disappeared! A healing had occurred, one so complete that the ultrasound did not even indicate scarring in the tissue that the tumor had invaded. As the camera backed away from the computer screen, the patient, still awake and conscious, appeared to be relieved by what she heard in the room. The nurse and the three men conferred among themselves, then nodded in agreement; their process had been successful. Politely, each bowed from the waist and softly clapped his hands, acknowledging their accomplishment.

At first, our conference room was silent. Then I heard sighs that gave way to gasps and cheers for what we had witnessed. What had just happened? How had a cancerous tumor, three inches in diameter, disappeared from inside the woman's body without even the telltale scars of such a condition, in a matter of moments?

Why is it that Western science has no mechanism to explain such an occurrence?

Both of the previous stories are important for two reasons. First, each illustrates a shared experience in the presence of a group, rather than the unique experience of one individual. Whatever happened to our perception of time on that day in the Sinai Desert of Egypt, it happened to many people of varying backgrounds, beliefs, and faiths. There were Muslim and Christian guards as well as Muslim, Buddhist, Jewish, and Christian travelers in our group as we made our way across the Sinai Peninsula. All of us had our own beliefs about our relationship to this world, and our own reasons for being in the desert that morning. Likewise, the disappearance of the cancer was witnessed by four people in the presence of the woman with the tumor. Additionally, it was recorded by a cameraman, bringing to five the number of people immediately present. This was a group experience as well.

For our group on the bus, the anticipation of being in Cairo, sealed inside the Great Pyramid for four hours of private access, was the dominant theme of the day. For many of our circle of friends, this was the culmination of a dream that began in childhood and had been made possible through hard work and months of planning. The key to this story and the healing of the woman's cancer is that the group's focus was on the *feeling of the outcome* rather than on the *feeling of how long it was taking* for the outcome to occur. This is a subtle yet powerful distinction that will be of even greater significance in later discussions.

The second reason I have shared these stories is that the events in each instance are unaccounted for in Western science at present. How are we to explain an occurrence that we have personally experienced, such as time compression or instantaneous physical healing, in the absence of a belief system that allows for such an event? Perhaps the way to answer these questions is to explore the nature of time through the eyes of our ancestors as well as modern science.

## The Mystery of Time

Since humankind began recording the accounts of our experience in this world, time has appeared to us as a concept of intrigue. Our only method of exploring the mysterious quality that we experience as time has been to speculate about its nature. Without the ability to capture, photograph, or record time itself, we are left with relative measurements of events that occur *within* time. Such measurements are often described as "now" and "then" or "before" and "after" the event. Indigenous traditions sometimes view time as a river, flowing in a single direction, with the experiences of humankind in some way inextricably bound to the life of the flow. Other traditions consider time as a road, transcending the membranes of space, that may be traveled in two directions. This perspective suggests that time originates somewhere and ends somewhere, leaving us to travel and experience the points between.

Regardless of how we perceive the space between "then" and "now," time has become the dominant factor in the way we view our lives. Our days consist of preparing for our future as we plan the events of the next moment, the next day, and the following year. From seemingly insignificant events, such as where we will have lunch in twenty minutes, to monumental milestones, such as the rendezvous of two craft from two different nations in space, time is the common thread that weaves us together through the synchronization of experiences in our world.

In light of the prophecies regarding future possibilities, our understanding of time may be of greater significance now than at any other point in recorded human history. *There is an ancient school of thought, a belief that has persisted for at least five thousand years, suggesting that time and the events of our future are not only inextricably related, but are consistent and knowable as well.* Furthermore, this line of reasoning suggests that the catastrophic events of prophecy, those with the potential to threaten the very existence of our species, may be known and avoided, or, at the very least, prepared for. A fresh body of research, conducted by the leading physicists and mathematicians of our day, now lends credibility to this line of reasoning. One thing appears to be certain: To understand prophecy as events that happen within time, we must first understand the nature of time itself.

## Conflicting Science

Surprisingly, much of the same science that scoffs at miracles and prophecy has yet to reach agreement on even the basic nature of our world. Though our technology may have placed mechanized sensors on the surface of other worlds and extended our senses to the edge of our known universe, we are still uncertain about who has come before us, and even about the age of the earth itself.

For nearly one hundred years, for example, the science of physics has been embroiled in a struggle to define the forces responsible for the events of our everyday world—the same forces that changed the appearance of the woman's tumor and compressed our sense of time in Egypt. It is believed that, once discovered, the mechanism responsible for the events of our daily lives ultimately will describe the workings of the cosmos. Divided into two main camps of thinking, the theories of classical physics and quantum physics make up the landscape of these two possibilities.

Classical physics is the set of laws that were used to explain our world until approximately the 1920s. Sir Isaac Newton's laws of motion, Maxwell's theories of electricity and magnetism, and Einstein's theories of relativity, for example, had been successful in explaining the observations of everyday events until that time. Developing technologies, however, allowed scientists to look beyond everyday events, and there they saw expressions of nature that could not be explained by classical physics. From the world of subatomic particles and distant galaxies, a modified physics began to emerge to account for newly observed phenomena. Proposing science-fiction-like theories of time travel and parallel universes, the mathematics of such possibilities became the science of quantum physics.

In some instances, the two schools of thought were in opposition. One of the keys to the controversy was whether the experiences of our world were produced by a predetermined sequence of events that may be known, or whether a degree of randomness was inherent in the process of life. In other words, if we could identify all of the events leading up to a given moment, would we have the information necessary to predict the outcome of the moment, or was there another agent of change that could not be accounted for in such knowledge? Stated in the present tense, can an event already set in motion change for no obvious physical reason, with no apparent force acting upon it?

The idea that a given outcome occurs only because of prior events is called *determinism*. Attributed to the German philosopher Gottfried Leibniz, determinism states that everything witnessed or experienced in our world, regardless of its random appearance, happens because of the events that preceded it. The theory is best described in Leibniz's own words: "Nothing takes place without a sufficient reason; that is to say, if one has sufficient knowledge, one may always explain why anything else happens as it does."[1]

In recent times, deterministic thinking has been further clarified by esteemed scientists such as Jacques Monod, Nobel Prize winner in biology in 1965. Monod describes his viewpoint by stating that "anything can be reduced to simple, obvious, mechanical interactions."[2] From these perspectives of determinism, the apparent healing of the cancerous tumor occurred as the result of events leading up to the moment of healing. If we had insight on each of those events, our sense of a miracle would disappear, and we would see the healing as the logical outcome of a known sequence of events.

In the world of quantum mechanics, however, an event such as the compression of time or the healing of a tumor offers a very different prospect. The additional agent has been identified as "free will."

## A New Physics

The key to quantum physics may be found in the very name of the science itself. *Quantum* is defined as "a discrete quantity of electromagnetic radiation." Physicists now speak of creation as being nonsolid and noncontinuous. The science of quantum physics has demonstrated that our world actually occurs in very short, rapid bursts of light. What we believe we see as the swing of a baseball batter on home plate, for example, in quantum terms is actually a series of individual events that happen very fast and very close together. Similar to the many still images that make up a moving film, these events are actually tiny pulses of light called *quanta*. The quanta of our world occur so rapidly that although our eyes are capable of doing so, our minds do not discern individual bursts. Instead, the pulses are averaged together into what we see as one continuous event—in this instance, the swing of the batter. Quantum physics is the study of these minute units of radiating waves, *nonphysical* forces whose movements create our *physical* world.

In recent years, scientists have turned to observations in the quantum world of the atom to explain mysteries that have been witnessed at the farthest reaches of the cosmos. The thinking is that if an event is observed on a small scale, then perhaps the same mechanism may be applied to understand events on a larger scale. Quantum physics now allows for "miracles" such as the disappearing tumor and our experience of lost time, possibilities that were previously considered impossible. For example, did the vehicles and our group merely change our perception of time, or did something even more amazing occur? Is it possible that on that morning in the Sinai Desert we participated in an event that challenges the very limits of our imaginations, the possibility of experiencing multiple realities and jumping from one outcome into another without even knowing that the jump occurred?

If time does, in fact, travel as a road in two directions, is it possible that the road has multiple lanes? *Could the events that begin along one lane of time arrive at a given point in a different lane with a different outcome?* Can we begin one course of events and "leap" midstream into a new outcome? If so, this implies the possibility of multiple outcomes for an event that has already begun. The implications of this kind of thinking give a new meaning of hope to predictions of worldwide destruction and global suffering and, at the same time, invite us to consider the choices we make in our daily lives as direct links to future experiences.

The existence of many outcomes for a given event has been predicted by quantum physicists for nearly eighty years. In recent times, scientists such as Fred Alan Wolf and Richard Feynman have brought a new relevance to such esoteric possibilities by linking quantum possibilities to daily life. Of all the uncertainties in a universe of many outcomes, two components are clear. First, for multiple outcomes to be considered implies that *each possibility is already created and present in our world.* Perhaps in a form that we have yet to recognize, somewhere in creation, as an embryonic mix of the physical and nonphysical, each outcome awaits to be called into the focus of our awareness. Second, as one outcome gives way to another, for a brief moment *the two must occupy the same space at the same time.* As one event is brought into the focus of our senses, it must be capable of overlapping a second event, if only for the fraction of a second that it takes the two to slide past one another.

Quantum physics has a name for the reality that occurs during the time that two atoms occupy the same point, in the same space, at the same time. Such an outcome is called a *Bose-Einstein condensate,* honoring the authors of the equations that predict such an occurrence. *These condensates have now been observed and documented under laboratory conditions.* Jeffrey Satinover reports that Bose-Einstein conditions have occurred with "condensates of up to 16 million merged beryllium atoms" formed in the laboratory in the late 1990s.[3] Moreover, Satinover reports that the material created from the experiments is "large enough to see with the naked eye and has been photographed." From these studies alone, although the events experienced in the Egyptian desert and witnessed on our videotaped healing appear contrary to the laws of nature, they fall within the predicted behavior of natural laws suggested by quantum physics.

Perhaps the consideration of multiple possibilities offers insight into one of the great mysteries of the creation sciences—why much of our universe appears to be "missing." Using supercomputers to trace the steps of creation back to the Big Bang at the beginning of time, a mysterious phenomenon quickly develops. Shortly after the instant that scientists believe our universe began, approximately 90 percent of it "disappears," leaving only 10 percent of the universe accounted for within the models.[4] At the same time, researchers in the life sciences ask us to consider a second mystery. Studies of the human brain suggest that for a given individual, only a fraction of the individual's brain is used—approximately 10 percent. The function of the remaining 90 percent is unaccounted for and is believed to be dormant. Certainly there are theories as to "multiple, redundant biological circuits" and a yet-to-be realized state of evolution when our brain will be utilized more completely. The numeric estimates, however, remain unexplained. Only 10 percent of the human brain is utilized, and only 10 percent of the mass of the universe can be accounted for. Where is the remaining 90 percent of creation, and what is the purpose of our brain's "unused" 90 percent? Is it by chance that these percentages correlate so closely? What are the computer models and biologists showing us—or failing to show us?

Neither the model nor the life scientists of the past are taking into account one of the most fundamental and possibly least understood dynamics of creation, the component of *dimensionality*. In our ever-changing view of creation, many scientists now believe that all we know as our world is ultimately made of the same substance, tiny packets of light (quanta) vibrating at different speeds. Some light vibrates so slowly that it appears as rocks and minerals. Other forms of light vibrate more rapidly to appear as the living material of plants, animals, and people, while even faster vibrations make up our television and radio signals. Ultimately, each may be reduced to a quality of vibrating light.

The observations of the physicists and the life scientists fail to take into account the parameters of dimensionality—events occurring at such high vibratory rates that they appear beyond our range of physical perception. New research suggests that our world does not end with the vibrations noted on conventional charts of cosmic waves, vibrating at over $10^{22}$ cycles per second. Cosmologists now suspect that shortly after the moment of creation, the universe was expanding so rapidly that its vibration could no longer express within the laws of three-dimensional experience. According to this theory, 90 percent of the universe literally vibrated itself into higher states of expression! It is this 90 percent that may represent the place where the parallel universes of quantum theory live.

## In and Out of Time: Choice Points

Often referenced in discussions of parallel possibilities are the theories of Hugh Everett III, a pioneering physicist from Princeton University. Everett developed the ideas of parallel universes as an answer to the puzzles of quantum realities. In a 1957 paper titled "Relative State Formulation of Quantum Mechanics," Everett went so far as actually to give a name to the moments in time where the course of an event may be changed. He called these windows of opportunity "choice points."[5] A choice point occurs when conditions appear that create a path between the present course of events and a new course leading to new outcomes. The choice point is like a bridge making it possible to begin one path and change course to experience the outcome of a new path.

From this perspective, in the moment that the three practitioners and the patient chose the view affirming that the tumor did not exist, they were moving through a choice point into a new outcome. By changing their belief system, they went beyond any attempt to "heal" the physical expression of an event that had already occurred. Rather, they addressed the nonphysical origins of the tumor and assumed the thought, feeling, and emotion from a place where it never existed. Their actions became the *attractor* for a choice point, allowing the quantum leap from a course of events already under way, to a new course with a different outcome. The tools that make such a jump possible are found in their beliefs: the thoughts, feelings, and emotions that the new reality was already in place. Contrary to the suggestion that such change occurs slowly, over long periods, the new possibility was brought into focus, and the original released, in two minutes and forty seconds!

Choice points may occur more often than we think. In our definition of quanta as the small pulses of light that create our reality, we opened the door to a tremendous possibility: a new definition of time! Just as physicists now believe that matter is made of many short bursts, rather than being one continuous field, the ancients believed that time occurred in a similar fashion. It is during each burst of light that we experience the events of our world. The more bursts of light we string together, the longer the duration of our experience becomes. Conversely, the fewer the bursts, the briefer the overall experience.

For there to be an end to one pulse of light before the next pulse begins, there must, by definition, be a space in between. Viewing our experience on earth as a small metaphor for the large-scale experience of the cosmos (as above, so below), the Essenes made similar reference to the breath of our lives and the breath of the cosmos. In the Essene Gospel of Peace, for example, we are reminded that "in the moment betwixt the breathing in and the breathing out is hidden all the mysteries. . . ."[6] In Essene philosophy, the spaces between quantum bursts may be viewed as small expressions of the stillness between each breath. It is in the spaces between, in the silence between the pulses of creation, that we have the opportunity to "jump" from one possibility to the next. This space is where the miracles occur.

## When Time Slows Down

The winter of 1977 seemed to have arrived suddenly in Missouri. Having been accepted at a university in northern Colorado to complete my degree in the earth sciences, nothing had prepared me for the seemingly endless flow of errands and paperwork that filled each day before my departure. Perhaps it is for this very reason that one event remains clear, standing out from all others in those very full days of preparation.

In the week before my classes were to begin, I witnessed three separate auto accidents on the roads and highways near our home.

Though never directly involved in any of the accidents, I was the first on the scene at all three. In each instance, I could see what was about to happen and felt powerless to do anything about it.

During the third of the three incidents, I was stopped at a traffic light entering a four-way intersection. Suddenly, from my left, I saw a small blue car accelerate while the surrounding vehicles were slowing to honor the signal. I glanced at the light and immediately knew what was about to happen. The woman driving the car was attempting to squeak through a yellow light. Suddenly the light changed, and I saw something that I had not seen earlier. Another vehicle was in the same turn lane, traveling in the *opposite direction*, toward the woman's car. As the light changed to red, the car waiting in the intersection began the turn, just as the blue car raced through. In an instant, the whole scene had played out.

Though the entire event lasted only seconds, my experience of the moment was much longer. A strange mixture of helplessness and fascination came over me as I watched from the safety of my own vehicle. In slow motion, I saw the two cars touch and then merge into one another. The woman driving the blue car had an infant in the backseat, apparently with no harness or seat belt. My fascination turned to horror as I saw a tiny child, clothed in a down jacket, with her head covered in a stocking hat, become airborne and sail limply over the front seats. In slow motion the infant slammed into the windshield, then slid down the glass to the dash, falling into a crumpled heap on the seat. For those brief seconds, I felt the world slow to a strange crawl. Like a video playback, advancing frame by frame, the scene was so vivid, so lucid, so real.

Many people have reported similar experiences, under a variety of conditions. I share this particular experience for a reason. During the week of the three accidents, culminating with the one just described, I recognized a theme common to each experience. It was clear that I determined *how* I saw each event by the way I *felt* about what I was seeing. On the day of the third accident, for example, my *emotions* of horror merged with my *thoughts* of fascination for what was occurring, and slowed my vision of the event to a snail's pace. It was as if someone had shown me the entire scene imprinted upon a deck of cards, with each image slightly different from the one before it. In such instances, the faster the deck is flipped, the faster the action appears. The accident reminded me of precisely this metaphor, with the powers that be flipping through the deck, very slowly. In this molasses-like effect, I witnessed the accident and remember specific details that, in all probability, would otherwise have gone unnoticed. On that day, my experience of quantum science transcended theory and what-ifs, to become the reality of a very tangible experience of seeing the events as well as the spaces in between.

## The Butterfly Effect

As strange as the ideas of quantum theories may sound, they account for observations in subatomic experiments with such success that they have been unmatched in nearly eight decades. It is such experiments that pave the way for new considerations of our role in history and the fate of humankind. From reports in the open literature, it is obvious that researchers have seriously studied the possibility of observing time and influencing outcomes. What are we to do with such information? How does knowledge of this magnitude affect our lives, day in and day out?

To bring such abstract information into a meaningful role in our lives, we must, at the very least, have a conceptual understanding of how the principles work. Applying our new physics to the ancient gift of prophecy, we now have an expanded vocabulary to describe the visions of ancient seers and the role of their visions in our lives.

Without the benefit of such language and conceptual models, ancient prophets were often left with little more than a glimpse into a future so far ahead of their time that they did not even have the words to describe what they had seen.

Perhaps our consideration of time as a roadway, moving in two directions, may help in applying the concepts of prophecy previously suggested. A prophet standing in the middle of such a roadway might apply his gift of prophecy by projecting his senses along the road to the front, or in the opposite direction behind. Rather than *looking* to the horizon for as far as the eye can see into time, the prophet's perceptions *actually travel* the road into another experience of space and time. While his body may appear in the present moment, sitting in the chair before the fireplace of Nostradamus's study in 1532, for example, the awareness of the prophet has actually navigated the road of time into the reality of a distant future. The key to understanding prophecy is that the future being observed is *the logical outcome of the circumstances at the time of the prophecy.* Between the moment of the present and the time of the future, if anything were to change, then the outcome of the prophecy must reflect that change.

Quantum physics has given rise to a wonderful new vocabulary to describe precisely such experiences. Descriptions that may at first appear to have very little to do with the science being discussed have an eloquent way of making complex ideas easy to understand. The "butterfly effect" is one of those descriptions. Used to describe the relationship between the moment of change and the possible outcomes stemming from that change at a later time, the butterfly effect is formally known as *sensitive dependence on initial conditions.* Briefly, the effect states that tiny changes in initial conditions can lead to big changes in a later outcome. Similar to the way complex ideas were described by simple stories in the past, a parable is used today to illustrate the butterfly effect. The single sentence suggests,

"If a butterfly flaps its wings in Tokyo today, a month later it may cause a hurricane in Brazil."[7]

Reminding us of how significant thoughts and actions of the moment may become, the power of the butterfly effect may be graphically illustrated as a localized error with global consequences. Is it possible that one seemingly insignificant mistake, such as a wrong turn by the driver of a foreign dignitary, for example, could ignite a global war? History witnessed precisely such an effect in the early part of the twentieth century. The year was 1914, and the dignitary was Archduke Francis Ferdinand of Austria. A documentary film about the origins of the First World War noted, "A wrong turn by the archduke's driver brought the heir to the Austrian throne face to face with [his assassin] Gavrilo Princip." What if the driver had turned down another street, or perhaps not even driven on that day? Although the archduke's assassination may well have come about at another point in the timeline of history, it probably would not have occurred on that day, in that manner. Perhaps the same mistake at a later time would have found our world in a political climate where such a mistake would have remained precisely that, just a mistake.

Such perspectives may serve as reminders not to underestimate the power of the butterfly effect because of the gentleness of its namesake. Viewing prophecies from thousands of years in our past, the butterfly effect may explain why some appear to have been accurately fulfilled, while others seem to have missed the mark entirely. When we consider that *any change* within the lifetime of the prophecy affects its outcome, it is amazing that visions of our time seen thousands of years ago have any resemblance whatsoever to the original vision of the prophet.

Continuing with our road analogy, what the ancient prophets may or may not have known is that running in a parallel path beside each time-road that they navigated is another road, moving at the same time, in the same direction. Next to that road is another, and beside that another. Each road is transparent to the others. Each road is occupied by an *overlay,* subtle copies of the same places, events, and people in the same cities, countries, and continents. The difference between the roads is that the experience of each one changes slightly in relation to its neighbor. The farther the roads become from the one the prophet is standing on, the greater the changes. For those close by, the differences may be so slight that one road of time is nearly indiscernible from another. The important thing here is that, however subtle, a difference exists.

Referencing passages from the prophets of the Dead Sea Scrolls and the Bible Code, we are reminded that to change the outcome of any prophecy for the future, we must change the expression of our lives in the present. Quantum physics suggests that the opportunity to redefine outcomes may come only at specific intervals where the roads of time *bend their courses* and approach other roads. Sometimes the roads move so close that they touch one another. These points of touch are the choice points discussed earlier.

In light of ancient as well as present-day prophecies, this concept of jumping from one road to another at key choice points becomes the solution to our mystery of miracles, healing, and time compression. Additionally, this ancient science, now well-based in modern physics, offers new hope in the presence of catastrophic predictions for our future. The outcome previously described in the Bible Code for the year 2012, for example, is accompanied by the words, "Will you change it?" In a matrix of possibilities that began playing out over three thousand years ago, the possibility of redirecting a potentially tragic outcome was recognized even then. The "change it" of the Bible Code, the tragic readings from Nostradamus, Edgar Cayce, and the prophets before them, followed by apparently conflicting scenarios of peace and redemption, are the markers of choice points along the road of time.

## Quantum Futures of the Hopi

In terms that may seem more relevant to modern times, the Hopi relate similar visions of our future, with similar opportunities to choose which outcome we experience. Discussed briefly in an earlier chapter, Hopi traditions of peace, viewed through the eyes of quantum understandings, offer new possibilities for our lives today.

Long ago, the Hopi, whose name means "People of Peace," were given the diagram of a life plan that would guide them through this time in history. Eloquently simple, their plan consists of two parallel paths, parallel possibilities representing the life choices of humankind. In the beginning, both paths appear very similar. The upper path, however, gradually turns into a broken zigzag that ends nowhere. Those who choose this path are represented with their heads detached, hovering over their bodies. They will experience the great shift as a time of confusion and chaos leading to destruction. The lower path continues as a level line, strong and even. Those choosing this path live to advanced ages and their crops grow strong and healthy.

Approximately two-thirds of the way along the paths is a vertical line connecting the two. Until this intersection point is reached, the Hopi say, we may move freely back and forth, exploring the two paths. Following this point in time, however, the choices are made and there is no return. In the words of quantum physics, this portion of the prophecy describes a choice point, an opportunity for humanity to experience the paths of both worlds and choose which is true for them. In the words of the prophecy, "If we hold fast to the sacred way as he [the Creator] devised it for us, what we have gained, we will never lose. But still, we have to choose between the two ways."[8] Mother Nature tells us which is the right way. "When earthquakes, floods, hailstorms, drought, and famine will be the life of every day, the time will have then come for the return to the true path."[9]

The record-breaking extremes of nature witnessed in our world today suggest to the Hopi that the time of purification is upon us. The severity of our cleansing is being determined, as our individual responses to life challenges create the collective outcome. In a text written by a group of elders from the Hopi Nation,[10] specific events in our world are viewed as barometers of our progress in the unfolding of a greater scenario. Among the indicators are these:

- widespread starvation and malnourishment
- increases of crime and violence
- loss of clean, abundant water resources
- unprecedented breach and expansion of the ozone layer above Antarctica
- effects of technology (loss of rain forest, depletion of wildlife, and spread of nuclear weapons)

It is during our time, the time indicated by phenomenal events in the world around us, that the belief systems of individuals and entire populations will be tested. The elders of the Hopi clans described a scenario of three "great shakings" of the earth. The first two were interpreted by elders of the tribe to represent the first two world wars; the third shaking remains a mystery. It is unidentified, as the nature of this shaking is still being determined by humankind. "The prophecy says the Earth will shake three times: first the Great War, then the second one, when the swastika rose above the battlefields of Europe, to end in the Rising Sun sinking in a sea of blood." The third shaking "will depend on which path humankind will walk: the greed, the comfort and the profit, or the path of love, strength, and balance."[11]

Clearly, such traditions recognize a direct relationship between the way we address the challenges of our world each day and the kind of world we experience in our future. The chaos of change is our opportunity to refine our beliefs, honoring the portions that work, and gracefully releasing those that may no longer serve us. It is our new, finely honed worldview of the present that will carry us gracefully through the times of future challenge.

As with the prophecies of the Essenes and Edgar Cayce, the Hopi leave us with a message of hope. Their vision of our future concludes by admonishing us to be responsible in the way we use the powers of our bodies and our machines. Once again we are reminded that the choices made each day will determine the duration and severity of our days of tribulation. With simplicity and eloquence, Hopi prophecy reminds us that the way we live our lives determines which path we follow. The choice is ours.

# Bending Time

A common denominator in considering many possibilities and multiple outcomes is the reference to a substance that makes up the very fabric of creation and the force that acts upon this substance. If there are parallel worlds of possibility, precisely what are these worlds made of? The Nobel Prize–winning physicist Max Planck shocked the world with his references to the unseen forces of nature. In accepting the Nobel Prize for his study of the atom, he made a remarkable statement: "As a man who has devoted his whole life to the most clear-headed science, to the study of matter, I can tell you as the result of my research about the atoms this much: 'There is no matter as such!' All matter originates and exists only by virtue of a force which brings the particles of an atom to vibration and holds this most minute solar system of the atom together. . . . We must assume behind this force the existence of a conscious and intelligent mind. This mind is the matrix of all matter."[12]

It may be that Planck's "force" is the key to redirecting the outcomes postulated by science and predicted by ancient prophets. Perhaps Nobel laureate Richard Feynman best described the potential of predicting our future in his now-famous quote, "We do not know how to predict what will happen in a given circumstance. The only thing that can be predicted is the probability of different events. We can only predict the odds."[13] In light of this kind of thinking, it is clear that science is seriously investigating the relationship between nonphysical forces of the cosmos and their effect upon our physical world.

The way that we attune to our possible outcomes is through our viewpoint on life. From this perspective, every life-threatening condition of each body is already healed, peace is already present, and every child, woman, and man of our world is already fed. Now we are invited to choose the quality of thought, feeling, and emotion that allows us to "bend" the waves of time and bring these conditions into the focus of the present.

And one day the eyes

of your spirit shall open,

and you shall know all things.

—*THE ESSENE GOSPEL OF PEACE*

5

# THE ISAIAH EFFECT

## *The Mystery*
## *of the Mountain*

In modern biblical texts, the first visions into our future are described by the Old Testament prophet Isaiah. In the Dead Sea Scrolls, the completeness of the Great Isaiah Scroll allows us to view the works of Isaiah as a template for understanding the apocalyptic prophecies of other traditions as well as glimpses of our future from the biblical prophets. In doing so, we eliminate the tedious task of examining in their entirety each of the four major and twelve minor books of biblical prophecy. This generalized approach makes it possible to view these ancient traditions from a high level and search for *patterns of ideas,* rather than focusing upon the specifics of each individual vision and how they compare to one another. As we do so, an interesting, and perhaps unexpected, possibility surfaces.

In earlier chapters we hinted at a pattern in the prophecies of Isaiah that forecast a time of destruction, catastrophic changes, and nearly unfathomable loss of life, followed by a time of peace and healing. The elements of such a forecast are clearly present. A specific portion of his prophecies, named the Apocalypse of Isaiah, offers even greater insight into the dual nature of the prophet's visions. He describes a time in his future when "the earth is polluted because of its inhabitants, who have transgressed laws, violated statutes, broken the ancient covenant. . . . Therefore they who dwell on earth turn pale, and few men are left."[1] Isaiah goes on to describe violent movement on earth as well as unusual behavior of our sun and moon: "The foundations of the earth will shake. The earth will burst asunder, the earth will be shaken apart, the earth will be convulsed. . . . Then the moon will blush and the sun grow pale. . . ."[2]

Following the darkest moments in his vision of earth's future, the Apocalypse of Isaiah takes an interesting and unexpected turn. With little indication of the change that is about to occur, Isaiah abruptly begins to describe a very different time in his future vision, a time affirming joy, peace, and life. In the next portion of his insight, still considered by scholars to be apocalyptic in nature, he describes a time when "a new earth" is created, along with "new heavens." It is during this time that "the things of the past shall not be remembered or come to mind. Instead there shall always be rejoicing and happiness . . . no longer shall the sound of weeping be heard . . . or the sound of crying. . . ."[3]

Following this sequence of events, we are led to believe that the joyous events follow the tragic events, *that one must precede the other* in the order suggested by the text. Why do the prophecies of Edgar Cayce, Nostradamus, the Native American elders, and others appear to be so contradictory at times, offering what may be perceived as a mixed message of hope and possibility along with terrifying glimpses of death, decay, and catastrophic destruction *for the same period of time?* Is it possible that such ancient glimpses into our future offer another possibility so empowering and so overwhelming that even the prophets did not realize the implications of their own visions?

This is precisely the sense we get as we review the prophecy of Daniel in a later chapter of the Old Testament. Having been offered a rare glimpse into the future of a distant time, it appears as though Daniel did not fully understand what he had been shown. With no frame of reference for the things that he witnessed in his future, how could he? Toward the completion of his excursion through time, the guide that has led him into the future simply suggests to him, "As for you, go your way till the end. You will rest, and then at the end of the days you will rise to receive your allotted inheritance."[4]

As he shared his visions, was Isaiah forecasting actual events that would occur with certainty, or was he describing *insights into a quantum possibility* with a meaning so unexpected that it has remained hidden until the twentieth century? When viewed through the eyes of our new physics, Isaiah's description of vastly different futures for the same point in time correlate surprisingly well with modern descriptions of quantum outcomes. In such discussions, the futures envisioned by Isaiah become waves of possibility rather than factual outcomes. Additionally, quantum science allows for individuals in the present to change such catastrophic outcomes of the future. The key is to understand when and how the opportunities for change present themselves.

The example given in chapter 1 of the mass prayer of peace on the eve of an airborne military campaign against Iraq offers a wonderful example of such choices. To some observers, the order to begin the attack, followed within minutes by an order to abort the mission, made little sense, but from the perspective of the thin veil between quantum possibilities, the events of the day make perfect sense.

On that evening thousands of people, in at least thirty-five countries on six continents, had already agreed to join in a mass vigil of peace that was heard around the world. Coordinated through the Internet and the World Wide Web,[5] the prayer was supported by families, organizations, and communities as a voice of peace that transcended the political boundaries of governments and nations. The vigil was not a protest *against* the bombing of Iraq or any policy, government, or situation existing anywhere in the world. Rather, the call of thousands of hearts and minds to honor the sacredness of life became a single, unified choice echoing a simple message: peace in all worlds, in all nations, for all life.

Within hours of the vigil, the course of events in Iraq had changed. On that day, in full view of the world, we witnessed the power of human consciousness as it rearranged the building blocks of events that were already in motion. Rather than scattered pleas from individuals asking for divine intervention in a situation that appeared to be inevitable, the synchronized choice of many people, coordinated through the miracle of the Internet, slipped between the veils of quantum possibilities into an outcome affirming life through peace.

In our uniqueness as nations, families, and individuals, on Friday, November 13, 1998, we shared a common experience. Hidden in the deepest recesses of our collective memory like a family secret, taboo for so long that the details had been lost, our prayer of peace opened the door to vast opportunities of healing, international cooperation, and our greatest expressions of love for those whom we hold dear. On that November evening we breathed a collective sigh of relief as we rewrote an outcome that appeared inevitable. In doing so, we witnessed our power to end the suffering of our world.

How may we prove scientifically that during the prayer of thousands of people, a new possibility replaced the events of war that were already in motion? At the same time, what power other than peace could possibly have moved forward in the presence of such a prayer? With this experience in mind, what are the implications of similar choices for the future of our world?

## Isaiah's Mystery Decoded

For nearly three millennia, scholars have sifted through the clues left by Isaiah for insights into what we may expect as our future. As cultures have changed, our interpretation of his prophecy has changed as well. Translations made during the time of the Spanish Inquisition, for example, reflected the stringent limits imposed by the Church upon mystical interpretation. Today the language of quantum science offers a new and expanded view of Isaiah's glimpses into our future.

Perhaps the mystery of Isaiah's prophecies was anticipated at the time of their writing. As if inviting the people of a future time to look beyond the obvious, he writes, "For you the revelation of all this has become like the words of a sealed scroll. When it is handed to one who can read, with the request, 'Read this,' he replies, 'I cannot; it is sealed.'"[6] In this rare passage, one of the few of its kind, Isaiah makes a subtle observation about the attitude of generations to come regarding his visions into time. He knows that the people of his future, those who "can read" his prophecy, have the ability to understand its message. They do not recognize it, however, because the *context* has never been revealed to them.

Could Isaiah's "seal" be our discovery of the fundamental laws of creation, the very nature of time itself? If he was, in fact, offering such insights to a generation of his distant future, how could Isaiah's vision be understood without the elements of twentieth-century physics? At the same time, what words could he possibly have used in his day to convey such an empowering yet abstract message to future generations? The prophet offers us a clue to this apparent mystery, as he describes how the inhabitants of the earth's distant future may choose which of his visions they experience. In doing so, Isaiah opens the door to a path that may forever change the attitudes of humankind and, in turn, accomplish nothing less than rewriting the course of human history.

Carefully, Isaiah outlines a form of behavior that allows us to escape the darkness that he has witnessed. He begins by referring to a mystical key through which the people of any generation may redirect the events that lie ahead in their probable future. The key is identified in his vision as a "mountain."[7] It is within his mountain that Isaiah describes a "refuge to the poor, a refuge to the needy in distress; shelter from the rain, shade from the heat."[8] In a particularly interesting passage, the prophet tells of a time when, in the presence of the mountain, "the veil that veils all peoples, the web that is woven over all nations," will be destroyed. Herein we find one of the first clues to this particular prophecy. Clearly he is referring to the mountain as the key of refuge and empowerment. *Precisely what is the mountain of Isaiah's prophecies?*

Some researchers believe that the reference is to a physical location, a place of power and sanctuary for those fortunate enough to discover it. Others suggest that Isaiah's mountain was intended as a code of sorts, a time lock to ensure that his message would be revealed only when the principles for using such wisdom were understood. While both of these may be a possibility, perhaps the mystery of the prophecy may be explained more simply. The identification of Isaiah's mountain may be a beautiful example of how the passage of time and the evolution of cultures has eroded the original context to such a degree that the message has become lost, or at least obscured, in the process.

Often, in modern references to ancient biblical texts, we find specific words marked by a marginal note indicating that there may be additional uses, interpretations, or meanings of the word. Such is the case with the mountain of Isaiah. In addition to the possibility of translators and languages introducing error, at this point yet another factor disguises the original meaning: the use of metaphor and symbols. Scholars indicate that during the time of the writings, the word *mountain* was, in fact, symbolic and used to represent the "heavenly Jerusalem."[9] Rather than a physical location—in this instance the city of Jerusalem—the footnotes clearly show that the word *mountain* is a metaphoric reference. Still, the meaning of a "heavenly city" remains somewhat nebulous, until further research reveals an additional clue. Our modern-day Bible is the product of earlier translations from the original Hebrew. Cross-referencing this phrase with the precise wording in its original language, we discover an unexpected, though perhaps not surprising, meaning for the reference.

In Hebrew, the word for Jerusalem is *Yerushalayim*. Here, the definition becomes very clear: it means "the vision of peace."[10] At last the mysterious meaning of Isaiah's message becomes clear. Isaiah's mountain is not a physical place, but a reference to the power of peace! With this clarification, we may read his prophecy, *"The vision of peace provides a refuge to the poor, a refuge to the needy in distress; shelter from the rain, shade from the heat. In the presence of the vision of peace, the veil that veils all peoples, the web that is woven over all nations, will be destroyed."*

This new understanding of Isaiah's prophecy offers a fresh insight into the power of his ancient message. Having peered into key moments of our future, he witnessed two very different and distinct possibilities: one a time of healing and one a time of destruction. Just as we would do today, the great prophet described his vision in the only words that he knew, alerting us to a possibility in our future based upon a given course of events. At the same time, he admonished those who would eventually read his prophecy to reconsider choices that they make in their lives and, in so doing, to avoid the suffering that he witnessed as a possible future.

# The Isaiah Effect

Clearly, we are entering a new era of understanding the inner sciences of prayer, prophecy, and the agents of change that Isaiah and others acknowledged in their writings. Deceptively simple, Isaiah's prophecies remind us of two things. First, through the science of prophecy we may glimpse future consequences of choices made in the present. Second, we embody the collective power to choose which future we experience. It is through our consideration of others in our daily lives that we piece together the experiences that bring our futures into focus. This is the Isaiah Effect—the expression of an ancient science stating that we may change the outcome of our future through the choices that we make in each moment of the present.

Quantum physics now gives us the language to give this sophisticated technology meaning in our daily lives. In doing so, we empower our families, our communities, and those that we hold dear with the simple and effective message of honoring all life in our world. Through our choice of peace in our lives, we ensure the survival of our species and the future of the only home we know. We have already witnessed the power of the Isaiah Effect. We know that it works. Now the question becomes, How do we implement this quantum principle of choice in our daily lives as a global family?

When prayer and meditation are used

rather than relying on new

inventions to create more imbalance,

then they [humanity] will also

find the true path.

—ROBERT BOISSIERE,
*MEDITATIONS WITH THE HOPI*

# MEETING WITH
# THE ABBOT

## *The Essenes in Tibet*

In my studies of esoteric traditions from Peru, Tibet, Egypt, the Holy Land, and the American Southwest, a theme arises that is both fascinating and curious. Prophecies from each of these cultures appear malleable, like soft clay in the hands of a sculptor. Just as the final shape of a sculptor's clay is determined by the choices and movement of the artist, the theme of these ancient traditions suggests that we are shaping the outcome and eventual fate of humankind in each moment of our lives.

Interestingly, I have found some of the clearest references to these traditions in documents from the Middle East, specifically the Qumran scrolls from the Dead Sea area. The references speak of a lineage of wisdom so ancient that it was already old during the time of classical Egypt, over three thousand years ago. My sense has been that if such information did in fact exist, what better location to preserve such wisdom than in the remote spiritual retreats of a land untouched by modern technology. It would be in such a place that traditions lost to the West long ago might still remain as the daily rituals of local inhabitants. Isolated from the outside world until 1980, the secluded monasteries of the Tibetan Plateau appeared to afford precisely such an opportunity.

In April 1998, I had the privilege of facilitating a pilgrimage into the highlands of Tibet in search of such traditions. Ironically, it was not until I returned from the journey that my suspicion was confirmed in writing. Within days of arriving home in the States, I received a recently translated manuscript of the Nazirines, a sect of the ancient Essenes. This particular text stated that pockets of information, like ancient time capsules, had been strategically hidden by the Essenes during the first century A.D., to preserve the wisdom for future generations. Among the places clearly mentioned as a repository for such texts were the remote monasteries and nunneries of Tibet.

With the aid of an expert on Asian cultures whom I had met in England four years earlier, our group was skillfully led through the Tibetan countryside into isolated villages, hidden monasteries, and centuries-old temples. For twenty-one days we were immersed in the presence of the Tibetan people, the sacredness of their lives, and the rugged magnificence of their homeland. We crossed shallow rivers on flat board rafts, negotiated washed-out roads, and experienced the euphoria of mountain passes over 17,000 feet above sea level. Two-thirds of the way into our trip, we even found ourselves abandoning the safety of our bus for an open-bed fruit truck waiting on the other side of an impassable snow slide over four stories tall.

Nearly one-third of our journey was in the mountainous area of the western plateau. Among remote villages, nunneries, and monasteries seldom seen by people outside of Asia, the people live today as they have for centuries, honoring the traditions of their ancestors. Each time we walked into the courtyard of a temple complex, it was is if we had entered into a living snapshot of Tibetan traditions frozen in an ancient time. With each step of our journey, we were greeted with an openness and warmth exceeding any that we could have imagined in the strange beauty that imbues such desolation. The purpose of our pilgrimage was to witness, experience, and document living examples of an inner technology that I suspected was lost to the West nearly two millennia ago. Today we know a fragment of this science as the inner technology of prayer.

## Blessed by the Abbot

A shaft of light beamed from somewhere high above the temple floor. The single ray had a curious three-dimensional quality, as if I could close my hands around it and climb to its source. With precision, the light sliced its way through the cool, misty air that was heavy with the smoke of countless butter lamps and incense. I turned my head to see where the light was coming from. Following the beam from the point where it touched the slick, oil-laden floor to its source, my eyes focused on an opening high above our heads. Through a small, square window I could see the intense blue of the Tibetan sky outside. Except for a miniature flashlight that I had taken from my backpack, this ray of direct morning sun was the only light in the maze of twisted corridors and dead-end passageways. I made a mental note of the opening overhead. It would be my reference to the outside in the event there were no other corridors leading back.

With a group of twenty, my wife and I had journeyed across the rugged terrain of the Tibetan highlands and negotiated rock and dirt roads that were little more than jeep trails, to be in this very place. For years, personal research into the traditions of those who have come before us had hinted at a lineage of wisdom forgotten in Western societies. Lost after the time of Christ, the teachings of mystery schools, sacred orders, and esoteric sects all pointed to a common lineage of wisdom lost approximately seventeen hundred years ago. Perhaps the clearest evidence of these traditions is found today among the records of the mysterious communities described in earlier chapters, the ancient Essenes.

Persistent references to the Essenes eventually led me to a series of journeys in search of direct, tangible evidence of their teachings and their relevance in our world today. By the mid 1980s, I found myself in the deserts of Egypt, trekking the high Andes of Peru and Bolivia, and upon numerous sojourns into the deserts of the American Southwest in a search for modern evidence of their lost wisdom. My reasoning was that a teaching so universal would have been left as more than a single isolated text or manuscript, such as the Dead Sea Scrolls. As significant as any ancient manuscripts may be, the real evidence would be found in the history, teachings, and traditions of the people themselves. Perhaps the possibilities are so obvious that they have been overlooked in recent times.

Rather than speculate *about* two-thousand-year-old texts and what the translations may be alluding to, in the presence of indige-nous peoples living the lost wisdom, we could actually *witness* their practices today. During our time together, we could hone our ques-tions and verify our answers with a clarity never possible in the trans-lations of temple walls and crumbling manuscripts. Additionally, we would gain a new respect for the caretakers of our lost wisdom, a new understanding of their culture and lives.

The key to such wisdom is to find records accurate enough, held by a people long enough to remain virtually intact and undistorted today. If there really were such a place, if it still exists today, I rea-soned, Tibet would be a good place to begin. Isolated as Tibet has been from the rest of the world until 1980, many of the teachings and records have remained precisely where they were placed cen-turies ago. Tucked away high upon the "roof of the world," in

The Isaiah Effect

monasteries and nunneries 1,500 years old, the wisdom of the ancient Essene lineage should remain in plain view, preserved as the rituals, lives, and customs of the people living there. Here we were, shuffling through the darkened corridor of one of those monasteries to search for ourselves.

Though we had acclimated over fourteen days, the quick movements of my glance from side to side still created a dizzying effect. I made a conscious effort to inhale deeply, as I noticed that my breathing had become shallow and fast. Without giving my eyes time to readjust, I cautiously stepped forward toward a dim light near the end of the smoke-filled corridor. Huge figures towered beside me, creating a gauntlet of sorts, as my light created a faint path toward the opening. Without stopping, I turned first to one side and then the other, illuminating the humanlike forms carved in monstrous proportions. The glow of my light hinted at massive paintings behind each figure, murals reaching into the darkness toward a ceiling that I could only guess was there.

Suddenly my attention was drawn away from the looming figures to a faint yet familiar sound in the distance. Beginning as a low drone of many closely related sounds, the notes merged into one continuous tone. It appeared to be coming from everywhere at once. I continued, stepping carefully over the lumpy floor, slick from six hundred years of spilled oils. Monks scurrying through this passageway with their urns of yak butter had created a treacherous route. It was the only route to the most sacred room of the monastery. The sound grew louder as I crossed a raised wooden threshold. Stepping down to the cold floor, once again I gave my eyes a moment to adjust.

The three walls of this tiny chamber surrounded me with the flickering of small flames. Hundreds of yak butter candles in tarnished brass lamps illuminated the room with an almost surrealistic glow. Though each lamp was small, their combined heat made the room remarkably warm. A young monk sat in front of me, rhythmically pounding a trancelike beat as he chanted a song from the prayer book in front of him. The voice of Xjinla,* our translator, whispered in my ear. (In the Tibetan language, the suffix -la is added to the end of a name as a sign of honor and respect. Thus, the name *Xjin* becomes *Xjinla.*)

"This is the room of the protectors," Xjinla said. Anticipating my question before I even asked, he continued. "The protectors are deities invited to discourage dark forces that may be interested in advancing into the next room."

Following monastery etiquette, we respectfully made our way to the left, past the monk, to the doorway of the next room. I was the second to enter, following the lead of our guide. Little more than a small cube, the space seemed to be dwarfed even more by a support beam in its center.

There, in the pale glow of a half-dozen or so candles, was the reason that we had journeyed halfway around the world, traveled over two continents, crossed ten time zones, and adjusted to some of the most rarefied air on earth. Seated with his legs skillfully positioned on thick woolen pads beneath his robes was the abbot of the monastery, the spiritual elder of this sect of monks. I felt honored to have even a few precious moments in the presence of this man. To my astonishment, those first moments were the opening of a time shared together that would last for nearly an hour!

The formalities came first. Each of us had been given a white linen scarf to offer as a gesture of honor. We had been instructed how the scarf, called a *kata,* should be carefully folded, handled, and presented to the abbot. Upon receiving his gift, the abbot would either accept the scarf as a gift, or bless it and return it to the offerer.

*The names of our guides and translators have been changed to honor their privacy.

If he kept them, I remember wondering, what this man would do with our twenty-two scarves in his tiny office!

Xjinla set the example as he offered his *kata* first, kneeling to the level of the frail-looking man seated on the pads. Bowing his head, this native Tibetan presented his scarf as a gesture of honor, open palms up. The abbot accepted, removed, and blessed the scarf, then returned it to Xjinla, placing it around his neck as he was still bowed in reverence. I was next.

Approaching the abbot seated before me, I suddenly had an eerie sensation of timelessness, that feeling which occurs during a moment when the world slows to a dreamlike crawl. In slow motion, I bowed respectfully, presented my *kata,* and waited for the abbot to return my offering. What seemed like many seconds had passed, certainly longer than it should have taken for the prescribed ritual. Curious, I lifted my head just in time to meet the forehead of the abbot coming toward me. Lifting his arms to position the scarf around my neck, he gently cradled my head in his palms and touched his forehead to mine.

Immediately, I felt a kinship with this man whom I had seen for the first time only moments earlier. The kinship quickly turned to trust, as I took the liberty to raise my eyes and look directly into his. What I know were only seconds became timeless. Knowing that I had deviated from the custom of keeping a bowed head throughout the ceremony of offering, I was uncertain how my eye contact would be received. The awkwardness lasted only briefly. The abbot demonstrated his mastery by replacing the uncertainty of the moment with grace and ease. Looking back into my eyes, he offered a warm, gracious smile. With his gesture of openness, I knew that my time with the ceremony was complete. I also knew that an opening had occurred, an opportunity to explore this man's memories and the experience of his teachings. It was time for the next person.

# Secret of the Prayer

Following twenty similar blessings, the abbot sat back quietly on his pads, closed his eyes, and focused on our meeting. This was the time that we had waited for. I had asked for an audience with this holy man specifically for the purpose of tapping into his ancient lineage of wisdom. If the Essenes had, in fact, migrated into Tibet after the time of Christ, elements of Essene traditions should be recognizable in the Tibetan rituals of today. Under Xjinla's skilled guidance, I posed the questions that I had journeyed halfway around the world to ask.

"Xjinla," I began, "please ask the abbot about the prayers that we have witnessed during our time in the monasteries. Will he describe for us what is involved during a prayer, and how each prayer is accomplished?" Xjinla looked at me, as if waiting for the rest of the question.

"Is there more?" he asked. "Perhaps I am not understanding the question that you have asked."

There are many words in the Tibetan language that do not translate directly to a single word in English. To communicate concepts, it is often necessary to create a phrase or short sentence in our language to describe the Tibetan equivalent. I sensed that this was one of those moments. Gathering my thoughts, I restated the question in the simplest English that I could muster without changing the intent of my question: "Specifically, when we see the chants, tones, mudras, and mantras on the outside," I asked, "what is happening with the person praying, on the inside?"

Xjinla turned to the abbot, who was patiently awaiting my question, and the process began. Sometimes the abbot would close his eyes and discourse for many minutes at a time in response to a single sentence from Xjinla. At other times he would mutter a short phrase accompanied by a gesture or a sigh. Xjinla did his best to convert the abbot's explanation of a subtle experience into the

English equivalent before sharing the translation. Hearing our revised question, the abbot looked at me with the hint of a grin on his face. There are some sounds that need no translation.

"Aaaahhhh . . . ," he said in a thoughtful tone.

I knew from the tone of his voice that our question had cut directly to the very crux of what was practiced in his monastery and others that we had seen throughout our journey. His grin became a smile as he pursed his lips and made a different sound.

"Mmmmmm . . ." I watched as his eyes rolled toward the ceiling, which was blackened from the soot of uncounted butter lamps, over hundreds of years. He fixed his gaze on an invisible place above. Using the spot on the ceiling as a point of focus, the abbot searched for the words to acknowledge the essence of my question. I remember thinking that what I had asked was the equivalent of asking someone to describe the meaning of life in twenty-five words or less. This man, who had no knowledge of my background, spiritual foundation, religious orientation, or intent, was searching for a way to honor my question. He was looking for a place to start.

"Now we are getting somewhere," I thought to myself. "What can I do to help the abbot be more at ease with my question?" Thinking back to translations of Essene manuscripts from the Dead Sea, I considered the language that was used twenty-five hundred years ago to describe the lost technology of prayer. The focus of their texts was on the actual elements of prayer: thought, feeling and body. The last thing that I wanted to do was suggest an answer to the abbot. Carefully, I restated my question.

"Xjinla," I asked, momentarily interrupting the abbot's train of thought, "more specifically, I am interested in *how* the prayer is created. When we see the outward expressions of prayers in the chanting halls, what is the result? Where are the prayers taking them?"

The abbot looked on, anxious for Xjinla to share with him my new, rephrased question. Quickly, in a remarkably short sentence,

Xjinla did precisely that. I knew that our persistence was getting us somewhere. Without even thinking, the abbot exclaimed a single word. Then he said the word again, followed by a burst of Tibetan language sounding very different from phrases that I had studied in the language books. Quickly, I gave up my attempts at translation. While I watched the abbot and gave him my eyes, the attention of my mind was focused upon Xjinla. I could almost see the process in his mind. Rather than convert each of the abbot's words from Tibetan into English, he would listen to the theme of the idea and then punctuate the response with specifics from the abbot.

"Feeling!" Xjinla said. "The abbot says that the object of each prayer is to achieve a feeling." The abbot's head was nodding up and down as if he understood Xjinla's translation. "The outward motions that you see are a display of movements and sounds that are useful in achieving the feeling," Xjinla continued. "They have been used by our ancestors for centuries."

Now the smile was on *my* face. While I had suspected that the nebulous force of "feeling" was a factor in the Tibetan prayers, for the first time my belief was being confirmed. The abbot was telling us that feeling was more than just a factor in prayer. He emphasized that feeling is actually the focus of each prayer!

Immediately, my mind raced back to the Essene texts. In the words of their time, those ancient writings brilliantly describe an experience that we consider today as a form of prayer. Just as the teachings of the Essenes referred to the creative forces of our world as angels, the language that they used to speak to the angels they named "communion." Today we call the same language "prayer." Through the lost texts of the Essenes we are reminded that through our communion with the elements of this world, we are afforded access to the great mysteries of life. "Only through communion with the angels of the Heavenly Father will we learn to see the unseen, to hear that which cannot be heard, and to speak the unspoken word."

A silence fell over the tiny room as we thought about the abbot's words. It would take a nun or monk years of training, scholarship, and direct experience before he or she would be allowed to have a similar conversation. The abbot seemed a little surprised at the questions that we were asking. As if he had heard my thoughts, once again Xjinla spoke before I had formulated my next sentence.

"Your questions are very different from those of others who have found this monastery," he said.

"Really?" I answered, somewhat amazed. "If others have taken the time to travel from the West into Lhasa, acclimate over two miles above sea level for a week or so, then breathe endless clouds of dust while navigating jeep trails carved into the sheer face of cliff walls to find this monastery at fifteen thousand feet in the Himalayas, what other kinds of questions would they ask?"

Xjinla laughed at the intensity of my question. The sound of his voice broke the silence as his laughter echoed off of the walls and reverberated through the countless chapels that continued from our room down the hallway.

"Normally, questions are in regard to the age of the monastery, what the monks eat, or the age of the abbot himself!"

With that, we both laughed and looked back to the abbot, automatically estimating his age in our minds. I thought to myself, *This man has no age. In these mountains, in this monastery, age has no meaning for him. He simply is.* I looked back to Xjinla. Following our last exchange, the abbot had remained in his position, seated with his legs drawn up underneath his heavy robes. The air in the room was cool, although my body was hot from the exhilaration of our dialogue. I looked at the miniature keychain thermometer dangling from the zipper flap on my wife's backpack. It read fifty-five degrees Fahrenheit. I wondered if it could be correct.

An attendant chose the opportunity of silence to relight the mounds of incense that provided relief from the pungent odor of spoiled yak butter smoldering in the lamps and dishes. Slipping a hand under my jacket, I touched the three layers of clothing that I had worn from the bus outside. I was amazed. My shirts were soaked! Each day in Tibet is like summer and winter: summer in the sun and winter in the shadows, shade, and inside of monasteries. I looked behind me just in time to see a gust of wind howl down the dimly lit corridor, whipping piles of straw and dust into small heaps in the corners.

# The Abbot's Message

My hand reached up to wipe the perspiration from my eyes as I asked Xjinla the next question. I began by explaining why we had come to the abbot's monastery, and our intent in asking what we had asked. Looking directly at the abbot, I concluded with a single question.

"If there was one message that he could share with the people of the earth," I began, "what would the abbot like for us to carry to the world outside of Tibet on his behalf?"

Even before Xjinla had finished translating, from his cramped position at the end of our poorly lit sanctuary, the abbot began speaking. I felt Xjinla's intensity, sometimes bordering upon frustration, as he searched for the English to convey what the ageless man was saying. On several occasions I would ask that the words be repeated or clarified. Often I would restate the translation in my own words, allowing Xjinla's expertise to help me through any inaccuracies. Turning to me specifically, his eyes betrayed what was happening within him. I sensed within Xjinla an acute awareness of his responsibility to communicate the abbot's words accurately. Together the three of us worked through the next few moments to be certain of what the abbot was offering.

"'Each time we pray individually,' the abbot says, 'we must *feel* our prayer. When we pray, we feel on behalf of all beings, everywhere.'" Xjinla paused as the abbot continued his reply. "'We are all connected,' he said. 'We are all expressions of one life. No matter where we are, our prayers are heard by all. We are all the same one.'"

Rather than answering my question directly, I sensed that the abbot was paving the way, laying the foundation for his response. Nodding in agreement, my body language conveyed what my skills of Tibetan language did not: I heard, I understood, and I was prepared for the rest of the answer. As to what message we could carry to the world outside of Tibet, the abbot responded passionately. Though his words were being conveyed through Xjinla, his tone and the language of his body were clear. Motioning toward us with a palms-up gesture from his heart, the abbot's hands spoke a language of their own. He looked directly at me as I listened to Xjinla carefully.

"Peace is of the greatest importance in our world today," he continued. "In the absence of peace, we lose what we have gained. In the presence of peace, all things are possible: love, compassion, and forgiveness. Peace is the source of all things. I would ask the people of the world to find peace in themselves, so that their peace may be mirrored in the world."

Each word became a source of amazement to my intellect, as well as a source of joy to my soul. The answers that the abbot shared were the same concepts, *in some instances nearly the same words,* as were recovered from the Dead Sea texts of the Essenes, written over 2,500 years ago! Through the Essene Gospels of Peace, for example, the Essenes begin a lengthy discourse on peace by opening with a single eloquent passage. The teaching simply begins with the statement, "Peace is the key to all knowledge, all mystery, all life."

It was clear to each member of our group how important it was to the abbot that he be heard and understood. His patience with our direct and sometimes redundant questions was remarkable. For nearly an hour he remained cross-legged in a lotus position, seated upon the small stack of thin, maroon-colored pads that insulated him from the cold stone floor of the ancient monastery. The rapid-fire questioning eventually gave way, once again, to the silence of pondering our exchanges. For each person in the room, our time together had been both intense and heartfelt.

Our audience with this holy man, who had devoted his entire life to pursuing wisdom in an ancient monastery high in the Himalayas, became our invitation to reconcile the experience within our lives. This man had graciously received us into the tiny quarters of his private study, and his patience with our questions touched me deeply. Again a silence filled the room. The abbot's eyes closed. This time, however, his chin dropped to his chest as he placed his hands in a position of prayer, palms and fingertips touching, pointed toward the ceiling. Holding the position with his hands, he touched his thumbs lightly to his forehead and held the position. That is the last image I have of the abbot.

He appeared to be fatigued, perhaps from entertaining these twenty-two Westerners who had appeared unannounced in his monastery. As if a silent signal had been given, we knew that our time with the abbot was complete. Almost in unison, we began to untangle ourselves from the intricate positions that had allowed each person in the room a direct view of this beautiful man of ancient lineage. One by one, we stood silently, stretched, and, after speaking our respectful "Namaste," filed out into the darkened hallway.

## Room of Knowledge

As we retraced the footsteps that had led us to the abbot's quarters, again we heard the sound of a low, almost indiscernible drone in the distance. It was the now-familiar sound of many monks in a resonant room, creating the monotone chant used in Tibetan prayer.

Each person perceives the sound differently. For me the tone hovers between the threshold of hearing through my ears and actually feeling the sound in my body. It appears to vibrate from somewhere in the center of my chest. Once one has heard the sound, it is unmistakable. In this moment, it sounded far away.

Sunlight illuminated the end of the hallway as we approached a narrow ladder of wooden stairs. There was no railing for support, and we immediately assumed the position that had worked well in similar instances at other monasteries. Strapping down our backpacks and handing cameras, bottles of water, and loose gear to one another, we freed our hands to go down the rough-hewn timbers of each step, backwards. The stairs were at such a steep angle that few were willing to look down as they descended the ladder in a forward position. Modesty sometimes goes right out the window during such maneuvers. Traveling with a small group under primitive conditions for days on end, the modesty of new friendships had already given way to familiarity within our virtual family. Those on the ground reached up to guide the person on the ladder to a place of safe footing, often supporting whatever portion of the body descended the ladder first. One at a time, each person was lowered to the hardened mud floor below.

A young monk perhaps fourteen years old had been waiting for us in a small antechamber behind the ladder. As the last person touched the ground and readjusted himself, we addressed the monk with the traditional greeting of *t'ashedelay*. The monk surprised us with a few sentences of broken English. He was very interested in our audience with the abbot, just moments before. Apparently our visit was rare, and it was difficult even for the monks in residence to be graced with such an opportunity.

By this time, Xjinla had found his way down the ladder as well, and took charge of the conversation. Following a few moments of formalities, I asked about the existence of ancient libraries within this particular monastery. I knew that among the many gifts that the Tibetans have kept safe in our world, they are meticulous recordkeepers. The beauty of this is that they appear to document without placing judgment on what they are recording. Perhaps it is their ability to live compassion in all that they do that allows their unbiased recording of the world around them. In the absence of a "right" or "wrong" regarding the events that they have experienced, they simply record what they have witnessed. Through their documentation of the events that were meaningful in their lives, I suspected that perhaps there would be written records of the wisdom that the abbot had shared. I was particularly interested in the mode of prayer based in feeling.

We were led through a series of passageways to a darkened room behind the myriad altars. Massive statues representing the many aspects of Buddha flanked each hallway and continued into yet another "room of the protectors." Here we could barely make out the figures of immense proportions upon the walls that glistened with the residue of butter lamps. Knowing that this monastery was over fifteen centuries old, I suspected that the soot had accumulated for at least several hundred years. For a radius of eighteen feet or so, the flickering strobelike effect of each lamp betrayed a scene of demons and dark forces. Closer inspection showed that each was engaged in combat with the forces of light, in ancient metaphors mirroring the tests, successes, and failures of every human through our earthly life.

Stooping through an opening into another dimly lit room, my eyes adjusted to a very different scene. Of all the beauty and experiences that had filled our days for the two preceding weeks, what I witnessed in this moment was worth the entire journey. Stacked from the floor to the ceiling, perhaps thirty feet above my head, disappearing into dark corridors and scattered among shelves covered with dust measured in fractions of an inch, were books. Rows upon rows of books. Some were neatly stacked. Some were haphazardly thrown upon others, falling into random heaps. Many of the books were so jumbled and disorganized that it was impossible to tell where one row ended and another row began. Noticing my amazement at the disarray, the young monk spoke to Xjinla. Except for the gasps of awe and amazement, these were the first words that we had heard since entering the room. I suspected he was offering an explanation. Xjinla turned to me and spoke. "The soldiers ransacked this room looking for jewels and gold."

"The soldiers!" I exclaimed. "Do you mean the soldiers from the revolution in 1959? Surely others have been in this room since that time. It has been nearly forty years."

"Yes," Xjinla answered, "those are the ones. Others have come to these rooms. They have been few. The monks believe that the soldiers brought bad fortune. Their spirits are left here, held in place by the protectors."

My eyes searched for a meaningful place to begin investigating as I stepped forward into one of the corridors. Holding my flashlight up high, for as far as my eyes could see there were hundreds of manuscripts, texts printed and bound in traditional Tibetan fashion. Each book began as a long, narrow cover of wood or animal hide. The rigid coverings varied in size, averaging perhaps twelve inches long by three to four inches wide. Another cover of similar description formed the top of the book, with the pages stacked between the two, as loose sheets of cloth, paper, or yak hide. The entire text was bound to keep the pages from falling out. Sometimes the bindings were elaborate, with brightly colored silk and linen. Sometimes they were simply held together with leather thongs.

The young monk nodded with approval as I reached up to examine one of the texts. I had chosen a book that was already unwrapped, so as to disturb as little as possible in the library. To my disappointment, and not to the monk's surprise, the pages of the book were so delicate that they crumbled at my touch. Our young guide was obviously moved by our excitement at his library. Apparently few people knew of its existence, and even fewer visited it. I turned to Xjinla and asked what were contained within these documents. Were they simply many copies of a single text, perhaps the teachings of Buddha? Was there more? By this time, our group had spread out. Each person was exploring a different aisle of different texts, sensing that something rare and wonderful was held in the pages of these ancient books. Without turning to face the monk, Xjinla shouted my question out loud. Without hesitating, the young monk smiled. He and Xjinla exchanged a few words before Xjinla offered a response to my question.

"Everything," he said. "The monk says that within the writings in this particular room are records of everything."

Stopping to face Xjinla, I held my light to show just enough of our faces so that we could see one another speak. "What do you mean, 'everything'?" I asked. "What does 'everything' include?"

Xjinla began, "Written into the pages of these books are the teachings and experiences that have touched the people of Tibet for centuries. As far back as anyone can remember, the wisdom of great mystics has found its way here to be preserved for future generations. In the pages of these books lie the foundations of many philosophies, from Tibetan Bon and Buddhist writings to Christian ones, and those explained by the abbot. All is recorded here in the books that surround us as far as our eyes can see."

I knew that each monastery was a school of sorts. Designed to preserve the secret traditions of the ages, each school specialized in one particular form of wisdom. Our journey had already taken us to monasteries that focused on the traditions of combat and martial arts, for example. Other monasteries preserved the wisdom of telepathy and psychic studies, debate, or the healing arts. The focus of this particular school was the preservation of knowledge.

Without prejudice or judgment, information was simply recorded and stored upon the fragile pages of countless numbers of books, such as the ones we were seeing before us.

*This is the reason that we have come,* I thought to myself. *Here we have seen the traditions of prayer and have the opportunity to document them through texts written by those practicing these traditions nearly two thousand years ago. This moment is worth the entire journey, and I know that there is more to come!*

In their texts, the Essenes had referred to a mode of prayer that is not accounted for by prayer researchers today. Here, in a cold monastery located in the remote mountains of western Tibet, I had witnessed this prayer and was shown sources documenting its history and origin. As the translations continued that day, my sense was confirmed that the Tibetans were continuing, at least in part, a lineage of wisdom whose elements predated history. How would I share this ancient yet sophisticated technology with others?

All matter originates and exists only by

virtue of a force which brings the

particles of an atom to vibration and holds

this most minute solar system of the

atom together. . . . We must assume

behind this force the existence of a

conscious and intelligent mind.

This mind is the matrix of all matter.

—MAX PLANCK

# THE LANGUAGE
# OF GOD

## *The Lost Science
of Prayer and Prophecy*

Ancient traditions suggest that the effect of prayer comes from something other that the words of the prayers themselves. Perhaps this offers a clue as to why so many people appear to have lost their faith in prayer. After the biblical edits of the fourth century, details underlying the *language* of prayer gradually faded from the traditions of the West, leaving only the words behind. During this era, many began to believe that the power of prayer lived in the spoken word alone. Revelations from the pre-fourth-century texts, however, remind us that there are no magic codes of vowels and consonants that open doorways into forgotten realms. The secret of prayer lies beyond the words of praise, the incantations, and the rhythmic chants to the "powers that be." Through texts such as the Dead Sea Scrolls, we are invited to live the *intent* of our prayer in our lives, for if the words are "spoken only with the mouth, they are as a dead hive . . . which gives no more honey."[1]

## To Speak the Unspoken Word

The power of prayer is found in a force that cannot be spoken or transmitted as the written word—the *feelings* that the prayer's words evoke within us. It is the feeling of our prayers that opens the door and illuminates our paths to the forces of the seen as well as the unseen. Though other ancient references often allude to this aspect of our communion with creation, the abbot in Tibet actually confirmed the feeling element of prayer during our private audience.

In answering my question about what was happening within the monks and nuns as we witnessed the outward expression of their prayers, the abbot had responded with a single word: *feeling*. The outward expressions of prayer that we witnessed in the monasteries of Tibet were a display of the movements and sounds that the nuns and monks used to achieve the feelings within. Carrying his answer one step further, the abbot then said to us that feeling was more than just a *factor* in prayer. He emphasized that *feeling is the prayer!*

Through our communion with the elements of this world, we are given access to the great mysteries of life, the opportunity "to see the unseen, to hear that which cannot be heard, and to speak the unspoken word." In its purest form, prayer has no outward expression. Though we may speak a prescribed sequence of words handed down for generations, they must generate a quality of feeling within us in order to touch the world around us. At best, any words that we choose to speak our prayers out loud can be only an approximation of the feeling they describe within. How could the great masters teach of such feelings two thousand years ago? How are we to share them today?

Often, when I am asked to speak to groups about the possibility of prayer, a question arises that reminds me of a conversation I had with my mother years ago. One evening, as we spoke on the telephone between brief visits and across several time zones, I was sharing insights into a new workshop that I had prepared on the science of compassion. As I offered a definition of prayer involving feeling and emotion, my mother asked a question that has been echoed by many people in many situations since that time. Openly and innocently, she simply said, "What is the difference between emotion and feeling? I always thought that they were the same."

I was interested to hear my mother's understanding of these sometimes nebulous experiences that play such a key role in defining our lives. Not surprisingly, her explanation resembled the definitions commonly accepted in the West today. For example, some dictionaries consider the two words nearly interchangeable, using each one to define the other. In *The American Heritage Dictionary of the English Language,* the word *feeling* is defined as "an emotional state or disposition; a tender emotion." (In the same text, *emotion* is defined in one place as "a strong feeling" and in another as a synonym for feeling.) While these definitions may serve the purposes of today's world, the ancients recognized a distinction between them. Further, though closely related, thought and feeling are identified as discrete elements, keys, which may be focused to effect change in the conditions or our bodies, our world, and beyond.

## As Above . . .

In an account twenty centuries old, the people of the Holy Land asked their leaders a question that continues to ring in our minds today. Except for specifics of the conditions, the question remains hauntingly similar. With regard to peace in our world, those who have come before us asked, "How, then, may we bring peace to our brothers . . . for we would that all of the Sons of Men share in the blessings of the angel of peace?"[2] Essene masters offered a reply illustrating the role of thought, feeling, and the empowering nature of prayer.

Defying the logic of today, their words remind us that peace is more than simply the absence of aggression and war. Peace transcends the end of a conflict or a statement of policy. While we may force the *outward appearance* of peace upon a people or a nation, it is the *underlying thinking* that must change to create a true and lasting peace. In words that sound surprisingly Buddhist as well as Christian in nature, the Essene masters replied that "three are the dwellings of the Son of Man. . . . They are his body, his thoughts, and his feelings. . . . First shall the Son of Man seek peace with his own body. . . . Then shall the Son of Man seek peace with his own thoughts. . . . Then shall the Son of Man seek peace with his own feelings."[3]

The ancients offered eloquent insight into a way of thinking that allows us to redefine *what we experience on the outside* by addressing *what we have become on the inside*. Similar in some respects to the philosophies of Western health practices, one school of medicine brings about change by attacking the condition of illness itself. This approach eliminates foreign bodies with chemicals, or surgically removes the organs and tissue that appear diseased. A second school of thought looks beyond the outward expression of our body's appearance to the underlying factors that may be source of the condition, where the unseen forces of thought, feeling, and emotion become the blueprint to understanding and changing the conditions of our lives that no longer serve us.

To change the conditions of our outer world, we are invited to *actually become* the conditions of our desire from within. When we do so, the new conditions of health or peace are mirrored in the world around us. This is essential to the Essene passage offered previously. To bring peace to those whom we love in this world, we must first *become* that very peace. In the language of their time, the authors of the Dead Sea Scrolls even offer insights into the technology that allows this healing quality of peace: it must occur in our thoughts, feelings, and bodies. What a powerful and empowering concept!

As I share the Essene passages in group settings, I watch the faces of the audience from my vantage point at the front of the room. The change begins slowly at first. While some people simply record the words in their notebooks with little display of emotion, others become excited as they immediately grasp the significance of the ancient teachings. There is a magic that occurs in validating current ideas through manuscripts left by those walking the same path and seeking the same validations over two thousand years ago.

Through their insights, the Essene elders made clear distinctions among emotion, thought, and feeling. While closely related, thought and emotion must first be considered independently, then merged into a union of feeling that becomes the silent language of creation. The following descriptions of each experience are keys leading us into the heart of our lost mode of prayer.

## EMOTION

Emotion may be considered the *source of power* that drives us forward toward our goals in life. It is through the energy of our emotion that we fuel our thoughts to make them real. In itself, however, the power of emotion may be scattered and without direction. It is in the presence of thought that our emotion is given direction, breathing life into the image of our thoughts.

Ancient traditions suggest that we are capable of two primary emotions. Perhaps more accurately, we may say that through our lives we experience various conditions that resolve to a single emotion. Love is one extreme of such conditions. Whatever we have come to believe is love's opposite is the second extreme, often described as fear. The quality of our emotion determines how it is expressed. Sometimes flowing, at other times lodged within the tissues of our body, emotion is closely aligned with *desire,* the force that drives our imagination to resolution.

THOUGHT

Thought may be considered the *guidance system* that directs our emotion. It is the image or idea created by our thought that determines where our emotion and attention are directed. Thought is closely associated with imagination. Surprisingly to many people, in itself thought alone has little energy; it is only a possibility with no energy to give it life. This is the beauty of pure thought. In the absence of emotion, there is no power to make our thoughts real. It is our gift of thought in the absence of emotion that allows us to model and simulate the possibilities of life harmlessly, without creating fear or chaos in our lives. It is only in our love or fear for the objects of our thoughts that we breathe life into the creations of our imagination.

FEELING

Feeling may exist only in the presence of thought and emotion, for it represents the union of the two. When we feel, we are experiencing the desire of our emotion merged with the imagination of our thoughts. Feeling is the key to prayer, as it is our feeling world to which creation responds. As we attract or repel the people, situations, and conditions that we find in our experience, we may look to our feelings to understand why.

To have a feeling, by definition we must first have both an underlying thought and an emotion. The challenge in developing our highest levels of personal mastery is to recognize what thoughts and emotions are represented as our feelings.

From these three brief and possibly oversimplified definitions, it becomes apparent why it is impossible to "think away" frightening and painful experiences. Thought is only one component of our experience, the "seeing" in our mind of possible outcomes. Pain, however, is a feeling, the product of our thought fueled by our love or fear for what our mind believes has occurred. With this formula in mind, the Essene masters invite us to heal the memories of our most painful experiences by changing the emotion of the experience itself.

As an ancient basis for the modern axiom "energy follows attention," a concise parable from the lost Gospel Q describes this concept: "Whoever tries to protect his life will lose it." These few deceptively brief words explain why we sometimes attract into our lives those experiences that we least choose to have. In this example, as we prepare and defend ourselves against each possibility and every situation where we could lose our lives, the model suggests that we are actually drawing attention to the very experience that we are choosing to avoid. In the not wanting, we create the conditions that allow it to be. Rather than focusing our attention on what we do not want, a higher choice is found in identifying that which we choose to bring into our lives, and living from that perspective. Affirmations provide a beautiful example of precisely this principle.

In recent times, affirmations have become very popular with followers of some spiritual and esoteric teachings. In these traditions it is suggested that by affirming the things that we choose to experience in our lives, often many times each day, they will come to pass. As a rule of thumb, the less cluttered the affirmation, the clearer the effect. The words of our affirmations often echo a desire for life change, such as, "My perfect mate is manifesting for me now," or "I am abundant, now and in all future manifestations."

I know people who carry their affirmations to the level of a serious discipline. They begin preparing for their day in the bathroom with Post-it notes all around the mirror, reminding them of their

E

Gregg Braden

affirmations. As they drive to work in the morning, the notes continue on the dashboards of their cars and hang from their rearview mirrors. In their offices at work, on their desks, bulletin boards, and stuck to the screens of their computers are even more notes, each note serving as a vigilant reminder of those things that they chose to have, change, or bring into their lives.

Clearly, affirmations have opened powerful doors for some people. For the first time, individuals have begun to feel empowered and responsible with regard to the events of their lives. For some people, their affirmations have obviously worked. For many, however, they have not. After months of countless reiterations of creative reminders with no result, they have simply stopped saying affirmations. Our ancient model of thought, emotion, and feeling may help those people to understand what has happened or failed to happen.

# When Prayer Doesn't Work

Recently I conducted an informal survey among seminar participants regarding prayer. The results of each survey were used to provide a modern-day example of the nature of prayer for that particular audience. I began each survey by simply asking the audience, "When you pray, what do you find yourself praying about?" Standing in front of a flip chart, I recorded the many and varied scenarios that members of each group described. After six months of these informal surveys, from audiences representing a cross-section of ethnic, geographic, and age-defined backgrounds, four broad categories of prayer emerged from the descriptions: more money, better jobs, better health, and better relationships, in precisely that order.

| Prayer For | Thought | Feeling | Emotion |
|---|---|---|---|
| 1. More money | ? | ? | ? ? ? ? |
| 2. Better jobs | | | |
| 3. Better health | | | |
| 4. Better relationships | | | |

Applying our model of prayer as thought, feeling, and emotion, we may explore why our prayers work and what happens when they do not. For example, at the top of our list, the most common prayer noted was for "More Money." To have a prayer *about* "more money," we must first have perceptions about the money that we already have. Filling in the blank spaces as we move across the table to the right offers insight into the quality of those perceptions.

When I asked the audiences to describe their thoughts about money when they ask for more in prayer, the answers flew back to me from throughout the room. Not surprisingly, they were similar in nature. Such phrases as "not enough," "need more," and "running out" were common. Quickly I recorded the words that the audience shared under the heading "Thought."

Earlier, we identified thought as our guidance system, the directional program for the energy that we move in our world. Without the power to fuel our thought, it may exist indefinitely as a possibility in our mind. *The potential of thought in the absence of the energy to fuel our thought, we know as a wish.* For our thought to become empowered, we must give it energy. Perhaps this is the answer to why our prayers sometimes appear to go unanswered. In the absence of the power to bring our affirmations and prayers to life, they may exist indefinitely as potential: well-intentioned wishes.

It is our gift of emotion that empowers the possibility of our wish. Recognizing that we may choose love or fear as the emotion that fuels our thought, more often than not our perceived need for anything is based in fear. When we say we "need more," that there is "not enough," or that we are "running out of," fear is generally the emotion driving such statements. Acknowledging that there may be exceptions, I placed the word "fear" at the head of the "Emotion" category in our chart. From these outwardly simple elements of prayer, we gain tremendous clarity into the mechanism of how and why our prayers work as they do.

Addressing each audience with the results of its chart, I would pose a question:

"When we merge the *emotion* of fear into the *thought* of 'not enough,' what is the feeling that we get?"

The response was usually silence. I was not surprised, because the feeling is different for everyone. The word that we use to describe the feeling is unimportant. What is important is the feeling.

"Go ahead," I ask again, "what does it feel like when you think that you have no money and your emotion is one of fear?

"Yuck!" I hear from somewhere in the room.

"Crummy!" someone else exclaims.

"Precisely," I reply. "That is precisely the point." We choose the conditions of our lives through our feelings, the invisible union of our thoughts and emotions. As we imagine an outcome in our mind's eye and become aware of the emotion that is fueling our imagination, our feeling is created. To understand what we have created, we are invited to simply look at the world around us. How are we to create money, relationships, and health if the feelings that empower our creation are "crummy" and "yuck"? Feelings of unworthiness fuel the creation of the very experience we least choose to have in our lives, the expression of not being worthy. Nearly every person in the room has heard the principles of the exercise before. What is new, perhaps, is the opportunity actually to understand what has happened to our prayers in the past. That is where our healing begins.

Working through such exercises together, on an inexpensive flip chart, in less than ten minutes, it becomes possible to illustrate the mechanism for what may be the greatest power in creation. Lost to the West a millennium and a half ago is the joy that comes from remembering our power to bring wellness, abundance, health, security, and joy to our lives, and have fun doing it! In addition to identifying *how* our inner technology of prayer works, we now have a way to *change* the elements of our prayer to better serve us in the future.

Immediately the realization would settle over each audience. First I would hear a sigh. Then another, and another. Each became punctuated with giggles of nervous laughter—perhaps an unconscious effort to dispel the intensity of the moment. Looking into the faces of each audience, I had the privilege of watching the miracle begin.

## The Soup of Creation

I have learned many things from many people, in a variety of settings over the years. Though each audience is unique, there are consistent threads that appear to be universal, weaving each group within each city into the common experience of one family. The asking of a question is one of those threads. As one person finds the courage to ask a question, others in the room are asking the same question as well, perhaps on unspoken levels. Some people may be aware of their question, but are simply shy about asking in a group setting. For others, it is not until they hear the words that they respond, "Yes, I've wondered about that, too." I savor those moments. The opportunity to interact and draw new clarity from one another is where our great moments of communication begin.

During one of the first opportunities that I had to present the concepts of prayer in a workshop situation, a gentleman close to the front of the room let out a moan that the whole room could hear. He had definitely gotten my attention! Looking his way, I saw a grimace of uncertainty on his face. Searching for a way to acknowledge the man's frustration without singling him out specifically and, perhaps embarrassing him, I turned to the audience in general and asked, "Are there questions?"

The man in the front of the room immediately seized the opportunity. Perhaps in his mid-thirties, he had one elbow on the table that he shared with the others in his row. His chin was resting casually on his hand, palm up, opened under his jaw. As I walked in his direction to honor his question, he placed his pencil on the table next to his notebook. I glanced quickly at the page that was facing up. It was covered with notes, diagrams, and scribbles. I could see that this man had been very busy. With a deep sigh, he began.

"I have heard all this before," he said, with his chin still resting on his hand. "I've been on the 'path' for over twenty years, with many teachers. In one way or another, they have all said the same thing. What you are saying is nothing new. Still, you have touched on something that has never quite clicked for me. How do our feelings *inside* have any effect on what happens in the world *outside* of our bodies?"

I thought back to the discussion I had shared with my mother, months earlier. The idea that the nonphysical component of thought, feeling, or emotion could have any effect whatsoever upon the physical world of molecules, atoms, and cells was the mystery that my mother, as well as this gentleman, had asked me to address. I began with an explanation that I have used as an analogy many times over the years. It comes from an experiment that I remember performing earlier in my life to prove to myself the principles that we were discussing.

The Isaiah Effect

"The soup of creation exists as a state of possibilities," I began. "All of the components for all of the things that we could ever conceive of, including life itself, exist as this state of possibility. Although the components are there to build them, there has been no trigger to 'nudge' them into motion. The idea is very similar to creating rock candy from a jar of water saturated with sugar. We may place many tablespoons of sugar into the water and watch as the sugar dissolves and disappears. Though we no longer see the sugar, we know there are several tablespoons hidden somewhere in the water.

"The sugar remains in the same state—invisible—until something comes along and changes the conditions of the water. We call this a catalyst, something that triggers a new opportunity for the sugar and water to interact. The trigger can be as simple as placing a fibrous string into the water. As the sugar-laden water seeps into the string, it evaporates, leaving behind the sugar. In the absence of the water, the sugar now crystallizes into a new expression of itself, the shiny crystals that follow the laws of air rather than the laws of water. Different temperatures and pressures represent different laws and produce different crystals.

"When we create feelings about the things that we choose to experience in our world, our feelings are like the string in the sugar solution. Into the possibilities of creation, we place a *feeling picture,* just enough energy to allow for a new possibility. The key to this system, however, is that creation gives back precisely what our picture has shown. The picture tells the soup of creation where we have placed our attention. The emotion that we attach to our picture attracts the picture's possibility. When we 'don't want' something—an emotion based in fear—our fear actually fuels what we claim not to want. These laws invite us to empower our choices by focusing upon the positive experiences that we choose, rather than by preparing for the negative things that we don't want. Creation simply

157

allows us the consequence of our feeling, by perpetuating what we have shown a picture of. This is the ancient secret of a lost mode of prayer, forgotten in the fourth century A.D."

I saw the man's expression change before my eyes. In a matter of seconds, this simple experiment, replicated today in mayonnaise jars bathed in the sunlight of countless windowsills in unnumbered classrooms throughout the world, explained a possibility that had mystified him for years.

## How Do We Pray?

Following our exercise of affirmations and prayer, I asked the audience members if they felt that their prayers of the past had been answered. At first there was a silence, a hesitancy to answer. Slowly, people began to raise their hands to say "no" or "only sometimes." These people were telling me that for the categories of prayer regarding money, jobs, relationships, and teachers, many felt that their prayers had not been answered.

My next question was "Why?" Where do we turn to understand the sophisticated technology of prayer, and how do we apply it in our lives? For purposes of study, prayer researchers divide the many applications and methods of prayer used in the West into broad categories. For example, Margaret Paloma, a sociology professor at the University of Akron, Ohio, identifies four classes, or modes, as described below:

### Colloquial Prayer

We speak to God in our own words, informally describing problems or giving thanks for the blessings in our lives: "Dear God, please, this one time, if you allow my car to get to the gas station at the next exit of the freeway, I promise that I will never let the gas tank of my car get this low again."

*Petitionary Prayer*

In this type, we claim our good from the creative forces of our world for specific things or outcomes. Petitionary prayer may be formal or in our own words: "Mighty 'I Am' presence, I claim the right to heal."

*Ritualistic Prayer*

Here we repeat a predetermined sequence of words, perhaps on special occasions or at prescribed times. Bedtime prayers such as "Now I lay me down to sleep" or the "God is great, God is good" of mealtimes are familiar examples.

*Meditative Prayer*

A meditative prayer is a prayer beyond words. In meditation we are silent, still, open, and aware of the presence of the creative forces within our world and our bodies. In our stillness, we allow creation to express itself through us in the moment.

To many people, the practice of meditation is beyond the scope of prayer. In the strictest sense of the word, if the meditation involves a thought, a feeling, and an emotion, it may be defined as both meditation and prayer.

The above four modes, used individually or combined with one another, constitute the bulk of prayer modalities used in the West today.

Throughout my experience of the indigenous and esoteric traditions, there have always been references to a mode of prayer that has never seemed to fit into any of these categories. Journeys into some of the most sacred places remaining on earth today have revealed a mode of prayer that is reserved for initiates and serious students of spiritual studies. The temple walls of Egypt, the customs of Native Americans in the North and the *curanderos* (healers) in the mountains of Peru have all demonstrated a form of prayer that does not appear to be accounted for in Western traditions. Is it possible that a *fifth mode* exists which allows us to merge our thoughts, feelings, and emotions into a single, potent force of creation? Furthermore, is this the force that opens directly to the healing processes of our bodies and our world? Ancient texts, as well as modern studies, suggest that the answer is yes.

The examples of the healed cancer, the disappearing neck wound, compressed time in the Sinai desert, and the mysterious reversal of the intended bombings in Iraq offer clues to the secret of our lost mode of prayer. Through our new understandings of time and choice points, quantum physics allows for the possibility of each of these apparent miracles as outcomes that already exist. The secret of our lost mode of prayer is to shift our perspective of life by feeling that the "miracle" has already happened and our prayers have been answered. Indigenous peoples of the world share this memory of prayer in their most sacred texts and oldest traditions. Now we have the opportunity to bring this wisdom into our lives as prayers of gratitude for what already exists, rather than asking for our prayers to be answered.

## David's Prayer

I reached over my shoulder and pulled a fresh bottle of water from my backpack. It was only eleven o'clock in the morning and already the high desert sun had penetrated the thick nylon, sapping any remaining coolness from the bottle. For weeks now, the warnings had been issued: no campfires, no burning of refuse. Even tossing a cigarette from the window of a moving vehicle could subject a person to a hefty fine. This was the third year of drought in the American desert Southwest. Though it was a time of weather extremes everywhere, it seemed as though the mountains of northern New Mexico were especially affected. Ski areas had not opened that year, and the Rio Grande slowed to a trickle before merging with the Red River near Questa.

Opening the bottle, my grip on the soft, warm plastic forced a small trickle to erupt around the cap. I watched, fascinated, as the water splashed to the ground. The surface was so parched that the droplets merged into a pool before rolling into a small depression nearby. Even in that shallow pit, they did not spread and soak into the ground. To my amazement, the entire pool evaporated within seconds.

"The ground is too thirsty to drink," David said softly from behind me.

"Have you ever seen it this dry before?" I asked.

"The old ones say that it has been over one hundred years since the rains have left us for so long," David replied. "That is why we have come to this place, to call to the rain."

I had met David years earlier, before I actually moved into the high desert north of Santa Fe. We had each been on a sacred journey away from our homes, families, and loved ones. His people called such a journey a "vision quest." For me, it was an opportunity to escape my corporate commitments and live close to the land, a periodic evaluation of my purpose and direction in life. Five months after our first meeting, I found myself living full-time in the mountains that I had previously visited for solitude. Though David and I seldom saw one another, when we did it was as if we had spoken only the day before. There was never any awkwardness or need to apologize for our lack of correspondence. We each knew that we had to place priorities on the events of our lives that demanded our attention in the moment. In the present moment we were together, sharing a hot morning in the summer desert.

After a long, warm drink from my bottle, I stood up and began walking toward David. Already he was a good twenty steps ahead of me. I followed him along an invisible path that only he could see. Our pace quickened as we made our way through thick stands of knee-high sage and chamiso bushes. I watched the ground in front of me. Each of his footsteps kicked up a small puff of dust that disappeared in the hot, dry breeze. Behind us there was not a trace of the trail that we were creating. David knew exactly where he was going, to a special place that had been known to his family and their ancestors for many generations. Year after year, they would come to this very place for their vision quests and rites of passage, and on special occasions such as this day.

"Over there," David said. I looked where he was pointing. It looked remarkably similar to the other hundred thousand or so acres of sage, juniper, and pine that surrounded us in the valley.

"Over where?" I asked.

"There, where the earth changes," David replied.

I looked closer, studying the land. Scanning the tops of the vegetation, my eyes searched for irregularities in spacing and color. Suddenly it leaped out at me, like a hidden image in one of those three-dimensional charts with a picture disguised among the dots. I looked closer and saw that the tips of the sage bushes were spaced differently. Walking toward the apparent anomaly, I could see something on the ground, something large and unexpected. Stopping to position myself in the shade created by my body in the sun, I could make out a series of stones, beautiful stones of all kinds, arranged in perfect geometries of lines and circles. Each stone was situated perfectly, betraying the precision with which ancient hands had placed it hundreds of years before.

"What is this place?" I asked David. "Why is it here, in the middle of nowhere?"

"This is the reason we have come," he laughed. "It is because of what you call 'nowhere' that we are here. Today there is only you, me, earth, sky, and our Creator. That is all. There is nothing else here. Today we will touch the unseen forces of this world, speaking to Mother Earth, Father Sky, and the messengers of the in-between.

"Today," David said, "we pray rain."

I am always amazed at how quickly old memories can flood the present. I am equally amazed at how quickly they disappear. Immediately my mind raced to the images of what I expected the next moments to look like. In my mind I recalled prayer scenes that were familiar to me. I remembered going to neighboring villages and seeing native peoples dressed in garments of the earth. I remember studying them as they moved rhythmically to the beat of wooden mallets pounding on drums of elk hide stretched tightly over pine frames. Nothing in my memory, however, prepared me for what I was about to witness.

"The stone circle is a medicine wheel," David explained. "It has been here for as long as my people can remember. The wheel itself has no power. It serves as a place of focus for the one invoking the prayer. You could think of it as a road map."

I must have had a puzzled look on my face. David anticipated my next thought, and answered before I had finished formulating the question in my mind.

"A map between humans and the forces of this world," he replied to the question that I had not yet asked. "The map was created here, in this place, because here the skins between the worlds are very thin. From the time I was a young boy, I was taught the language of this map. Today I will travel an ancient path that leads to other worlds. From those worlds, I will speak with the forces of this earth, to do what we came here to do: to invite the rain."

I watched as David removed his shoes. Even the way that he untied the laces of his tattered work boots was a prayer—methodical, intentional, and sacred. With his feet bare to the earth, he turned his back and walked away from me toward the circle. Without a sound he navigated his way around the wheel, taking great care to honor the placement of each stone. With reverence for his ancestors, he placed his naked feet onto the parched earth. With each step, his toes came within fractions of an inch of the outer stones. Never once did he touch them. Each stone remained precisely where the hands of another had placed it, from a generation long departed. As he rounded the farthest rim of the circle, David turned, allowing me to see his face. To my amazement, his eyes were closed. They had been closed the entire time. One by one, he was honoring the placement of each round, white stone by feeling the position of his feet! As David returned to the position closest to me, he stopped, straightened his posture, and moved his hands into a praying position in front of his face. His breathing became nearly indiscernible. He appeared oblivious to the heat of the midday sun. After a few brief moments in this position, he took a deep breath, relaxed his posture, and turned to me.

"Let's go, our work is finished here," he said, looking directly at me.

"Already?" I asked, a little surprised. It seemed as though we had just arrived. "I thought you were going to pray for rain."

David sat on the ground to put his shoes back on. Looking up, he smiled.

"No, I said that I would 'pray rain,'" he replied. "If I had prayed *for* rain, it could never happen."

That afternoon the weather changed. The rain began suddenly, with a few splats on the deck facing the mountains to the east. Within moments the droplets grew larger and more frequent, until a full-fledged thunderstorm was under way. Huge black clouds hovered over the valley, obscuring the Colorado mountains to the north for the rest of the afternoon and into the evening. The water accumulated faster than the earth could absorb it, and before long, local fears of flooding became a reality. I stared out at the eleven miles of sage between me and the mountain range to the east. The valley looked like a vast lake.

Later in evening, I watched the weather reports on the local stations. Though not surprised, I remember feeling a sense of awe as the colored climate maps flashed across the screen. Animated arrows indicated a typical pattern of cool, moist air angling down from the Pacific Northwest, across Utah, and into Colorado, as it often did for the summer months. Then, unexplainably, the jet stream changed its course and did something unusual. I watched, amazed, as the air mass dipped with precision into southern Colorado and northern New Mexico before looping tightly back to the north, resuming its path across the Midwest. With the dip came low pressure and cool air to mix with the warm, moist air moving up from the Gulf of Mexico, the perfect recipe for rain. From the reports, it sounded as though there would be rain, and a lot of it. I called David the following morning.

"What a mess!" I exclaimed. "Roads are washed out. Homes and fields are flooded everywhere. What has happened? How do you account for all of this rain?" The voice on the other end of the phone was silent for a few seconds.

"That is the problem," David said. "That is the part of the prayer that I have not figured out yet!"

By the following day, the ground was wet enough to accept more water. I drove through several small villages on my way into the nearest town. People were ecstatic with the coming of the rain. Children were playing in the mud. Farmers were at the feed and hardware stores, resuming the business of livestock and agriculture. The crops had sustained minimal damage. Cattle had water in livestock ponds, and it looked as though northern New Mexico would be spared the heartache of drought, at least for the remainder of one more summer.

## Gratitude: Breathing Life
## into Our Prayers

David's story beautifully illustrates the inner workings of the mode of prayer forgotten by our culture nearly two thousand years ago. Following his brief ceremony inside the medicine wheel, David had looked at me and simply said, "Let's go, our work is finished here." The remainder of my time with David that day now makes much more sense and has much greater relevance.

Now I knew what David's response, "I came to pray rain," meant. The rest of the story is perhaps best shared in David's own words.

"When I was young," he had said, "our elders passed on to me the secret of prayer. The secret is that when we ask for something, we acknowledge what we do not have. Continuing to ask only gives power to what has never come to pass.

"The path between man and the forces of this world begins in our hearts. It is here that our feeling world is married to our thinking world. In my prayer, I began with the feeling of gratitude for all that is and all that has come to pass. I gave thanks for the desert wind, the heat, and the drought, for that is the way of it, until now. It is not good. It is not bad. It has been our medicine.

"Then I chose a new medicine. I began to have the feeling of what rain feels like. I felt the feeling of rain upon my body. Standing in the stone circle, I imagined that I was in the plaza of our village, barefoot in the rain. I felt the feeling of wet earth oozing between my naked toes. I smelled the smell of rain on the straw-and-mud walls of our village after the storms. I felt what it feels like to walk through fields of corn growing up to my chest because the rains have been so plentiful. The old ones remind us that this is how we choose our path in this world. We must first have the feelings of what we wish to experience. This is how we plant the seeds of a new way. From that point forward," David continued, "our prayer becomes a prayer of thanks."

"Thanks? Do you mean thanks for what we have created?"

"No, not for what we may have created," David replied. "Creation is already complete. Our prayer becomes a prayer of thanks for the *opportunity* to choose which creation we experience. Through our thanks, we honor all possibilities and bring the ones we choose into this world."

In his way, in the words of his people, David had shared with me the secret of communing with the forces of our world and our bodies. Though I had heard with my ears and understood what he had said, his words have even more meaning today.

## Our Lost Mode of Prayer

Following my time with David, again I searched in the texts, some ancient, some contemporary. I discovered that many groups, organizations, and philosophies had hinted at our lost mode of prayer. Many continue to do so today, with techniques suggesting that we "think like our prayers have come to pass" or "come from the place that our prayer is accomplished." As I have searched further into their technologies, however, almost universally the element of feeling is absent.

In the mid-twentieth century, the man known simply as Neville brought the lost mode of prayer to the forefront of contemporary thinking through his pioneering work in the laws of cause and effect. Born in Barbados, West Indies, Neville eloquently described his philosophy of bringing our dreams alive through the use of feeling by inviting us to "make [our] future dream a present fact by assuming the *feeling* of [our] desire fulfilled."[4] Additionally, Neville suggests that it is our love for our new state that empowers its birth into existence. "Unless you, yourself, enter the image and think from it, it is incapable of birth."[5] Examining a specific prayer, such as a prayer of peace, may add a degree of concreteness to these some-times nebulous concepts.

Much of our conditioning in Western traditions has invited us to "ask" that peace come to pass in specific circumstances of our world. In asking for peace to be present, for example, we may unknowingly be acknowledging the lack of peace in our world, per-haps inadvertently reinforcing what may be viewed as a state of non-peace. From the perspective of our fifth mode of prayer, we are invited to create peace in our world through the quality of thought, feeling, and emotion in our body. Once we have created the image of our desire in our mind and felt the feeling of our desire fulfilled within our heart, it has already happened! Though the intent of our prayer may not have appeared in full view of our immediate senses, we assume that it is so. The secret to the fifth mode of prayer lies in acknowledging that when we feel, the effect of our feelings has occurred somewhere, upon some level of our existence.

Our prayer, then, originates from a very different perspective. Rather than *asking* that the outcome of our prayer come to pass, we acknowledge our role as an active part of creation and give thanks for what we are certain that we have created. Whether we see imme-diate results or not, our thanks acknowledge that somewhere in cre-ation our prayer has already been fulfilled. Now our prayer becomes an affirmative prayer of thanks, fueling our creation, allowing it to blossom into its greatest potential. Following is a summary of our prayer of peace, through the traditional asking and from the per-spective of our lost mode of prayer.

| *Prayer of Asking* | *The Fifth Mode of Prayer* |
| --- | --- |
| 1. We focus on conditions where we believe that peace does not exist. | 1. We witness all events, those that we see in the absence of peace, without judgment of good, bad, right, or wrong. |

2. We ask for intervention from a greater power to change the conditions.

2. Through our technology of thought, feeling, and emotion, we create the conditions from within that we choose to witness in our outer world. For example, "Graceful change on earth, healing to all life, and peace in all worlds." Our feeling that it is already so empowers our prayer and brings its outcome to focus. In doing so, we have created a renewed memory of a greater possibility.

3. In the asking, we may be acknowledging that peace and graceful change are not already present in these places.

3. We acknowledge the power of our "inner technology" and assume that our prayer has come to pass; peace and graceful earth changes are already here.

4. We continue to ask for this intervention until we see the change actually come to pass in our world.

4. Our prayer now consists of
   a. acknowledging what we have chosen,
   b. feeling that it is already accomplished,
   c. giving thanks for our opportunity to choose, and, in doing so, breathing life into our choice.

Recent translations of original Aramaic texts offer new insights as to why references to prayer may have been so ambiguous in the past. Twelfth-century manuscripts reveal the degree to which liberties were taken to condense sentence structure and simplify their meaning. Perhaps one of the most obvious and, at the same time, subtle of these references is a prayer that students of religious studies and in Sunday school classes have been taught for generations. This fragment of our lost mode of prayer invites us to "ask" that our heart's desire come to pass and we shall "receive" the benefit of our prayer, as in the familiar admonition "Ask and you shall receive." A comparison of the expanded Aramaic text with the modern biblical version of the prayer offers powerful insights into the possibilities of this lost technology.

The modern, condensed version:

*Whatsoever ye shall ask the Father in my name, he will give it*
   *to you.*
*Hitherto have ye asked nothing in my name:*
*ask and ye shall receive, that your joy may be full.*[6]

The original, retranslated Aramaic version:

*All things that you ask straightly, directly . . . from inside my name, you will be given. So far you have not done this. Ask without hidden motive and* be surrounded by your answer. Be enveloped by what you desire, *that your gladness be full. . . .*[7]

Through the words of another time, we are invited to embrace our lost mode of prayer as a *consciousness that we embody,* rather than as a prescribed form of *action that we perform* on occasion. In inviting us to be "surrounded" by our answer and "enveloped" by what we desire, this ancient passage emphasizes the power of our feelings.

In the modern idiom, this eloquent phrase reminds us that to create in our world we must first have the feelings of our creation already fulfilled. Our prayers then become prayers of giving thanks for what we have created, rather than of asking that our creations come to pass.

## A New Faith

I cannot say for certain that David's prayer played any role in the storms that followed our time together. What I can say is that the weather in northern New Mexico changed that day. From weeks of drought, failing crops, and dehydrating cattle, in one day the weather shifted into torrential rains that gave way to a pattern of daily showers lasting until the autumn frosts. Further, I can say that there was a synchronicity between the unexpected shift in the weather and the experience I had shared with David. The time between the events was a matter of hours. How are we to prove an event of such magnitude and significance?

The people of the native villages in the desert Southwest need no proof; beyond doubt, they *know* that within each of them lives the power to commune directly with the creative forces of this world and beyond. They do so without expectations, without judging the outcome of their communion. For example, if the rains had not come, David would have viewed the absence of rain as a part of his prayer, rather than as a sign of failure. His prayer was without condition. He placed no time frame on the outcome of his communion with the forces of nature. David had shared a sacred moment with the powers of creation, planted the seed of a possibility through his prayer, and given thanks for his opportunity to choose a new outcome. His unwavering faith that his prayer had accomplished something is the key to embracing our lost mode of prayer.

In our modern world, we often find ourselves expecting quick gratification and a rapid response. The processing time of our computers, for example, is more than fifty times faster than when microcomputers were first introduced in the early 1980s. We thought that they were fast then. Waiting for more than a fraction of a second after typing our command into the keyboard often evokes anxiety from a response that was state-of-the-art only a few short years ago. Microwave ovens have halved the time required to boil water with conventional electricity or gas. Now, we wait impatiently as the digital counter marks down the seconds until our water boils. There has been a tendency to view the results of prayer in much the same way. If results are not immediately forthcoming, we may feel that our prayer has not worked. The ancients knew better.

When David prayed rain, he knew beyond any doubt that his prayer had invited a new possibility to be present. He also knew that his prayer was a possibility only. Perhaps the effect was not immediately visible to our eyes. As he and I stood in the sage field, high in the deserts of northern New Mexico, the fact that we did not immediately see rain was of little consequence to David. He was confident in his ability to choose a new outcome, and his confidence came naturally for him.

David's certainty that he had planted a seed of possibility somewhere in the ethers of creation, leads us to reexamine a word that may have lost meaning in recent times. That word is *faith*. Though it is defined in *The American Heritage College Dictionary* as "belief that does not rest on logical proof or material evidence," the ancient and indigenous peoples of our world accept a much broader definition of faith. Their understandings remain as valid today as in generations past, when faith was the key to communicating with the unseen forces of our world. Through their wonderfully integrated view of our role in creation, *faith becomes the acceptance of our power as a directive force in creation.* It is this unified perspective that allows us to move forward in life, trusting that through our prayers we have planted the seeds of new possibilities. Our faith allows us to rest assured that our prayers are accomplished. In this knowledge, our prayers become expressions of thanks, giving life to our choices as they blossom in our world.

The paths of the Infinite Garden

"must be traversed by the body,

the heart and the mind as one. . . ."

—*THE ESSENE GOSPEL OF PEACE*

# THE SCIENCE
# OF MAN

## Secrets of Prayer
## and Healing

In the fourth century A.D., our relationship to the forces of the world around us, as well as within us, began to change. When the words validating these relationships were edited from the texts that had preserved them, we began to view ourselves as observers, passively *witnessing* the wonders of nature and the functions of our bodies. Traditions such as those of the Essenes and Native Americans suggest that our relationship to the world extends far beyond the role of observer, reminding us that we are a part of all that we see. In a world of such interconnectedness, it is impossible to watch passively as a leaf falls from a tree or an ant races across the ground. The very act of observing, places us in the role of participant.

The physicist Niels Bohr offered a theory in the late 1920s that suggested this very relationship, and described a similar view in modern terms. It had been noted that on the atomic level, matter sometimes behaved strangely, in contradiction to accepted theory. In simplified terms, Bohr's theory, known as the Copenhagen View, postulated that the observer of any event becomes part of the event, *just by the act of observing.* In the very small world of atoms, the observation takes on a greater significance as "atom-sized objects are disturbed by any attempt to observe them."[1] From this line of thinking it is clear that modern science is searching for a language to describe the relationship of unity that the Essenes employed as the basis of their prayers.

Viewing ourselves as independent of the world around us has precipitated a sense of separateness, an "in here" versus "out there" attitude. From the time of our childhood, we begin to believe that the world "just happens." Sometimes good things occur, at other times things that are not so good. Our world appears to happen all around us, often for no apparent reason. In preparing for the what-ifs of life, we spend much of our time building strategies to survive and navigate whatever challenges may come our way. New research into the relationship between the power of our feelings and the chemistry of our bodies suggests that the implications of such "us" and "them" viewpoints are far-reaching and, at times, unexpected.

Science has demonstrated, for example, that specific feelings produce a predictable chemistry in our bodies that corresponds to that particular feeling. As we change our feelings, we change our chemistry. We literally have what may be viewed as "hate chemistry," "anger chemistry," "love chemistry," and so on. Biological expressions of emotion appear in our bodies as the levels of hormones, antibodies, and enzymes present in our state of wellness. Love chemistry, for example, affirms life by optimizing our immune system and the regulatory functions of our body. Conversely, anger, which is sometimes directed inward as guilt, may be expressed as a suppressed immune response.

In the summer of 1995, Glen Rein, Ph.D., Mike Atkinson, and Rollin McCraty, M.A., published a paper in the *Journal of Advance-*

*ment in Medicine.* Titled "The Physiological and Psychological Effects of Compassion and Anger," it focused upon the study of salivary immunoglobulin A(S-IgA), an antibody found in mucus, which defends our upper respiratory, gastrointestinal, and urinary tracts from infection. The essence of the paper stated that "higher levels of S-IgA are associated with decreased incidence of disease to upper respiratory infections."[2] The abstract of the paper concluded that "anger produced a significant increase in total mood level disturbance and heart rate, but not S-IgA levels. *Positive emotions, on the other hand, produced a significant increase in S-IgA levels.* Examining the effects of a six-hour period, we observed that anger, in contrast to care, produced a significant inhibition of S-IgA from one to five hours after the emotional experience"[3] (my emphasis). Further studies point to specific qualities of emotion as a powerful factor in hypertension, congestive heart failure, and coronary artery disease.

Living as if the world "out there" were somehow separate from us opens the door to a belief system of judgment and the chemical expressions of that judgment in our bodies. Thus we tend to see our world in terms of "good germs" and "bad germs," and use words such as "toxins" and "waste" to describe the by-products of the very functions that give us life. It is in such a world that our bodies may become a combat zone for forces at odds with one another, creating the biological battlegrounds that play out as illness and disease.

The holistic perspective of the Essenes, on the other hand, sees all facets of our bodies as elements of one sacred and divine force moving through creation. Each is an expression of God. In a world where all that we may know and experience originates from such a unified source, bacteria, germs, and the by-products of our bodies work together to imbue our bodies with strength and life. This view invites us to redefine the tears, perspiration, blood, and products of digestion that we have known as "waste" as sacred elements of the earth that have served us, rather than abhorrent by-products that must be eliminated, discarded, and destroyed.

# Why Prayer?

The voice came from somewhere toward the back of the room. My eyes darted to the left, searching each row to locate the source of the question. From the stage at the end of the ballroom, I looked out over the participants in our three-day program. I have always considered the opportunity to speak with an audience an honor as well as a sign of trust. An important aspect of honoring each audience is to acknowledge the questions that are certain to arise at the end of any meaningful discussion. I gazed into the faces focused upon me. A glaring bank of overhead lights illuminated the first few rows from the ceiling. As I looked toward the back of the room, each successive row became more faint, merging into a darkness that extended to walls I could not see. The only light visible across the room was the green glow of the exit signs over the doors.

"Who asked that question?"

Directed by the gestures of the audience pointing to the left, I stepped off the platform and walked to the aisle in the hope of eye contact. An audience facilitator with a microphone met me at the row where the fingers were pointing.

"Here I am," a frail voice echoed.

"Good," I said. "I see you now. What is your name?"

"Evelyn," the tiny voice whispered awkwardly into the microphone. "My name is Evelyn."

"Evelyn, would you please repeat your question?" I asked.

"Certainly" she replied. "I simply asked, 'Why prayer?' What good does it do, really?"

I heard the question that Evelyn was asking. I sensed an innocence underlying her question as my mind listened to the words themselves. In the circles of my friends and conversations, the role of prayer and prayer's relevance were common themes of our everyday discussions. Over long-distance conference calls and worldwide vigils coordinated on the Internet, we discussed the applications, origins, and techniques of prayer. Often our conversations were directed to the specifics of global events unfolding in the moment. In my recollection of our conversations, however, we had never discussed the actual *purpose* of prayer. Not really. Evelyn was doing her work well. By asking her question, she was inviting me to draw an answer from deep within myself to a question that I had never been asked.

It was one of those moments that occur only rarely. Somehow her question threaded its way through the sentries of logic and reason, slipping into the reality of the moment. I had little idea of what I was about to say. In response to Evelyn's question, I opened my mouth to reply, trusting implicitly in the process unfolding between us. One by one, the words tumbled from my mouth, in the precise instant that each was formed. Though not particularly surprised, I was in awe of the process, how easily each word flowed, how concise my reply.

"Prayer," I began, "is, to us, as water is to the seed of a plant."

That was all! My response was complete. A silence fell over the room. Together the audience and I paused to consider the power and simplicity of those thirteen words. I thought about what I had said. The seed of a plant is whole and complete unto itself. Under the right conditions, a seed may exist for hundreds of years simply as a seed, a rigid shell protecting a greater possibility. Only in the presence of water will the seed realize the greatest expression of its life.

We are like those seeds. We come into this world whole and complete unto ourselves, carrying the seed of something even greater.

Our time with one another, in the presence of life's challenges, awakens within us the greatest possibilities of love and compassion. It is in the presence of prayer that we blossom to fulfill our potential.

A smile came over Evelyn's face. I sensed that she already knew the answer that she had masterfully drawn from me. It was as if she had known that the room would benefit from hearing the words that, apparently, I would not otherwise have spoken that day. Early in the twentieth century, the prophet and poet Kahlil Gibran stated that the work we do in our lives is our love made visible. In her courage to stand in a room of several hundred people, most of whom were strangers to her, and speak timidly into her microphone, Evelyn drew from me a response that served each of us in that moment. Since that day, the same response has served many people in many cities. In those moments, Evelyn and I did our work—our love made visible—well together.

## Beyond the Words

I remember praying a lot as a child. I said my prayers in the way that I had been taught, at mealtime, bedtime, during holidays, and on special occasions. It was during these moments of prayer that I would give thanks for the good things in my life and reverently ask God to change the conditions that hurt me, or caused suffering in others. Often my prayers were for animals. I have always felt especially close to the animal kingdom, and took the liberty of sharing our family home with the wildlife that I would find in the wooded areas near our house in northern Missouri. Not allowed in the house proper, my animal friends would often compete for space with the family station wagon in our single-car garage. At any given time, nearly every class of animal was represented in the garage-sanctuary, a part of our home that my mother came to call the "menagerie."

I remember feeling that our home was a refuge of sorts, a shelter until the inhabitants could fly, run, swim, or scamper back into their natural environment. Sometimes the animals were sick or injured. With broken bones, shattered beaks, or torn limbs, I would find them in the wild, left alone to fend for themselves. Looking back, I now know that some of my guests were just too slow to escape my well-intentioned "rescue."

Living within customized habitats—individualized containers, glass jars, and converted bathtubs—each animal had a label of its own, meticulously identifying species, location found, and favorite foods. In an effort to explain why some animals were abandoned by their own kind, friends and family gently reminded me that this was "nature's way." I remember wondering, "What if nature's way could use a little help? What if all this animal needs is a few days in a safe home with the right food to heal from its injury?" My reasoning was that following a brief time of healing, the animals could return to the wild for whatever life held in store for them. Whether they lived one more day or for many years was unimportant to me. What did matter was that the animal's suffering ended. Even if the creature became a meal for another animal the next day, in the meantime it would be strong, healthy, and free of pain.

I would pray for my animals every night—for their safety, for their healing, for their lives. Sometimes my prayers would work. Sometimes they did not. I never understood why. If God was everywhere, listening, why did he hesitate to answer? If he could hear all of my prayers and answer some of them, some of the time, why would he refuse to do the same for another animal at another time? The inconsistency made little sense.

I continued to pray as I got older. Though I believed that I was praying in more adult ways, the themes of my prayers never really changed. I still spoke with the "powers that be" on behalf of the animals in my life. For those running in the wild as well as motionless

# Gregg Braden

casualties crumpled along the roadside, I asked for the blessings of safe journeys and peace in their afterlives.

Though I had always prayed for people as well, during this time my prayers for others grew beyond the realm of familiar faces. In addition to family, friends, and loved ones, my prayers were often for people whom I had never met. I knew them only as nameless faces that would flash across the screen of the black-and-white television in our living room or stare back at me from the pages of *Look* and *Life*. For animals and people alike, I prayed for their lives, and a healing of the things that hurt them in this world.

Eventually, my feelings about prayer began to change. Specifically, *the feelings that I had while I was praying* began to change. I sensed that something was missing. Though the sacredness of the moment was comforting to some degree, I always had the feeling that there was more. Often I would notice a nagging sensation deep inside myself, an ancient feeling that the prayer I had completed in the moment was just the beginning of something greater. I felt that there was a time when we were closer to the unseen forces of our world, and to one another. In the absence of religion and ritual, I sensed that prayer itself was the key to our closeness. Somewhere in the mists of our ancient memory, I knew that there must be more to the silent language that allows us to commune with the forces of our world and beyond.

In the early 1990s, I received the first inkling as to why my prayers had felt incomplete. The clue appeared unexpectedly one day as I was leafing through a copy of an ancient text given to me by a friend. What set this document apart from similar works was that the translator had returned to the original language of the authors for his references, rather than reiterate the words of other scholars, possibly distorted over time. There, in fresh translations of the original Aramaic manuscripts, were the actual details of how to merge the three components of prayer into a single, empowering force in our lives.

The text that my friend had offered was compiled by a renowned scholar of ancient studies, Edmond Bordeaux Szekely, the grandson of Alexandre Szekely, who compiled the first grammar of the Tibetan language over 150 years ago. Working from the original Aramaic version of the Gospels, Szekely's translations illustrated the rich language of the original prayers and stories offered by Jesus and his disciples. Though not surprised, I am still in awe at the clarity that such translations continue to shed upon the teachings and science of prayer. A fresh look at these works from the viewpoint of quantum physics offers subtleties that have been lost in other translations throughout later times.

Through the eyes of the Aramaic authors, for example, the way that a course of events unfolds in our lives is a matter of perspective. Whether we consider global history or personal healing, ancient scholars remind us that all possibilities have already been created and are already present. Rather than *forcing solutions upon the events of our lives,* we are invited to *choose* which possibility we identify with, and live as if it has already occurred. Clearly, this is not to suggest that our "will" is imposed upon others in the form of prayer. Rather, it is our willingness to allow for all possibilities without judging any of them, and knowing that we may attract or repel each through the choices we make in our lives that provides the subtle difference. Choosing an outcome through prayer does not guarantee that it will come to pass; our prayer simply opens the door to the possibility of that outcome. The question now becomes, How may we bring specific outcomes into the focus of the present through prayer?

## When Three Become One

Through their writings we know that the ancient Essenes believed that we commune with our world through our perceptions and senses. Every thought, feeling, emotion, breath, nutrient, or movement, or combination of any of these, was considered to be an expression of prayer. From the Essene perspective, as we sense, perceive, and express ourselves throughout our day, we are in constant prayer.

Through the poetic grace and powerful metaphors of their time, Essene texts remind us that our body, heart (feelings), and mind work together in much the same way as a chariot, horse, and driver.[4] Though considered independently, the three work hand in hand to provide our experience of life. In this analogy, the chariot is our body and the driver is our mind. The horse represents the feelings of our heart, the power that carries the horse and driver over the road of life. It is through the strength of our physical body, the wisdom of our heart's experience, and the purity of our intentions that we determine our quality of life.

If prayer is, in fact, the forgotten language through which we choose the outcomes and possibilities of life, in a very real sense each moment may be considered as a prayer. In each moment of our waking and sleeping lives, we are continuously thinking, feeling, and emoting, contributing to the outcome of our world. The key is that sometimes our contributions are direct and intentional, while at other times we may be participating indirectly, without even knowing of our contribution.

Experience of the latter type may best be described by those who feel that life "just happens" to them. People having this experience often sense that they are "bystanders" simply observing the processes of life happening around them to their friends, family, and loved ones—even to the earth itself. Feelings of this experience range from the awe and wonder of the birth of a new baby to a sense of helplessness at the tragic loss of life in times of war or natural disaster. Watching the horrors of refugees driven from their homes in the Kosovo crisis of 1999, or the outrage of mass killings in a public school, are examples of such moments of feeling helpless.

Recently translated texts, some of them over two thousand years old, offer another way to participate actively, to "do something" during such experiences of life. Recognizing the effectiveness of prayer's silent power, the ancients describe a form of prayer known today as *active prayer*. As these components of prayer are merged into one, we are offered a bridge into the language of creation. Through this bridge we may choose the outcome of a given situation from a series of possibilities. Five hundred years before the birth of Jesus, the Essene masters invited us to focus the power of prayer's individual elements—thought, feeling, and emotion, experienced as our heart, mind, and body—into a single focused outcome. The key to such mastery is echoed in a single passage: "The paths are seven through the Infinite Garden, *and each must be traversed by the body, the heart and the mind as one. . . .*"[5] It is this unified force of heaven's language, spoken through our bodies, that imbues life into our prayers and assures us that "whosoever shall say unto this mountain, be thou removed, and be thou cast into the sea . . . that those things which he saith shall come to pass. . . ."[6]

Consider the effects of prayer through a simple model. Over fifty years ago, in 1947, Dr. Hans Jenny (pronounced "Yen-knee") developed a new science to explore the relationship between vibration and form.[7] Through well-documented studies, Dr. Jenny demonstrated that vibration produced geometry. In other words, by creating vibration in a material that we can see, the pattern of the vibration becomes visible in that medium. When we change the vibration, we change the pattern. When we return to the original vibration, the original pattern reappears. Through experiments conducted in a variety of substances, Dr. Jenny produced an amazing variety of geometric patterns, ranging from very complex to very simple, in such materials as water, oil, and graphite and sulfur powder. Each pattern was simply the visible form of an invisible force.

The significance of these tests is that Dr. Jenny proved, beyond any doubt, that vibration causes a predictable pattern in the substance that it is projected into. *Thought, feeling, and emotion are vibration.* Just like the vibrations in Dr. Jenny's experiments, the vibrations of thought, feeling, and emotion create a disturbance in the "stuff" that they are projected into. Rather than water, sulfur, and graphite, we project our vibrations into the refined substance of consciousness. Each has an effect.

In chapter 4 we discussed the science that suggests that our future may already exist as one of many "possibilities," dormant in the soup of creation. As we make new choices in our lives each day, we awaken new possibilities, and fine-tune the eventual outcome. This view implies that each time we *ask* for something in prayer, a possibility exists where our prayer is *already answered.* If this view of our world is correct, then in the garage menagerie of my childhood, for example, each shattered beak, torn limb, and broken bone was one possible outcome for that moment. In the same moment, another outcome existed where each animal in my care was already healed. Each outcome already existed. Each possibility was real.

The key to choosing one outcome from among many possible outcomes is our ability to feel as if our choice has already come to pass. From our previous definition of prayer as "feeling," then, stated another way, we are invited to find the quality of thought and emotion that produces such a feeling—living as if our prayer had already been answered. For how may we benefit from the effect of our thought and emotion, if each pattern is moving in a random direction? If, on the other hand, the patterns of our prayer are focused into union, how can the "stuff" of creation fail to respond to our prayer?

When thought, feeling, and emotion are not aligned, each may be considered as *out of phase* with the others. While there may be brief areas of overlap, much of the pattern is unfocused, working in

FEELING

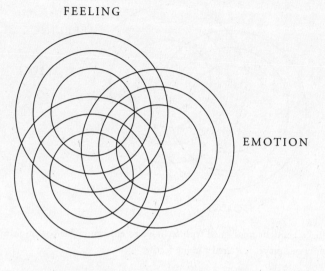

EMOTION

THOUGHT

Fig. 1. Thought, feeling, and emotion as unaligned patterns. In the absence of union, they may lose their focus.

different directions, independent of the rest of the pattern. The result is a scattering of energy.

For example, if our thought is "I choose the perfect mate in my life," a pattern of energy is released that expresses that thought. Any feeling or emotion that is not in sync with our thought is incapable of empowering our choice of a perfect mate. If they are misaligned through feelings that we are not worthy of having such a perfect partner or emotions of fear, our patterns may actually hinder our choice from becoming our outcome. In this nonaligned state we may find ourselves asking why our affirmations and prayers have not worked.

Through these simple examples, it becomes clear why prayer brings about the greatest change when the elements of prayer are focused and aligned with one another.

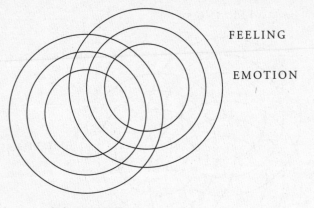

FEELING

EMOTION

THOUGHT

Fig. 2. Thought misaligned with feeling and emotion. This condition may render our prayer scattered and ineffective.

Without using the word *prayer*, and certainly in a less technical fashion, the idea of unifying thought, emotion, and feeling and living from the place of our heart's desire was offered early in this century using a very different language. Further affirming the use of our fifth mode of prayer, of assuming that our prayer has already happened, the work of Neville offers the following: "You must abandon yourself mentally to your wish fulfilled in your love for that state, and in so doing, live in the new state and no more from the old state."[8] Though effective, Neville's descriptions of our ability to change outcomes and choose new possibilities in our lives may have made little sense to the people of the early twentieth century. As with so many thinkers whose ideas are ahead of their time, little was known about Neville's work until after his death in 1972.

Understandings such as these allow us to view prayer as both a language and a philosophy bridging the worlds of science and spirit. Just as other philosophies are expressed through unique words and specialized vocabularies, prayer has a vocabulary of its own in the silent language of feeling. Sometimes an idea that makes perfect

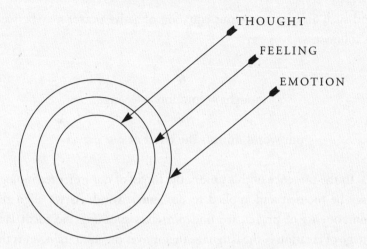

Fig. 3. ". . . whosoever shall say unto this mountain, Be thou removed . . . those things which he saith shall come to pass." (Mark 11:23). The key to effective prayer is the union of thought, feeling, and emotion.

sense to us in one language has very little meaning in another language that we are not familiar with. Still, the language exists.

The philosophy of peace, for example, may be expressed through languages as diverse as physics and politics, as well as prayer. For example, the greatest peace in physics may be described as the absence of motion in a system. In such a language, when frequency, velocity, and wavelength reach zero, the system is at rest and we have peace. In politics, peace may be interpreted as the end of aggression or the absence of war. Our prayers may be thought of in much the same way.

Through the language of prayer, peace may actually be described as an equation, bringing prayer even closer to our science that many have dared to believe. Rather than the equations of numbers and variables, however, logic, feeling, and emotion become the components in our equation of prayer. Taking the form of a standard mathematical proof—*if* such-and-such is so, *then* we witness such-

and-such an outcome—our equation of active prayer may be seen as follows:

$$If$$
$$\text{thought} = \text{emotion} = \text{feeling,}$$
$$then$$
$$\text{our world mirrors the effect of our prayer.}$$

In the presence of this union, the forces of our inner technology may be focused and applied to our outer world. As we align the components of prayer, we find ourselves speaking the silent language of creation—the language that moves the mountain, ends the wars, and dissolves the tumors.

The beauty of prayer is that it is not necessary to know precisely how it works to benefit from its miraculous effects. In this universal technology, we are simply invited to experience, feel, and acknowledge what our feelings are saying to us. Our prayers come to life as we focus upon the *feeling* of our heart's desire, rather than the *thought* of our knowing world.

## The Forgotten Key

I knew that the answer existed somewhere in the texts that surrounded me. Somewhere among the books, papers, documents, and manuscripts scattered on the floor around me were words that ancient masters had written over two thousand years ago, with moments just like this in mind. They knew that in some future generation the same questions would be asked that were posed to the masters in the first millennium A.D. Though it would be a different world, the questions would be the same, questions regarding our relationship to the cosmos, our Creator, and one another. Specifically, they knew that those in their future would reach a point of development where the achievements of their day would call to them, inviting them to remember the very foundation of human nature and reclaim the essence of their lives. I knew that clues into an ancient lineage of wisdom were left for us today, for a moment precisely like this.

It was two o'clock in the morning. I had been seated on the floor for hours, poring over the texts that surrounded me. I stood up and walked to one of the windows overlooking thousands of acres of high desert sage. In the moonless landscape, I could barely make out the silhouette of the mountain to the north, rising over two thousand feet above the valley floor. Taking a deep breath, I walked back to the center of the five-sided building, the largest room on the property. Looking to the ceiling, once again I pondered the mystery of the beams that appeared from each wall, angled toward the sky that met at a point above the center of the room. Apart from these square beams made of pine, there were no other signs of support holding the roof. I had always marveled at how each beam, eight inches square, was anchored into the earthen walls, twenty-four inches thick, to hold up the ceiling. The structure provided a very sacred space. It always felt as though I were in the womb of the earth when I found myself in the "dome," as some people in the valley liked to call it. It was perfect for evenings such as this one.

Taking a deep breath, I sighed and reclaimed my space on the floor. I had dedicated several weeks to piecing together fragments of an understanding that would describe what I believed were the elements of a science lost to the West nearly seventeen hundred years ago. Reaching for a document that I had seen hundreds of times before, once more I began to leaf through the pages. Suddenly my eyes focused on a sequence of words that I had skimmed just fractions of a second before. Something in that particular grouping, a pattern of words, caught my attention. I had probably seen the same words on many occasions. This time, however, they looked different and I found myself flipping through the book, scanning the text for words of familiarity. About three-quarters of the way down one page, I found them. The text that I was leafing through had converted the ancient language of the Middle East into English. It was there that I saw the one key that I was searching for: the single word *peace*. "How, then, may we bring *peace* to our brothers . . . for we would that all of the Sons of Men share in the blessings of the angel of *peace?*"[9]

The text in my hands echoed the question asked two thousand years ago, a question that is often heard repeated in public forums today. How are we to feed our hungry, house our homeless, heal our ill, and end our wars and suffering? Though relief aid, military solutions, and fragile treaties may address the outward expressions of suffering on a physical level, and it remains important to do so, the key to lasting change comes from shifting the thinking that allows these forms of suffering to continue. Perhaps in response to the same questions that modern seekers ask today, the visionaries and scribes of our past left us their understandings, explaining how to bring the power of prayer to bear upon the challenges of society.

Religious and spiritual practices in our time have asked us to weave the threads of prayer into the fabric of our lives. Seldom, however, have we been shown how. At very best, the well-intentioned instruction offered today is vague, inexact, and nebulous.

In texts carrying a lineage of wisdom that predates our history, we are shown the fine points of this powerful technology lost long ago. After identifying the elements of thought, feeling, and emotion, the Essenes actually show us how to merge the three components into a focused application! They do so by identifying a common denominator that links the end of suffering with aligning the elements of prayer. That thread may best be described by the masters of prayer in their own words:

*First shall the Son of Man seek* peace *within his own* body;
*for his body is as a mountain pond that reflects the sun when
it is still and clear. When it is full of mud and stones it reflects
nothing.*

*Then shall the Son of Man seek* peace *within his own*
thoughts. . . . *There is no greater power in heaven and earth
than the thought of the Son of Man. Though unseen by the eyes
of the body, yet each thought has mighty strength, even such
strength can shake the heavens.*

*Then shall the Son of Man seek* peace *with his own* feelings.
*We call on the Angel of love to enter our feelings, that they may
be purified. And all that was before impatience and discord will
turn into harmony and peace.*[10]

These were the words! These were the clues that the Essenes had
left for future generations. Not only did they share with us the possibilities that prayer may bring into our lives, they opened the door
to possibilities of prayer that Western science explains away as "miracles." Knowing that we would reach a point in our evolution where
we would be asked to redefine the role of technology in our world,
they left us the key to affirming life in the science and mystery of
life itself. Their secret is the ancient code of peace. Subtle and perhaps deceptively simple, the power of our lost mode of prayer is
found within the framework of peace!

I turned the pages excitedly, looking for further confirmation,
perhaps a hidden clue describing the role that peace may play in the
present day. Exceeding my expectations, the words nearly jumped
at me from the middle of the next page. "Seek the Angel of *peace* in
all that lives, in all you do, in every word you speak. For *peace* is the
key to all knowledge, to all mystery, to all life."[11]

In the tradition of their time, the Essene word for "angel" could
be translated a number of ways, including "powers or forces that

be." With this in mind, the words *power* or *force* may replace the word *angel* for those whose beliefs suggest that angels are a religious or Christian term. Clearly, the technology offered through the gift of prayer transcends any secular or religious orientation. The Essenes appear to be describing a universal technology that, in some instances, dates to five hundred years before the time of Christ. Revealing itself in all aspects of their lives, even the moments of greeting and departing were viewed by the Essenes as an opportunity to affirm the power of peace within their world. The last words spoken by members of the brothers and sisters of the Essenes were "Peace be with you."

Now the pieces were in place. Through these words, in the language of their time, we are offered insight into a sophisticated technology, often overlooked in the West today. Beyond the microcircuits and computer chips of modern appliances, the technology of prayer is based in components that are so sophisticated we have yet to duplicate them in our machinery. The components are logic and emotion, empowered through the operating system of peace!

As I marked the pages for future reference, I found I was almost dizzy with excitement. I had to share the results of my evening with someone. Glancing at the small digital clock across the room, I blinked in disbelief. It was nearly four in the morning, certainly too early to call anyone. Reaching for my quilted jacket, I stood up and walked toward the door. My wife was sleeping in our home, a rustic building several hundred feet from the office.

Opening the door to step outside, I felt a rush of heat from the woodstove behind me, escaping into the frosty air of the desert night. The thermometer beside the building was hovering at nearly twenty degrees below zero, typical for this time of year. With the first rays of the high desert sun, morning temperatures would quickly rise sixty degrees within an hour or two, creating a balmy afternoon in the mid-forties. Closing the door behind me, I walked across the loose gravel that formed a walkway between the buildings. For just a moment, I stopped. It was a precious moment.

With the exception of my breath, hanging in clouds of steam in front of my face, there was no sound. It was absolutely silent. There was no wind. The few leaves that had not fallen from the Russian olive trees beside me were curled and brown. The slightest motion of wind would have rustled them into the familiar sound of autumn. They were silent. I looked into the sky of a cloudless night, right through the edge of the Milky Way. I had seen it hundreds of times before. Tonight, everything seemed different. The ancients had shown us how to touch those stars, and beyond, through our inner science of prayer. The reach of our prayers, they reminded us, is mirrored in our beliefs concerning what we are capable of. In that silent moment, it all made sense.

I rushed up the flagstone walkway and across the deck, into the tiny house where my wife was sleeping. Excitedly, I sat on the edge of the bed and began to share with her my discoveries. She opened one eye to signal that she was hearing me, and I paused briefly. She smiled her warm, supportive smile. Quietly she asked, "Can we do this in the morning?"

"Of course," I said, a little embarrassed by my excitement.

"Good," she said. "This sounds important. I'd like to be awake to hear what you've found."

Though I was surprised at the intensity of my enthusiasm, I was not disappointed by my wife's response. Maybe it was time for me to sleep as well. After all, these texts had held their secrets for two thousand years. I knew that they could wait a few more hours until sunrise.

# Knowledge, Wisdom, and Peace

I see a subtle distinction between the qualities of knowledge and wisdom. Knowledge may be viewed as the element of our experience that deals with information. All of the data, statistics, and behavior patterns of our past or present may be shared as knowledge. Wisdom, on the other hand, is how we live our knowledge. Knowledge may be taught and passed down for generations as texts and traditions. The experience of wisdom must be lived by each individual of each generation to know the consequences of direct experience.

There was a theme that ran through each piece of Essene knowledge that I had found the previous evening. The common denominator was the ancient key of peace. I viewed the poetry, analogies, and parables left in 2,500-year-old texts just as I would the code in an instructional book today. The Essene code of peace is based in familiar qualities that we already experience in life: logic and emotion. In their way, the Essenes left us their knowledge of peace, reminding us of two things. First, we are shown the significance of peace throughout all of creation. Second, we are shown how applying peace to our inner world creates change in our outer world.

The scholars of the Qumran communities have reminded us of the potential that prayer may bring into our lives. Through their description of prayer's components, we are given the equation for moving electrical energy across the membranes of our cell walls, generating complex patterns in the substance of human consciousness, and creating specific chemistries within the laboratories of our bodies. In the presence of such power, is it possible that the image of "moving the mountain" is a literal description of the great power that lives as our greatest potential? In light of science's confirmation of prayer's effects, we must reconcile the possibility of such a power within our lives.

Of all the distortion that has occurred in the translations of our most sacred texts, the last key to our technology of prayer is one element that slipped through the fourth-century edits of the Nicean Council and remains with us today. Though the words may have been streamlined somewhat, enough of the original intent remains to usher a new perspective into our lives. Elements of this key exist today in our biblical texts as well as in the Essene manuscripts predating our Bible by several hundred years. Such "crossover" passages fuel the belief that the two documents arose from a common origin.

In some teachings, the lost code is known as the Great Commandment. The Book of Mark, chapter twelve, verse thirty solves the last mystery to merging the elements of prayer into focused union. To create this power, we are invited to love in a very specific way. "Thou shalt love thy God with all thy *heart,* with all thy *soul,* with all thy *mind,* with all thy *strength."* Perhaps the key to understanding this mysterious passage is to be found in the Essene view of our relationship with our Creator. From their perspective, we are one with our Father in heaven. "Beside the river stands the holy Tree of Life. There doth my Father dwell, and my home is in him. *The Heavenly Father and I are One."* [12] Within each person that walks this world lives the divine spark of creation and of our Creator. This understanding, then, becomes the great challenge to our mystery. To focus our prayer, we must love the creative principle of life itself, our Creator, with all of our heart, soul, mind, and strength. *Because we are one with our Father in heaven, in doing so, we have just loved ourselves.* Through these four specifics, we are reminded how to honor the love that the Essenes referred to as "the source of all things." The key is that it is only in the presence of this kind of love that the quality of peace may be found to reward the labor of our prayer. The words have been offered before. Precisely what do they mean? What does it mean to love in this way? How are we to love with all of our heart, soul, mind, and strength?

The lost code of the Essenes reminds us how this peace may be accomplished. It is through our body, heart, and mind that we experience our thought, feelings, and emotions. While we may sense little control over our perceptions, it is through our link to our perceptions that we may choose the quality of our experience. The last portion of our code, based in logic and emotion, is perhaps the final key in our quest to unify our prayers. *"Know* this peace with thy mind, *desire* this peace with thy heart, *fulfill* this peace with thy body."[13]

Through the logic of our mind, we must know peace to be true. We must prove it to ourselves, demonstrating the viability of peace in our lives and in our world. Through the strength of our hearts, we must then desire this peace in all that we experience. Peace already exists in our world. We are challenged to seek it out, to find peace even in places where it may look as if peace does not exist. It is through our bodies that we express our minds and our hearts. We choose the actions that we offer to the world. This passage reminds us to allow our actions to mirror outwardly the choices that we have already made within.

In this way the Essenes challenged us to a code of conduct, of sorts. Though others may choose actions in their lives that deny life in themselves or others, through these words we may hold ourselves to a higher standard. We are invited to create peace in each of these elements, to achieve the love that brings unity to our actions.

## Secrets of Prayer and Healing

We may look to pre-Christian traditions of the ancient Essenes for some of the least distorted records of our forgotten technologies.

Perhaps the greatest insight into the eloquence of such wisdom may be found in the Essene model of prayer and healing, which makes an assumption that begins where many modern therapies conclude. The fundamental tenet of Essene healing is that *we are already healed*. Within each moment of our time in this world we make choices either affirming or denying the life that already exists in our bodies.

Essene masters viewed the expressions of illness as powerful illusions, stemming from choices and actions made by the individual, rather than looking to external "causes." They believed that we determine our response to the conditions of our world—sometimes consciously, other times not. Through their most sacred writings, we know the Essene philosophy viewed the blueprint of our souls as a divine expression of our Creator, untouched and untainted by the experiences of life. Our souls are already healed, and seek to express that state through our bodies. Accepting our healing through our own beliefs and forgiveness, our healing is mirrored through our souls' expression in this world, our bodies.

This perspective invites us to view the conditions that we witness in our bodies as indicators of the quality of our choices. If we could distill the many proverbs, parables, teachings, and sayings into brief, concise summaries, we would discover that this thinking suggests that we affirm or deny life in our bodies through the quality of four assumptions or tenets. Each tenet contributes to our overall expression of health and vitality. Each testifies to the interrelated nature of spirit, matter, and life. We may view these tenets today, through twentieth-century idiom, as possible models offering insight into the choices that we make on a daily basis—their nature, our reasons for making them, and their possible outcomes.

On the following pages, each tenet is stated concisely, in a few words or a single sentence. An explanation follows, in the form of an example or a simple description. Then we examine the implications and consequences of the tenet, focusing on why it is important. Finally, we are shown how to apply a particular tenet in our lives today.

## TENET 1. WE ARE ALREADY HEALED.

*Explanation*

The key to understanding this tenet is same one that allows us to choose new outcomes for existing conditions. The understanding that we are already healed stems from our view of the world as an array of possible outcomes, and from our ability to choose which outcome we experience. Inherent in this faith is our acknowledgment of our role as an empowered force in creation, bringing new outcomes into focus while releasing those that have already served us. Our body is the feedback mechanism, mirroring to us the quality of our choices of thought, feeling, emotion, breath, nutrients, and movement, and our honoring of life.

In the example of the disappearing tumor (chapter 4), rather than imposing the will of healing upon the condition of the cancer, the practitioners chose to feel, think, and emote from an outcome in which the tumor had never been present. In doing so, they attracted the new outcome, the overlay of a quantum possibility mirroring their beliefs of the moment. In two minutes and forty seconds, the new belief replaced the old belief. The ancients knew the power of such technology as a mode of prayer, transcending any religious, mystic, or scientific principles.

*Implications*

To accept the tenet that we are already healed, we are invited to allow for the possibility that there are many outcomes for a given condition. The act of making new choices in our lives is the technology that allows us to select new possibilities. From the viewpoint that defines prayer as a quality of feeling, prayer also becomes our language to fine-tune life-affirming choices of health and relationship.

The tenet that we are already healed reminds us that each time we *ask* to be healed in one outcome, a possibility exists where our prayer is already answered in another. With this possibility in mind, each time we are diagnosed with a condition of ill health or life-threatening disease, we are being shown only one of many possible outcomes for that moment.

The diagnosis of a condition is not necessarily either incorrect or correct. In the absence of allowing for other possibilities, it is simply incomplete. In the same moment, another outcome must exist in which the ill health, disease, or condition is not present. Each possibility already exists. Each outcome is real. Through the eyes of this tenet, the difference between outcomes is a matter of our perspective.

### Applied to Our Lives

In each moment, we make choices that affirm or deny life in our bodies. Consciously or unconsciously, we choose the quality of six parameters: thought, feeling, emotion, breath, nutrient, and movement. For each of the parameters, we must ask whether we provide ourselves the highest quality of each that we are capable of. In the event that we discover conditions within our bodies that we choose to change, our quality of health is our signal to look at one or a combination of the six parameters of life.

Applying our lost mode of prayer to the tenet that we are already healed, our prayer becomes a clarification of the condition(s) that we choose to portray to the world, rather than a plea for a change in our present condition. Feeling and living from the knowledge that new conditions are present tunes us to the outcome of our new choice.

## TENET 2. THERE IS ONLY ONE
## OF US HERE.

*Explanation*

Global census figures indicate that there are approximately 6 billion people living on earth today. This tenet reminds us that each person is a unique, individualized expression of a single, unified awareness. Within this oneness, the choices and actions of each person affect all others to some degree.

*Implication*

The implications of this tenet are vast and, at the same time, tremendously relevant. In its broadest sense, our role within a unified awareness means that there can be no isolated actions, no "them" and "us." No longer can we view the conditions of our world as "their problems" and "our problems." In a field of unified consciousness, each choice that we make and every act we perform in each moment of each day must affect every other person in this world. Some actions produce a greater effect and some a lesser one. Still, the effect is there.

Each time we choose a new way to deal with the challenges of life, our solution contributes to the diversity of human will that ensures our survival. As one of us pioneers a new creative solution to the seemingly small challenges of our individual lives, we become a living bridge for the next person who finds himself or herself faced with the same challenge, and the next, and so on. Each time one of us faces the condition that others have faced in the past, we have more options from our collective response to draw from. Relatively few individuals may create possibilities that become choices for the whole.

Implied in such a world of unified awareness are the consequences of our actions. Each time we hurt others through our words or actions, in effect we have hurt ourselves. Each time we take the life of another, we have taken a part of our own lives. The very thoughts that allow us to hurt another limit our ability to express the will of creation through ourselves.

At the same time, each time we love another, we have just loved ourselves. Each time we create time for another, strive to understand another, make ourselves available for another, we have just done each of these things for ourselves. When we disapprove of the actions, choices, or beliefs of others, we witness through them those portions of ourselves that ask for a greater healing.

### Application

As others perform actions that we may judge negatively, we are invited to acknowledge their role in unity as the part of us that has chosen a different way. Without condoning, consenting to, or even agreeing with the actions of another, we are compassionately invited to bless the action as a possibility and move forward with our choice of a new way.

The key to our oneness is the leverage to transform our world. The power of our oneness allows for a relatively few individuals to affect the quality of life for an entire population.

## TENET 3. WE ARE IN RESONANCE, "TUNED" TO OUR WORLD.

### Explanation

We are a part of all that we perceive. As bundles of atoms, molecules, and compounds, we are made of precisely the same elements that our world is made of, nothing less and nothing more. The foundation of many ancient and indigenous beliefs, this tenet invites us to remember that through unseen threads and immeasurable cords, we are part of every expression of life. In a world of such resonance, every rock, tree, mountain, river, and ocean is a part of us. Whatever happens to the materials of our world is felt by our bodies.

The materials that surround us in our daily lives mirror the quality of choices that we have made in our lives. Without exception, our homes, our automobiles, our pets, and our earth mirror to us, in each moment, the quality, implications, and consequences of our life choices.

## Implication

As we learn to recognize what the conditions of our outer world are saying to us, we are shown empowering possibilities for creating change in our world through changes in our lives. Researchers have documented shifts in the earth in direct relationship to the changes in human consciousness. From the extremes of anger to the heights of compassion, sensors placed in the ground surrounding the individual experiencing the emotions detect the change in biological frequency.

What is the outward effect of many people, perhaps entire communities or cities, sharing common emotions of anger or compassion? Is it possible that the healing of emotions within the small world of our bodies has effects upon the world around us, on such things as weather patterns and earthquake activity?

## Application

In each moment of life, we are in relationship to the elements of our world. Through our friendships, romances, homes, vehicles, and the circumstances of life, we are offered powerful insights into our belief systems, judgments, and intentions. As we change our beliefs and find new ways to express ourselves, this tenet states that the world around us mirrors our choices. Turbulent systems become peaceful in the presence of our peace. Life-affirming choices within our bodies create conditions in our world that mirror our choices. Perhaps this is an explanation for the ancient suggestion that to heal our world, we begin by becoming the conditions of healing ourselves.

## TENET 4. THE TECHNOLOGY OF PRAYER ALLOWS DIRECT ACCESS TO OUR BODIES, ONE ANOTHER, AND THE CREATIVE FORCES OF OUR WORLD.

*Explanation*

Through our inner technology of prayer we commune with the unseen forces of our world. We have always had the ability to access and work through these forces to determine the quality of our life and our world.

*Implication*

The experiences of our outer world mirror the choices that we have made in each moment, with each breath. Sometimes we are aware of our choices, sometimes not. Recent research has documented that our emotions and feelings directly influence the expression of DNA in our bodies.[14] Additional studies now suggest that it is our DNA that influences the way atoms and molecules of our outer world behave as well![15]

We have witnessed the response of human tissue to specific qualities of feeling, as in the "healing" of lesions and tumors within moments. The link has been demonstrated, though the implications are beyond the framework of modern science. Our choice to recognize the relationship is a deeply personal one, inviting us once again "to think the thoughts of angels and do as angels do."[16]

## Application

Prayer may be the single most powerful force in creation. Individually, we are given the silent language that allows us to participate in the outcome of events and the challenges of our lives. Together, mass prayer is our opportunity to share in the outcome of our world.

Ancient traditions and modern scientists suggest that prayer is the sophisticated technology that allows us to recognize the possibilities of future outcomes and choose which outcome we experience. As we become the very conditions that we choose to experience in our world, we attract the outcome that mirrors our choice. In doing so, wars, disease, and suffering no longer simply "happen"; rather, we are shown a mechanism for their occurrence. At the same time, we are offered the power to choose again.

How ironic it is that the findings of twentieth-century technology, largely the product of defense and military applications, have led to the insights directing us to the powerful yet simple science of prayer. The foundation is now in place. The data have been measured and the experiments have been run. We have proved, at least under certain conditions, that thought and emotion produce feeling, and that feeling produces the vibratory patterns that affect our world. As we change the quality of our feeling, we change the pattern of the vibration, thus shifting patterns of our outer world.

The question now becomes how, and to what degree, do our patterns of feeling affect the world around us? If we can find a link between the invisible force of human feeling and the effect of our feelings on the world around us, then we have come full circle. Such a link would give new credibility to ancient traditions and the abilities of mystics and yogis reported over the years. Perhaps the work of Vladimir Poponin may offer some of the first evidence to confirm a direct link between matter and human DNA.

## Moving Mountains:
## The DNA Phantom Effect

In the early 1990s, Moscow's Russian Academy of Sciences reported a startling relationship between DNA and the qualities of light, measured as photons.[17] In a report detailing these early studies, Dr. Vladimir Poponin described a series of experiments suggesting that human DNA directly affects the physical world through a new and previously unknown field connecting the two. Recognized as a leading expert in the field of quantum biology, Dr. Poponin was on loan to an American research institution when this series of experiments was carried out.

The experiments began as the patterns of light in a vacuum were measured in a controlled environment. After all of the air was removed from a specially designed chamber, the patterns and spacing of the light particles followed a random distribution, as expected. These patterns were double-checked and double-recorded, to be used as a reference for the next portion of the experiment.

The first surprise came as physical samples of DNA were placed inside the chamber. In the presence of genetic material, the spacing and patterns of the light particles shifted. Rather than the scattered pattern that the researchers had seen before, the particles of light began to fall into a new pattern resembling the crests and troughs of a smooth wave. The DNA was clearly influencing the photons, as if shaping them into the regularity of a wave pattern through an invisible force.

The next surprise came to the researchers as they removed the DNA from the chamber. Fully believing that the particles of light would return to their original state of random distribution, something very unexpected occurred. The patterns were very different from those seen before the DNA was introduced. In his own words, Poponin described the light as behaving "surprisingly and counterintuitively." After rechecking the instruments and rerunning the experiments, the researchers were faced with finding an explanation for what they had witnessed. In the absence of the DNA, what was affecting the particles of light? Did the DNA leave something behind, a residual force of some kind, that lingered long after the biological material had disappeared?

Poponin writes that he and the researchers were "forced to accept the working hypothesis that some new field structure is being excited. . . ." To emphasize that the effect was related to the physical DNA molecule, the new phenomenon was named the "DNA phantom effect." Poponin's "new field structure" sounds surprisingly similar to the "matrix" of Max Planck's force and the effects suggested in ancient traditions.

This series of experiments is important because it clearly demonstrates, perhaps for the first time under laboratory conditions, a relationship that offers even greater credibility to the effect of prayer in our physical world. In this instance the DNA was more or less a passive collection of molecules unattached to the brain of a conscious living being. Even in the absence of direct feeling pulsing through its double-helix antenna, there was a force and a measurable effect in its immediate world.

Researchers suggest that the average-sized person, of average height and weight, has many trillions of cells in his or her body. If each cell, each antenna of feeling and emotion within an individual, carries the same properties affecting the world around them, how much is the effect amplified? Now, rather than random feelings coursing through the cells of that one person, what happens if the feeling is a result of a specific form of thought and emotion, regulated as prayer? Multiply the effects of this one individual, empowered through a specific mode of prayer, by even a fraction of the 6 billion or so people in our world today, and we begin to get a sense of the power inherent in our collective will. It is the power to end all suffering and avert the pain that has been the hallmark of the twentieth century. The key is that we must work together to achieve such a goal. This may prove to be the greatest challenge of the third millennium.

In our own language we have the vocabulary to describe our forgotten relationship to the forces of our world, the intelligence of the cosmos, and one another. Using some of the most sensitive devices of our time to measure fields of energy that we did not even acknowledge fifty years ago, our own science has now validated the relationship of which the ancients reminded us over two thousand years ago. We have direct access to the forces of our world, and we have come full circle. This is the language to move mountains. It is the same language that allows us to choose life over cancerous tumors, and create peace in situations where we may believe that peace does not exist. When we read of healing miracles in times past, no longer are we left wishing that the same miracles could occur today. The miraculous outcomes are already here; we are simply asked to choose them.

Today I continue to pray. For me, each moment of life has become a prayer. I still give thanks for the good things and now feel empowered to choose new conditions in place of those that have caused suffering in the past. My training in the hard sciences has shown me that there are few mysteries and little we cannot validate, if we dare to accept the "laws" that nature shows us in the miracle of each day.

Prayer has demonstrated to me that certain things *are*, regardless of our ability to prove them in the moment. For example, I know that some of the most sacred memories of our heritage have been scattered throughout the monasteries, churches, tombs, and temples of those who have come before us. I also know that the same memories live on in the customs and traditions of peoples that we may previously have judged as primitive. I know that we are capable of beautiful dreams, great possibilities, and unspoken depths of love. Perhaps most important, I know that a possibility already exists in which we have ended the suffering of all creatures by honoring the sacredness of all life. That possibility is already here and with us now. I know these things to be true, because I have seen them. The moment we allow for such possibilities on a mass scale becomes the first moment of new hope. It is that moment that we will always remember. It is the moment when we override the last day of prophecy.

Nation shall not lift up sword against nation,

neither shall they learn war any more:

For the former things are passed away.

—*THE ESSENE BOOK OF REVELATION*

# HEALING HEARTS, HEALING NATIONS

## *Rewriting Our Future in the Days of Prophecy*

Only moments earlier, I had been alone. Walking along the old road that paralleled the valley to the west, I threaded my way through chest-high stands of mountain sage, still wet from the morning frost. The ground was soft and dry beneath a thin layer of ice that crunched under my feet. With each step, my feet sank into the fragile mixture of clay and soil, leaving a perfect impression of my lug-soled work boots in the desert floor behind me. Searching in the glow of predawn, I could see someone walking toward me. As I squinted to adjust my eyes, I knew that it was Joseph. We had agreed to meet, as we often did, simply to walk, talk, and share the morning. The first rays of the winter sun cast long shadows from behind the Sangre de Cristo Mountains towering to the east. Together we stood with our backs to the rocks and gazed at the magnificent vista before us.

Standing on the rim of a valley containing over 130,000 acres of an especially fragrant sage, Joseph stopped and inhaled a deep breath.

"This entire field," he began, "as far as our eyes can see, functions as a single plant." His words formed brief clouds of steam as his breath merged with the chill of air still cold from the night.

"There are many bushes in this valley," he continued, "and every plant is joined to the others through a root system that is beyond our view. Though they are hidden from our eyes, beneath the ground, the roots still exist. The entire field is one family of sage. As with any family," he explained, "the experience of one member is shared to some degree by all others."

I listened to what Joseph was saying. *What a beautiful metaphor,* I thought, *of the way that people are connected to one another through life.* Though we see many bodies that we believe are strangers, living independent lives of unrelated tasks, there is a single thread of awareness that binds us as a family. Our connection is through a system that we do not see. Still, the connection exists as what some have called a "universal mind": the mystery of our consciousness. Like the sage plants, we are all related during our journey through this world. In consciousness, there is only one of us here.

Sometimes the great mysteries of life become clear only when we stop thinking about them. Though we may *know* information in our minds, the meaning of a mystery must be *felt* before it can be lived. In the innocence of the moment, sharing the experience of another sometimes becomes the catalyst to awaken new understandings within ourselves. Now I know why.

I often think back to that morning, awed by the eloquent simplicity with which Joseph described the relationship of the sage plants. In addition to understanding how we are connected, Joseph's explanation also described the possibilities of such a relationship. For example, when one area of sage develops a tolerance to an insect or a particular chemical, the entire family demonstrates the same tolerances. *The key is that many benefit from the experiences of just a few.* Recent studies into the effect of mass prayer—many people's feeling focused on a common theme—document similar relationships in human conscious-ness. The quality of life for an entire neighborhood has been shown to be affected by the focused prayer of a few individuals.

Almost universally, ancient traditions believe that the relation-ship runs even deeper between the world of every day and the inner world of our consciousness. Viewing our bodies and the earth as mir-rors of one another, they suggest that the extremes witnessed in one may be considered as metaphors for changes within the other. This thinking relates destructive weather patterns and storms, for exam-ple, to the unsettled consciousness of people where the storms occur. At the same time, such holistic views suggest that the extremes of earthquakes, life-threatening storms, and disease may be eased, or even eradicated through subtle shifts in our belief systems.

If in fact these relationships exist, then perhaps for the first time we may look to the twenty-first century with a new sense of confi-dence and trust. Beyond long-standing prophecies of a third world war, beyond predictions of catastrophic loss of life and end-of-century chaos, the 2,500-year-old secret of prayer may provide a rare oppor-tunity to define our time in a way that we have only seen in dreams. Rather than protecting ourselves from events that may appear to have power over us, we may actually *choose* the life-affirming conditions that transcend illness, suffering, and war in our future.

## Soft Temples

In the words of their time, Gnostic scholars appealed to future gen-erations to remember that the earth is in us, that we are in her, and that the two of us are intimately enmeshed in all that we experience. New translations of Essene documents from the Dead Sea caves illustrate even greater, and sometimes unexpected depths, of their authors' understanding. The motivation for the ceremonies, rituals, and lifestyle of early Essene communities was their deep conviction honoring the living thread that binds all life, throughout all worlds.

Essene masters viewed our body as a convergence point through which the forces of creation join to express the will of God. They considered our time together as an opportunity to share the very experiences of anger, rage, jealousy, and hatred that we sometimes shun and judge in our lives. It is through the same bodies that we hone the qualities of love, compassion, and forgiveness that elevate us to the greatest expressions of our humanness. For this reason, they regarded our body as a sacred place, a soft and vulnerable temple for our soul.

It is within our body-temple that the forces of the cosmos unite as an expression of time, space, spirit, and matter. More precisely, it is within the experience of time and space that spirit works through matter to find the fullest expressions honoring life. Interestingly, the Qumran scholars focused upon a particular place within the body, rather than on the body itself as the landscape of divine expression. In the words of a fragment found in the Dead Sea Scrolls, we are reminded that through our bodies we have "inherited a holy land . . . this land is not a field to be plowed, but a place within us where we may build our holy temple."[1]

Within the innermost recesses of ancient temples are found the most sacred portions of the sanctuary. In the temples of Egypt, for example, the holiest chapel is nestled deep in the interior of the complex. Timeworn scriptures refer to the single room, often small in comparison to the rest of the structure, embedded within winding corridors and preparatory shrines as the *beth elohim,* the holy of holies. It is in the holy of holies that the invisible world of spirit touches the physical matter of our world.

Carrying this metaphor from the hard temples of stone to the soft temples of life, our bodies must have a holy of holies as well. Perhaps in a manner yet to be recognized by the science of today, the innermost portion of our living temples represents the sacred place where the body of matter is touched by the breath of spirit. Does such a place exist within us?

In a report from the third annual conference of the International Society for the Study of Subtle Energies and Energy Medicine, scientists documented the nonphysical force of emotion *actually changing* the physical molecule of DNA. Based in rigorous testing of individuals capable of emotional self-management, as well as control subjects without any specialized training, the study reported that "individuals trained in generating focused feelings of deep love . . . were able to *intentionally cause a change* in the conformation [shape] of the DNA" (my emphasis).[2] Specific qualities of emotion, produced at will, determined to what degree and how tightly the two strands of the molecule of life were coiled!

This study is important for a number of reasons. The way that our basic building block of life is configured plays a key role in the way DNA repairs and reproduces itself in our bodies. The question has remained as to what determines the actual shape of the DNA molecule. Confirming the long-held suspicion that emotion greatly affects our health and quality of life, these reports now demonstrate, perhaps for the first time, that emotion is the missing link, a direct line of communication to the very core of life itself.

Could the Dead Sea Scroll references to a "holy land . . . a place within us where we may build our holy temple" be a description of the actual cells of our bodies? After all, this is the place where science has now witnessed the marriage between spirit and matter. If this is the case, then each cell within the temple of our bodies is, by definition, a holy of holies. Each cell must be considered sacred! The moment that our technology allowed us to witness spirit shaping the world of matter (emotion shaping DNA), we opened the door to a new era acknowledging the relationship between our beliefs and our experience.

The understandings gleaned from something as unlikely as 2,300-year-old texts, now validated by twentieth-century science, may be considered a kind of "biological unified theory." Such a theory offers a long-sought mechanism to describe our relationship to all life. Beyond science, religion, and mystic traditions, we have no name for our revised worldview as yet. Echoing the indigenous traditions of ages past, views of this kind are reminiscent of the words that our abbot left with us in Tibet. "We are all connected," he had said. "We are all expressions of one life. . . . We are all the same one."

Perhaps the similarity of his words to those of Joseph describing the sage, and to the Essene texts, is no coincidence. Records indicate that a particular sect of the Essenes, the Carmelites of Mount Carmel, transported copies of their most sacred writings into remote regions of the world to preserve them from the corruption that was befalling such texts following the time of Jesus. Native American elders describe tribal memories of emissaries bringing Essene traditions to North America nearly two thousand years ago.

Additional texts found their way into secluded monasteries of central Asia during the same period. One of these documents, known to historians as the Aramaic Gospel of Matthew, is also known as the Gospel of the Nazirenes, the Gospel of the Hebrews, and the Gospel of the Ebionites. All of these names refer to the same manuscript. This particular text is clearly documented as having found its way into isolated monasteries of Tibet during the first century A.D., and has been established as "considerably older" than the finished version of the New Testament.[3]

## Gateway Beyond the Worlds

An irony often appears with the development of an advanced technology. Generally, the simpler the technology appears to the user, the more complex the systems are behind the scenes to allow such simplicity. A beautiful example of this concept may be found in our picture-driven computers and "point and click" technology. Each time we move our computer cursor across the screen and click on the picture of a program that we choose, we have set into motion an amazingly complex series of operations. Internal pointers, machine language, shells of operating systems, and application programs are brought to life at the speed of electrons racing along pathways of microcircuits. All we did was point to a picture and push a button. Fortunately, we are not required to know any of the events occurring behind the scenes. In fact, it may be a relief not to know.

Our inner technology of accessing creation operates in much the same way. As we master certain experiences in our lives, it is those very experiences that open the doors to other worlds and possibilities that we may only have dreamed of in the past. Perhaps without even realizing the power of their writings, ancient scholars remind us that from the moment of our birth we are conduits of the easy-to-use, yet highly sophisticated, technology to transform our world. The teachings of the Ebionite and Nazirene communities hint at the lost language and forgotten power living within each of us. It is this silent language that allows us to become gateways, bringing the qualities of heaven to earth. The wisdom, peace, and compassion that we experience in our dreams, for example, may become the reality of our world by reflecting such qualities in our daily lives.

Through an excerpt from an Essene text, we are reminded of the possibilities of such a relationship: ". . . who doth build on earth the kingdom of heaven . . . shall dwell in both worlds."[4] Our lost language of prayer is the bridge linking the worlds of heaven and earth. "Only through the communions . . . will we learn to see the unseen, to hear that which cannot be heard, and to speak the unspoken word."[5]

As deceptively simple as our most advanced computer technology, the implications of these pre-Christian concepts touch our lives in ways that we may never suspect. They imply that we each participate in the outcome of global events as well as the health of our bodies and the quality of our relationships. Sometimes we are aware of our participation, and sometimes not. In light of these understandings, centuries-old references suggesting that our lifetime is a rare window of opportunity now take on new meaning and perhaps greater significance. It is during our time, through managing our choices, that we are invited to create an outer world that mirrors our innermost prayers and dreams.

## Miracle in the Andes

In the spring of 1998, the weather phenomenon known as El Niño was wreaking havoc throughout the world, in the form of extremes of temperature, rainfall, and winds. In the mountains along the west coast of South America, Peru was experiencing the brunt of storm systems moving onto the mainland from the Pacific Ocean. After massive rains of record proportions, the flooded lowlands ran together, forming a new lake covering 2,300 square miles. Rich farmlands that had been handed down in families for generations had changed into a permanent freshwater landform so large that the new lake is now visible on satellite photographs.

In other parts of Peru, however, El Niño created the reverse effects, with below-average rainfall and a drying of the dense jungle growth created from rains earlier in the year. The mountain highlands in the southern portion of the country became particularly susceptible to a rare period of extreme dryness and the danger of inaccessible forest fires. Located at an altitude nearly two miles above sea level, the ancient temple complex of Macchu Picchu, portions of which are now believed to have been built before the time of the Incas, is situated in the midst of some of the most luxuriant forest in the country. One of the most popular and mysterious archaeological sites remaining on earth today, the massive temple complex draws thousands of tourists each year and is a national treasure. The absence of rain, combined with the already low humidity of such elevations, created the conditions for fires that could become a disaster of catastrophic proportions.

I was guiding a prayer trek through the mountains outside of Cuzco in May of 1998, when our Peruvian guide and translator shared a story that touched each member of our group deeply. At the same time, her story confirmed our belief in the focus of our journey: to explore and embrace the lost science of prayer. Maria stood at the front of our tour bus as we wound our way through the narrow roads to the ancient site of Pissiac, with a temple complex situated over two miles above sea level. The next morning we would begin a four day trek through the Andes to our destination at the "lost city" of Macchu Picchu. In addition to the physical challenge of the trek, the purpose of our journey was to create experiences that would draw from us the strength, wisdom, and compassion to move through our lives with grace.

During each morning of our journey, we would begin our day with a meditative theme that would take on deeper and greater meaning as we faced the challenges of each day. These moments would become experiences to be carried back into the world of our families, careers, and the circles of those whom we love and hold most dear. For example, the strength required each night to carry our bodies into our campsite, located on a shelf at 14,000 feet, would become a model for the same strength that allows us to move forward in the face of life's greatest challenges. Each day of the journey became a reference point for one quality of prayer that held the potential of serving us in the presence of life's greatest challenges.

When lightning had ignited fires in the high Andean jungles earlier in the year, the local communities had organized to battle the blazes and save their villages. Despite their efforts, the fires had burned out of control, spreading for days as government officials and local people looked on, helpless and exhausted. The fires cut a widespread path of destruction, appearing to be burning in all directions at once. One afternoon the winds shifted and the fire headed directly toward the temples of Macchu Picchu. Mobilizing the few resources available, firefighters mounted an effort to smother the flames before they reached this most famous example of Andean history. With little equipment, railroads washed out, and trails blocked with mudslides from earlier rains, the only source of water was the narrow Urubamba River, in a canyon several thousand feet below. Efforts to rescue the temples were fruitless. The front line of the fire advanced, razing the peripheral sites of the multi-acre complex. As the flames scorched the outlying temples on the peak of nearby Wyannu Picchu, the situation looked hopeless.

Exhausting all other means of stopping the inferno, local villagers resorted to a technology that had been a part of their culture for centuries. In groups of families and as individuals, publicly and privately, they began to pray. Though the specific prayers varied, the underlying theme was consistent: they prayed to spare the temples of Macchu Picchu. Collectively they were directing their prayers to a common challenge. Within hours the people of Southern Peru witnessed an event that many consider to be a miracle. A low-pressure system developed over their portion of the Andes. A mass of moist, warm air from the coast merged with the cold, dry air of the mountains, the skies clouded, and it began to rain.

The rain became a downpour, soaking the dense forest where the fire had jumped from treetop to treetop. Rainwater poured down through gullies cut from the bare mountaintops, into the parched earth below. Mixing with the rich soil to create a thick black mud, the slurry steamed as it poured over heated rocks into the fire zone. Within hours the flames had disappeared, leaving smoldering tree trunks in the wake of the worst fire in the recorded history of the area. Outsiders looking on had witnessed what they believed was a fortunate coincidence. Government officials were mystified. Local villagers were simply relieved. To them there was no mystery. God had heard their prayers, and answered.

Similar stories have been shared regarding mass prayers accelerating the peace process in Northern Ireland, avoiding the loss of life from NATO bombing raids in Iraq, and the mysterious course change of an asteroid on a path to collide with earth in 1996. In each instance, circumstances that were certain to result in a tragic outcome, with the equally certain loss of human life, shifted unexpectedly. In each instance the shift was coincident with the effort of many individuals and groups coordinated in mass prayer. Western science has now validated that, at least to a degree, our outer world of atoms and elements mirrors our inner world of thought and emotion. Could creating peace and cooperation in our world be as simple as joining in unified prayers of the same?

For hundreds of generations the framework of prayer as a support system in times of joy as well as crisis has played a central role in the lives of individuals, families, and communities. Crossing the boundaries of culture, age, religion, and geography, the silent language of prayer is perhaps the most universal custom that we share as a species. It is almost as if somewhere, hidden in the mists of our collective history, we have a memory of this sacred language that speaks to the unseen forces of our world and one another.

Perhaps it is our deep and very personal views of prayer that has allowed our universal custom to become a source of our separateness as well. Even today, as we step into the first days of the third millennium, emotions run high as science and philosophy debate the power of prayer. To the ancients, to the indigenous people of our world, and in many Western households today, no physical proof of the power of prayer is required. Those who pray have witnessed the outcome of their prayers for generations in the absence of validation, measurement, or what many today may call scientific proof. To people of faith, the miracles in their lives are all the proof they need.

For others of our time, however, it is the ability to measure, document, and validate the wonders of life that have allowed them to build the technology that has brought us safely to this moment in our lives. Each path is valid. Both invite us to make the choices that define our future.

## What Would It Take?

Masses of people have always fascinated me. Gazing into hundreds of faces from the solitude of an airport café or a bench on the edge of a bustling city square, many times I have wondered what it would take to bring each person, independently carrying out seemingly unrelated tasks, together in a common moment of peace and cooperation. What event could possibly reach beyond the differences of appearance, past the concerns of daily routines, to awaken the memory of a common history, leading into a shared future in the only world that we know?

One school of thought suggests that as people and nations we have grown so separate from our earth and from one another that only a crisis of immense proportions will awaken our memories of oneness and renew the possibility of cooperation. Strangely, it appears that times of adversity draw from us our deepest knowledge, expressed as our greatest strengths, to triumph over our shared ordeals. During such times, a common goal takes precedence over any differences of ethnic origin, social class, and culture.

History demonstrates that diverse populations tend to pull together in times of crisis. During the Kobe earthquake in Japan, for example, the great fires in Mexico, or the unprecedented hurricane season of 1998, people of all walks of life abandoned their social status to offer assistance in places where it was most needed. Suddenly, corporate executives were standing beside street vendors in the remains of collapsed buildings to free children trapped in the rubble. Bank presidents were working with the national guard to shore up flooded levees. During one of the worst ice storms in recorded history, 5.2 million people survived without power for thirty-three days in the winter of 1998. In portions of Canada and the northeastern United States, communities where people had barely known one another only days before shared emergency kerosene heaters and cookstoves.

It may be that a similar scenario, perhaps on a global scale, will be the impetus to merge our inner technology of prayer, quantum thought, and the power of human emotion. The threat of a rogue asteroid hurtling toward earth, for instance, or a disease that cannot be stopped with conventional medicine, might be a catalyst for such cooperation. Fortunately, these examples are hypothetical, at least for now. Not so hypothetical, however, is a growing threat to the fragile peace that has graced our world since the end of the last world war, over fifty years ago.

## Nation Against Nation

At the birth of the twenty-first century, the conditions appear to be in place for a great polarization of world powers, bringing the threat of a global war well within the realm of possibility. Countries that have previously been viewed as less of a factor in global strategies are taking on new and unexpected roles in the unfolding drama that is reshaping our world.

The last two years of the twentieth century, for example, saw a number of new countries joining the exclusive ranks of those possessing nuclear arms. Of particular note were the surprise weapons tests of India and Pakistan. In spite of adamant pleas for restraint by the United Nations Security Council, Russia, and the United States, the two technological rivals have continued to test their weapons and delivery systems, defending their peacetime escalation of nuclear weapons in the interest of national security.

Though many scoff at the possibility of a global war, believing that the horrors of World War II are too fresh in our memory to allow such an event again, it is important to remain vigilant and discerning, and to recognize the significance of global events that, at first, may seem far away with little relevance to home.

The late-century crisis in Kosovo offered an example of just such events. Though they appeared to casual observers to have "come out of nowhere," the conflicts leading to the Kosovo crisis actually stem from centuries-old tensions in a portion of Eastern Europe that many analysts refer to as the "Balkan powder keg." Following the ethnic cleansing and wartime atrocities witnessed by the world in Bosnia less that a decade before, the nations of the West were unwilling to allow a similar tragedy to continue in Kosovo. The intent, duration, and form of military intervention, however, were factors that divided even the allied forces attempting to intervene. The struggle for power in Eastern Europe offers a clear study on how regional strife may unexpectedly polarize the great powers of the world into precarious positions on opposite sides of the negotiating table.

The Balkan area is only one example of a political situation with vast military implications. As the United Nations monitors the events unfolding in Europe, it also continues to enforce an embargo and military restrictions on Iraq. Threatened by the buildup of chemical and biological weapons, Iraq has been viewed as yet another powder keg, this one in the Middle East. Even that country's Arab neighbors, those traditionally considered to be its allies, disapprove of Iraq's new weapons capabilities and the destabilization of what was already a delicate balance of power in a volatile part of the world.

During a time that many have considered relatively peaceful on a global scale, the last twenty years have, in fact, been a time of tragedy and tremendous suffering on a localized basis. The death toll resulting from separatist movements and religious and civil wars is estimated to be over four and a half million lives, a number representing the entire population of the state of Louisiana or the entire country of Israel. When the conflict in Tibet is factored in, the loss of human life escalates by at least another million, and possibly more.

## LOCATIONS OF GLOBAL TENSIONS AT THE BIRTH OF THE THIRD MILLENNIUM.[6]

| Location | Description of conflict | Lives lost* |
| --- | --- | --- |
| Bosnia/Herzegovina | Serb opposition to Bosnian independence | 200,000+ |
| Kosovo | Kosovars struggle for independence | 2,000+ |
| Northern Ireland | Sectarian violence | 3,200 |
| Haiti | Civil war leading to 1991 coup | ? |
| Chechnya | Muslims battle Russians for independence | 40,000 |
| Sri Lanka | Tamils battling Sinhalese since 1983 | 56,000 |
| Rwanda | Hutu majority battling Tutsi minority | 800,000+ |
| Republic of Congo | Civil war | 10,000+ |
| Somalia | Civil war | 300,000+ |
| Sudan | Muslims battling Christians | 1.9 million |
| Angola | Civil war | 1.0 million |
| Sierra Leone | Civil war | 3,000 |
| Liberia | Civil war | 250,000 |
| Algeria | Civil war | 65–80,000 |
| Turkey | Civil war | 37,000 |
| Tibet | Conflict between China and Tibet | 1.0 million |

*Statistics as of first quarter, 1999.

These statistics certainly describe something other than a peaceful world! Until the late 1990s, however, such conflicts appeared to be localized and, though tragic, less relevant in the daily lives of the people of the Western world. Events late in 1998 and in 1999, however, changed our worldview, with mass media bringing the horror of regional conflicts and isolated wars into our homes and classrooms in a way never seen before. Additionally, situations such as the breakdown of peace negotiations between Israel and the state of Palestine, continued tensions in Northern Ireland, and a sudden leap in China's nuclear technology contribute to what many scholars believe are the precursors of well-known prophecies tumbling into place, the global positioning of a third great war. The sheer number of conflicts presents a threat to global stability that becomes a greater possibility as tensions increase.

## Visions of War

Ancient prophecies do, in fact, abound with visions of a millennial breakdown in governments, followed by a time of an especially widespread and horrible war. The apostle Matthew, for example, referred to our time in history as one when "you will hear of wars and reports of wars . . . nation will rise against nation and kingdom against kingdom."[7] Often included in such prophecies are a variety of interpretations as to the cause and nature of the outcome. Ranging from shortages of natural resources such as water and oil to disagreements over fertile land, many prophets have seen the birth of the third millennium as a time of unprecedented warfare between the great powers of the earth. A nearly universal theme of conflict pervades the end-of-century forecasts from the well-known visions of Edgar Cayce and Nostradamus to those of such lesser-known prophets as Bishop Christianos Ageda and a Bavarian visionary named Stormberger.

Born in the eighteenth century, Stormberger demonstrated remarkable precision in his prophecies of a twentieth-century world. Among his predictions were the specifics of a conflict that became World War II, the Great Depression, and a third global tribulation, another world war: "After the second great struggle between the nations will come a third universal conflagration, which will decide everything. There will be entirely new weapons. In one day more men will perish than in all the previous wars together. Enormous catastrophes will take place."[8]

Of particular interest in Stromberger's future vision is his comment that the war will come as a surprise to many. He sees those that do recognize what is happening as incapable of sharing their insights: "The nations of the earth will enter into these calamities with open eyes. They shall not be aware of what is taking place, and those who will know and speak will be silenced. The third great war will be the end of many nations."[9] Stromberger is unclear on whether the end of the nations will be due to their being absorbed by other powers or to their devastation from the new weapons.

In some of his clearest quatrains, Nostradamus describes his millennial vision of war as occurring in the year 2000. In Centuries X, quatrain 74, he writes: "In the year that the great seventh is completed [2000], there shall occur at the time of slaughter not far from the start of the grand millennium. . . ."[10]

Calling to mind the hundreds of thousands of refugees forced to flee the Balkan states in the last years of the second millennium, Bishop Christianos Ageda foresaw in his fourth-century prophecy a time when "there will be wars and fury that will last a long time; whole provinces shall be emptied of their inhabitants, and kingdoms shall be thrown into confusion."[11]

In a document that became know as the Prophecy of Warsaw, an eighteenth-century Polish monk described the great war as a time of "poisonous clouds, and rays which burn more deeply than the sun on the equator; armies will march encased in iron; flying ships full of dreadful bombs and arrows, and flying stars with sulfuric fire which exterminate entire cities in an instant."[12]

From the previous sampling, a clear thread of similarity emerges as each prophecy describes a time of tragedy, war, and death. While such prophecies are certainly open to interpretation, the fact that virtually every major belief system sees its prophecies being fulfilled in this era certainly warrants a close look at current situations. The key to reading such prophetic statements, some as old as India's epic poem, the Mahabharata,* is that they represent possibilities only, descriptions of events that have not played out as yet. Previous discussions offered an explanation of how accounts of such detail may have been inspired centuries before their time. Additionally, the discussions have offered a context within which to view these and other predictions as glimpses of a vast array of possible futures. Rather than discounting such visions as "millennial madness" or "apocalyptic jargon," perhaps we are better served by asking ourselves what we can learn from such insights.

Amid the ambiguity of ancient prophecies and predictions, one thing remains certain. For hundreds and in some cases thousands of years, ancient prophets have seen something in our future that disturbed them. Whether the prophecy was made fifty or 2,500 years ago, the visions of the prophets remain remarkably similar. In the words of their day, they have described their experiences in an effort to avert the tragedy of their visions. The opportunity of our time is to reconcile current events and determine the role and viability of

---

*Used to teach Hindu traditions, the Mahabharata is composed of approximately 100,000 dual-lined couplets describing dharma, or right action.

ancient visions in our modern lives. We must ask ourselves if the conditions of our world today fulfill the visions seen from another time. If so, perhaps our lifetime represents the days when "every secret thing shall be revealed"[13] and when at last we employ our forgotten technology of prayer to redirect the ancient visions of tragedy and suffering.

## Mass Prayer and Mustard Seeds

In addition to the written predictions of ancient prophets, the conditions that precede a time of great warfare are held in the oral traditions of many native peoples. Perhaps the events that pave the way for such tragedy are best summarized by the people of peace themselves, the Hopi. In a portion of their native prophecy, the Hopi eloquently remind us that each time humanity strays from the natural laws that affirm life in this world, our choices are mirrored in our societies and the systems of nature around us. As the hearts and minds of mankind become so separate that they forget one another, the earth acts to bring the memory of our greatest attributes back into focus. "When earthquakes, floods, hailstorms, drought, and famine will be the life of every day, the time will have then come for the return to the true path." In addition to offering the signs of such a time, the Hopi traditions go even further, recommending a course of action to bring the hearts and minds of man into alignment with the earth once again.

Deceptively simple, the prophecy reminds us that "when prayer and meditation are used rather than relying on new inventions to create more imbalance, then they [humanity] will also find the true path."[14] The words of the Hopi serve as simple reminders of the quantum principle which states that to change the outcome of events already in motion, we are invited to shift our beliefs regarding the outcome itself. In doing so, we attract the possibility that matches our new belief, and we release the present conditions, *even those already under way.*

Recent studies into the effects of prayer offer new credibility to ancient propositions suggesting that we may "do something" about the horrors of our world, both present and future. These studies add to a growing body of evidence suggesting that focused prayers, especially those offered on a large scale, have a predictable and measurable effect on the quality of life during the time of the prayer. Documenting statistical changes in daily life, such as specific crimes and traffic accidents, while prayers are offered, a series of studies shows a direct relationship between the prayers and the statistics. During the time of the prayers, the statistics drop. When the prayers end, the statistics return to previous levels.

Scientists suspect that the relationship between mass prayer and the activity of individuals in communities is due to a phenomenon known as the *field effect* of consciousness. Much like Joseph's description of the sage, where the experience of one plant affects the entire field, studies of specific population samples appear to bear out this relationship. Two scientists considered to have played a key role in the development of modern psychology clearly referenced such effects in studies offered nearly one hundred years ago.

In a paper originally published in 1898, for example, William James suggested that "there exists a continuum of consciousness uniting individual minds that could be directly experienced if the psychophysical threshold of perception were sufficiently lowered through refinement in the functioning nervous system."[15] James's paper was a modern reference to a zone of consciousness, a level of universal mind, that touches each and every life. By using specific qualities of thought, feeling, and emotion, we may tap into this universal mind and share in its benefits. The purpose of many prayers and meditative techniques is to achieve precisely such a condition.

In the words of their day, ancient teachings suggest a similar field of consciousness, accessed by similar methods. The Vedic traditions, for example, speak of a unified field of "pure consciousness" that permeates all of creation.[16] In such traditions, our experience of thought and perception are viewed as *disturbances,* interruptions in an otherwise motionless field. At the same time, it is through our path of mastering perception and thought that we may find the unifying consciousness as individuals or as a group.

This is where the application of such studies becomes crucial in global efforts to bring peace to our world. If we view conflict, aggression, and war in our outer world as indicators of stress in our collective consciousness, then relieving collective stress should relieve global tensions. In the words of Maharishi Mahesh Yogi, founder of the Transcendental Meditation (TM) programs, "All occurrences of violence, negativity, conflict crisis, or problems in any society are just the expression of growth of stress in collective consciousness. When the level of stress becomes sufficiently great, it bursts out into large-scale violence, war, and civil uprising necessitating military action." The beauty of the field effect is that *when stress is relieved within a group, the effects are registered beyond the immediate group,* into an even larger area. This is the thinking that led to studies of mass meditation and prayer during the Israeli-Lebanese War in the early 1980s.

In September 1983, studies were conducted in Jerusalem to explore the relationship between prayer, meditation, and violence. Applying new technologies to test an ancient theory, individuals trained in the techniques of TM, considered to be a mode of prayer by prayer researchers, were placed in strategic locations within Jerusalem during the conflict with Lebanon. The purpose of the study was to determine if a reduction of stress in the localized populations would, in fact, be reflected as less violence and aggression on a regional basis.

The 1983 studies followed earlier experiments indicating that as little as one percent of a mass population practicing unified forms of peaceful prayer and meditation was enough to reduce crime rates, accidents, and suicides. Studies conducted in 1972 showed that twenty-four U.S. cities, each with populations over ten thousand, experienced a statistically measurable reduction in crime when as few as one percent (one hundred people for every ten thousand) of the population participated in some form of meditative practice.[17] This became known as the "Maharishi Effect."

To determine how certain modes of meditation and prayer would influence the general population in the Israeli study, the quality of life was defined by a statistical index based on the number of fires, traffic accidents, occurrences of crime, fluctuations in the stock market, and the general mood of the nation. At the peak of the experiments, 234 participants meditated and prayed in the study, a fraction of the population of greater Jerusalem. The results of the study showed a direct relationship between the number of participants and the decrease of activity in the various categories of quality of life. When the numbers of participants were high, the index of the various categories declined. Crime, fires, and accidents increased as the number of people praying was reduced.[18]

These studies demonstrated a high correlation between the number of people in prayer and the quality of life in the immediate vicinity. Similar studies conducted in major population centers of the United States, India, and the Philippines found similar correlations. Data from these cities between 1984 and 1985 verified decreases in crime rates that "could not have been due to trends or cycles of crime, or to changes in police policies or procedures."[19]

# The Harvest Is Great,
# Though the Laborers Are Few

For centuries, prophets and sages have suggested that one-tenth of one percent of humanity, working together in a unified effort, may shift the consciousness of the entire world. If those numbers are accurate, then a surprisingly few individuals may plant the seeds of great possibilities. At present the population of our world is estimated to be approximately 6 billion people. One percent of our global neighborhood, then, is represented by 60 million, with one-tenth of that number approaching 6 million people. For scale 6 million people is roughly three-quarters of the population of Los Angeles.

Although these statistics may represent an *optimum* number to bring about change, the studies in Jerusalem and the other large population centers suggest that the numbers to initiate such change may be even smaller! The studies indicate that the first effects of the mass meditation/prayer became noticeable when the number of people participating in the prayers was greater than *the square root of one percent of the population.*[20] In a city of one million people, for example, this value represents only one hundred individuals!

Applying the localized findings of the test cities to a larger population on a global scale offers powerful and perhaps unexpected results. Representing only a fraction of even the ancient estimates, the square root of one percent of earth's population is *just under eight thousand people!* With the advent of the World Wide Web and computerized communication, organizing a time of coordinated meditation/prayer supported by a minimum of eight thousand people is certainly feasible. Clearly, this number *represents only the minimum* required for the effect to begin—a threshold of sorts. The greater the number participating, the greater the acceleration of the effect. Such numbers remind us of ancient admonitions suggesting that a very few people may make a difference to an entire world.

Perhaps this is the "mustard seed" of the parable that Jesus used to demonstrate the amount of faith required of his followers. Of such faith, we are reminded in the lost Gospel Q that "the harvest is abundant, but the workers are few."[21] With the evidence of such potential, what are the implications of directing such a collective power toward the great challenges of our time? Perhaps we have already witnessed the effect of such global choices in instances such as the peace prayer on the eve of the military action in Iraq in November 1998.

## To Think the Thoughts of Angels

Scholars, researchers, and scientists have identified the conditions that they believe will precipitate disasters of catastrophic proportions well into the twenty-first century. A combination of politics, social changes, and rogue weather patterns have already taken the lives of hundreds of thousands of individuals, primarily women and children, in the last days of the twentieth century. While well-intended efforts are under way to alleviate the present conditions, they have proven temporary at best.

Rather than viewing political treaties and military solutions as answers, perhaps now is the time to recognize them as bridges to a new way of thinking. It appears that we have reached a critical time in the evolution of governments and nations, when the pattern of demands followed by force simply does not work the way it did even fifty years ago. The wise use of force may serve us in isolated incidents of short duration. Each time we apply a military bandage, however, it is akin to placing our finger over a tear in the fabric of a balloon filled with water. What appears to be a "fix" in one place becomes a bulge somewhere else on the balloon. This is precisely the scenario that is unfolding with respect to global politics. *To change the conditions that allow war, oppression, and mass suffering, we must change the thinking that has allowed the conditions to be present.*

We live in a world of *collective consent.* The conditions of war and suffering on a large scale mirror the elements that make such conditions possible on a small scale. Sometimes consciously, and sometimes not, we consent to expressions of our group will in ways that we may never suspect. On levels that we may not even be aware of, our thoughts, attitudes, and actions toward one another each day contribute to the collective beliefs that agree to the wars and suffering of the world.

For example, the creation of a wartime mentality of expecting and preparing for conflict in our international world can happen *only if we allow for such conflict in our personal lives.* As we live individual episodes of "defending ourselves" in romance and personal relationships, "outsmarting" others in our schools, and "out-strategizing" co-workers and competitors, quantum physics reminds us that these individual expressions of our lives pave the way for similar expressions, amplified by many orders of magnitude, in another time and place. To know peace in our world, we must become peace in our lives. From the quantum perspective, it makes little sense to shove people impatiently out of the way to get to our parked vehicle, then dart in and out of traffic rudely cutting off other drivers as we race across town to a rally supporting global peace.

The subtlety of this concept became even clearer to me in the final moments of an interview that I was completing shortly after the crisis in Kosovo began in early 1999. On a syndicated radio station that was heard throughout the United States, the moderator had graciously set aside the first hour of a live program for us to develop concepts and offer broad brushstrokes of possibility before taking questions on a call-in line. I had just finished describing the quantum concepts of many outcomes and the power of prayer to choose our future, when the call came in. After introducing the caller, our host invited the gentleman on the other end of the line to ask his question. Following praise for our interview and compliments for the program, the caller began.

"Gregg, I understand what you have said about the power of prayer and how many people praying together have a greater effect than random prayers of individuals. Now," he continued, "my question is, why don't you organize a vigil, and let's use our power of prayer to cause a heart attack in the dictator responsible for all of this trouble in eastern Europe?" There was an awkward stillness on the air, as both the moderator and I reeled from the question.

"I suppose that would be my question to answer," I said, breaking the silence.

"It's all yours, Gregg," the moderator's voice replied.

"Taking the life of a world leader, even to stop the violence in his country, is to miss the point of our power of prayer. It is precisely this kind of thinking that has allowed the atrocities of war in the first place," I replied. "While we may deceive ourselves into believing that the taking of a life has solved the immediate problem, somewhere, in some part of the world, we will see the consequence of our actions, possibly in ways that we would never expect. Prayer transcends imposing our will upon others. Prayer represents our opportunity to become more than such cycles by employing our science of feeling to bring new possibilities to an existing situation."

"I think I understand what you are saying," the caller replied. "I hadn't thought of it quite in those terms. Maybe, instead of killing him, we can just hurt him. Maybe that will do the trick!"

The moderator interrupted with a commercial break, followed by an opportunity for me to summarize our interview and close out the program. For the rest of the evening and for days afterward, I thought about the caller and the pain that must have been in his life to lead him to such conclusions. While I believe that his question represented an extreme viewpoint, at the same time the caller demonstrated how deeply embedded warlike thinking has become in our culture. Why are we surprised at mass killing in our homes, offices, and schools when we agree to the same thinking on a larger scale in the name of peace?

Whether we view our world from the perspective of ancient traditions or quantum physics, we are invited to completely rethink the way that we have approached conflict in the past. Both paradigms, science and ancient philosophy, remind us that there can be no "us" and "them." There is only "we," and we have outgrown the conditions where it is effective to impose our will and ideas of change upon the lives of others. One look at the conflicts listed on page 229 reminds us that while such solutions may have appeared to work in the past, they have probably bought us time to recognize new choices rather than lasting solutions. As we choose to honor life in our everyday world, we witness the power of our choices to end war and render aggression obsolete.

Prayer has often been referred to as a passive act. On many occasions I have been asked what I am "really going to do," with regard to a particular world crisis. In these instances prayer was viewed as secondary to actually "doing something." From the perspective offered by ancient traditions and now supported by modern research, our ability to commune with the forces of the cosmos, to choose our path through time and determine our course of future history, may be the single most sophisticated and empowering force to grace our world.

Prayer is a concrete, measurable, and directive force in creation. Prayer is real. *To pray is to do "something!"* What else can we do? The solutions of the past are failing us in the present. Prayer is the act of redefining the foundation of hate, ethnic violence, and war. The doing simply occurs in a form very different from our idea of doing in the past. Could it be so easy? Is it possible that to mirror the peace of our hearts in the reality of our world, we are simply asked to choose such a reality by feeling the outcome as if it had already happened? Recent events, in the eyes of the world, appear to say that the answer is yes.

At the doorway to the twenty-first century, we stand on the threshold of a time when the survival of our species may actually depend upon our ability to marry our inner and outer sciences into precisely such technologies. As we redefine the roles of political affiliations, military alliances, and the boundaries of nations, the power of mass prayer cannot be discounted. The implications of applying our technology of prayer on a global scale are of immense, perhaps unfathomable proportions. Our lifetime represents a rare moment when, perhaps for the first time in our history, we can determine the outcome of this moment! Transcending science, religion, and mystic traditions, the Essenes suggest that it is during this time in history, through the use of our lost science of prayer and prophecy, that healing comes to all beings, those formed and unformed, and that peace prevails in all worlds. It is during our lifetime that the people of earth will know all of the secrets of the "angels in heaven."

Without judging the events of each day as good, bad, right, or wrong, we are invited to choose a new viewpoint, a higher option in response to the horror of such events. If the tenets of prayer and peace are valid, then the pain of those in Africa, the Balkans, the Middle East, and anywhere else where human life is suffering is our suffering as well. The ancient secrets of healing remind us that there is only one of us here in our world. As we alleviate the pain of others, we alleviate our pain as well. As we love others, we love ourselves. Each man, woman, and child of this world has the power to create a new possibility, to change the thinking that allows suffering.

Those who have come before us prepared us well for this time in our history. We have the opportunity to choose a new way in the presence of challenges that appear to be mounting on a daily basis. We are invited to think and do in our world as those of the heavens do in theirs. In so doing, we awaken a forgotten technology from the sleep of our collective memory and, at last, bring the conditions of heaven to earth.

In their own words, the scholars of Qumran recorded the teachings of their great masters preserved for moments such as this, when the encouragement of those who have come before us gives us the strength to live and love in this world, one more day. We are reminded that "to lift our eyes to heaven when the eyes of others are on the ground is not easy. To worship at the feet of the angels when others worship fame and riches is not easy. But perhaps the most difficult of all is to think the thoughts of the angels, to speak the words of the angels, and to do as angels do."[22]

# Completions

The story came to my attention only moments before I was to begin the first night of a conference that would last for the next three days. For the better part of the afternoon I had wondered how I would begin the program that evening. Though I had a good idea of what our time together would look like following the opening, precisely how the first moments of the night would unfold remained a mystery. In such moments of uncertainty, when it seems as if reasonable solutions exist only as glimmers of a distant possibility, I have found that there is usually a piece of the puzzle that is missing, something that has yet to come to my attention. My trust in that feeling, and knowing that there is more to come, often replaces anxious moments of panic with a strange calmness.

I walked into the dining area of our home and opened a large envelope that had been given to me earlier in the day. It contained several accounts of human triumph, one of which moved me so deeply that I found myself wiping the tears from my face before I had even finished reading the paper. Later that evening, I shared the story with a live audience of several hundred people. The story had the same effect on them. The paper that had come to me that day described an incident occurring at the Special Olympics of 1998.

The Special Olympics was organized as an opportunity for children and young adults to join together in the spirit of friendly competition. What makes these Olympic games different is that each individual competes with the challenge of physical or mental conditions that prevent him or her from participating in the International World Olympics that capture the world's attention every four years. This particular article was the story of nine children who had become friends during their time at the Olympic camp in 1998.

One morning they found themselves competing together on the same track, in the same event. At the sound of the starting gun, they were off toward the finish line at the other end of the course. It was a young boy with Down's syndrome that made this account so powerful. As the other competitors bounded down the track using whatever skills they had to work toward the finish, this special boy slowed down and looked back to the starting line. He saw that one of his teammates had fallen at the beginning of the race and was struggling to stand up.

The boy with Down's syndrome suddenly stopped, turned, and began walking back toward his friend. One by one, each of the other competitors realized what was happening, turned and followed, until they had retraced their steps to the point where they had begun. Lifting their friend to his feet, they locked arms, and together walked down the track to the finish. In that moment those nine children redefined the rules of the competition. With the clock still ticking away, they moved beyond the limits of time and sport to create an experience where they each finished in their own way, all at the same time. It made no sense for one of them to arrive at the finish without the others.

This story is important for two reasons. Each time it is shared, the image of the children working together elicits a powerful emotion. Rather than sadness or frustration, it is often described as an emotion of hope. That emotion opens the door to greater possibilities and new outcomes in our lives. Additionally, the account provides a beautiful example of how a group of young people, in the innocence of their love for one another, redefined the outcome of their experience by applying a new rule to an existing condition. In their own way, the children of the Special Olympics remind us of the great possibilities of our lives, as we move through a rare moment of history.

We have been shown that it is possible to redefine the parameters of prophecy for our future. The evidence reminds us that we intercede on our own behalf each time we respond to the challenges of our daily lives. Perhaps the best way to demonstrate such possibilities to ourselves is to explore the nature of compassion, time, forgiveness, and prayer through the eyes of those who have come before us. In the words of their time, we are reminded that there is only one of us here and, above all other reasons, we have come to this world to love.

# Notes

## INTRODUCTION

1. *The New American Bible, Saint Joseph Edition,* "The Book of Isaiah," chapter 24, verse 3 (New York: Catholic Book Publishing Co., 1970), 847.

2. Ibid., chapter 35, verses 6–7.

3. Ibid., chapter 29, verse 18.

4. David W. Orme-Johnson, Charles N. Alexander, John L. Davies, Howard M. Chandler, and Wallace E. Larimore, "International Peace Project in the Middle East," *The Journal of Conflict Resolution* 32, no. 4 (December 1988), 776–812.

5. Michael C. Dillbeck, Garland Landrith III, and David W. Orme-Johnson, "The Transcendental Meditation Program and Crime Rate Change in a Sample of Forty-Eight Cities," *Journal of Crime and Justice* 4 (1981), 25–45.

6. John F. Harris, "U.S. Launches, Then Aborts Airstrikes after Iraq Relents on U.N. Inspections," *Washington Post,* 15 November 1998.

CHAPTER 1. LIVING THE DAYS
OF PROPHECY

1. Matthew Bunson, *Prophecies: 2000: Predictions, Revelations and Visions for the New Millennium* (New York: Simon & Schuster, 1999), 31.

2. Ron Cowen, "Gamma-Ray Burst Makes Quite a Bang," *Science News* 135 (8 April 1998), 292. Originally reported by S. George Djorgovski of the California Institute of Technology in Pasadena in *Nature,* 7 May 1998.

3. Doug Isbell, Bill Steigerwald, and Mike Carlowicz, "Twin Comets Race to Death by Fire," NASA Goddard Space Flight Center (http://umbra.nascom.nasa.gov/comets/comet_release.html, and http://umbra.nascom.nasa.gov/comets/SOHO sungrazers. html), 3 June 1998.

4. Jonathan Eberhart, "Fantastic Fortnight of Active Region 5395," *Science News* 153 (9 May 1998), 212. Reported by Patrick S. McIntosh of the National Oceanographic and Atmospheric Administration's Space Environment Laboratory in Boulder, Colorado.

5. Joseph B. Gurman, "Solar Proton Events Affecting the Earth Environment," NOAA Space Sciences Environment Services Center (http://umbra.gsfc.nasa.gov/SEP/seps.html). From revision of 25 August 1998.

6. Richard Monastersky, "Recent Years Are Warmest Since 1400." *Science News* 153 (9 May 1998), 303. Originally reported by Michael E. Mann of the University of Massachusetts, Amherst, in *Nature,* 23 April 1998.

7. Richard Monastersky, "Satellites Misread Global Temperatures," *Science News* 154 (15 August 1998), 100. Originally reported by Douglas M. Smith of the United Kingdom Meteorological Office in Bracknell, in *Geophysical Research Letters,* 15 February 1998.

8. Richard Monastersky, "Antarctic Ice Shelf Loses Large Piece," *Science News* 153 (9 May 1998), 303. Originally reported by Ted Scambos of the National Snow and Ice Data Center in Boulder, Colorado.

9. Richard Monastersky, "Signs of Unstable Ice in Antarctica," *Science News* 154 (11 July 1998), 31. Originally reported by Reed P. Scherer of Uppsala University, Sweden, in *Science* 3 July 1998.

10. Matt Mygaff, "Sudden Occurrence of Radio Waves at Galactic Center Puzzles Scientists," reported in *Valley Times* (Livermore, California), from Associated Press report, 5 May 1991.

11. Tom Majeski, "Airport Renames 2 Runways as Magnetic North Pole Drifts," *St. Paul Pioneer Press,* 7 October 1997. Report of interview with Bob Huber, assistant manager of the Federal Aviation Administration's Airports District Office.

12. Richard Monastersky, "Earth's Magnetic Field Follies Revealed," *Science News* 147 (22 April 1995), 244. Originally reported by Robert S. Coe of the University of California, Santa Cruz, and Michel Prevot and Pierre Camps of the University of Montpelier in France.

13. Edmond Bordeaux Szekely, ed. and trans., *The Essene Gospel of Peace* (Matsqui, B.C., Canada: I.B.S. Internacional, 1937), 19.

14. Michael Drosnin, *The Bible Code* (New York: Simon & Schuster, 1997), 173.

15. David W. Orme-Johnson, et al., "International Peace Project in the Middle East," *The Journal of Conflict Resolution* 32, no. 4 (December 1988), 778.

16. Jeffrey Satinover, M.D., *Cracking the Bible Code* (New York: William Morrow, 1997), 244.

## CHAPTER 2. LOST WORDS OF
## A FORGOTTEN PEOPLE

1. *The Lost Books of the Bible and the Forgotten Books of Eden* (New York: New American Library, 1963).

2. Ibid., preface to Book One.

3. Ibid.

4. Ibid., introduction to Book Two.

5. Ibid., "The Gospel of the Birth of Mary," chapter 2, verse 10, 19.

6. Ibid., "The First Book of Adam and Eve," Chapter 1, Verse 1–2, page 4.

7. Edmond Bordeaux Szekely, ed. and trans., *The Essene Gospel of Peace,* Book Three (Matsqui, B.C., Canada, I.B.S. Internacional, 1937), 39.

8. Ibid., 11.

9. Szekely, *The Essene Gospel of Peace,* 39.

10. *The Dead Sea Scrolls,* translated and with commentary by Michael Wise, Martin Abegg Jr., and Edward Cook (New York: HarperSanFrancisco, 1999), 8.

11. Szekely, *The Essene Gospel of Peace,* Book Four, 34.

12. Ibid., Book One, 10.

13. James M. Robinson, ed., *The Nag Hammadi Library,* translated and introduced by members of the Coptic Gnostic Library Project of the Institute for Antiquity and Christianity, Clearmont, California (New York: HarperSanFrancisco, 1990), 279.

14. Ibid.

15. Ibid., 285.

16. Robinson, *The Nag Hammadi Library,* "The Thunder: Perfect Mind," 295.

17. Ibid., 297.

18. Ibid.

19. Burton L. Mack, *The Lost Gospel. The Book of Q and Christian Origins* (New York: HarperSanFrancisco, 1994), 295.

20. Robinson, *The Nag Hammadi Library,* "The Gospel of Thomas," 128.

## CHAPTER 3. THE PROPHECIES

1. Michael D. Coe, *Breaking the Maya Code* (New York: Thames and Hudson, 1993), 61.

2. Jose Arguelles, *The Mayan Factor* (Santa Fe: Bear & Company, 1987), 145.

3. Ibid., 126.

4. Richard Laurence, tr., *The Book of Enoch the Prophet,* chapter VII, verses 11–12, translated from an Ethiopic manuscript in the Bodleian Library (San Diego: Wizards Bookshelf Secret Doctrine Reference Series, 1983), 7.

5. Jim Schnabel, *Remote Viewers: The Secret History of America's Psychic Spies* (New York: Bantam Doubleday Dell, 1997), 12–13.

6. Ibid., 380.

7. John Hogue, *Nostradamus, The Complete Prophecies* (Boston: Element Books, 1999), 798.

8. Mark Thurston, Ph.D., *Millennium Prophecies, Predictions for the Coming Century from Edgar Cayce* (New York: Kensington Books, 1997), 5.

9. Ibid., 6.

10. Ibid.

11. Ibid., 35.

12. Ibid., 34.

13. Tom Majeski, "Airport Renames 2 Runways as Magnetic North Pole Drifts," *St. Paul Pioneer Press,* 7 October 1997. (Report of interview with Bob Huber, assistant manager of the Federal Aviation Administration's Airports District Office.)

14. Thurston, *Millennium Prophecies,* 34.

15. Ibid., 35.

16. Ibid., 110.

17. Laurence, *The Book of Enoch the Prophet,* 4.

18. Ibid., 1.

19. Ibid., 57.

20. *The New American Bible, Saint Joseph Edition,* Preface to the Book of Daniel (New York: Catholic Book Publishing Co., 1970), 1021.

21. John F. Walvoord, *Every Prophecy of the Bible* (Colorado Springs, Col.: Chariot Victor Publishing, 1999), 212.

22. Neil Douglas-Klotz, *Prayers of the Cosmos: Meditations on the Aramaic Words of Jesus* (New York: HarperSanFrancisco 1994), 12–13.

23. Edmond Bordeaux Szekely, *The Essene Gospel of Peace,* Book Two (Matsqui, B.C., Canada: I.B.S. Internacional, 1937), 114.

24. Ibid.

25. Ibid., 125.

26. Ibid., page 126.

27. Ibid.

28. Ibid., 127.

29. Ibid., 55.

30. Michael Drosnin, *The Bible Code* (New York: Simon & Schuster, 1997), 19.

31. Ibid., 174.

32. Jack Cohen and Ian Stewart, *The Collapse of Chaos* (New York: Penguin Books, 1994), 44–45.

33. Drosnin, *The Bible Code,* 155.


CHAPTER 4. WAVES, RIVERS, AND ROADS

1. Jeffrey Satinover, M.D., *Cracking the Bible Code* (New York: William Morrow, 1997), 233.

2. Ibid., 232.

3. Ibid., 244.

4. Eugene Mallove, "The Cosmos and the Computer: Simulating the Universe," *Computers in Science* 1, no. 2 (September/October 1987).

5. Fred Alan Wolf, *Parallel Universes: The Search for Other Worlds* (New York: Simon & Schuster, 1990), 33, 38.

6. Edmond Bordeaux Szekely, ed. and trans., *The Essene Gospel of Peace,* Book Two (Matsqui, B.C., Canada: IBS International, 1937), 37–39.

7. Jack Cohen and Ian Stewart, *The Collapse of Chaos* (New York: Penguin Books, 1994), 191.

8. Robert Boissiere, *Meditations With the Hopi* (Santa Fe: Bear & Company, 1986), 110.

9. Ibid., 113.

10. Thomas E. Mails and Dan Evehema, *Hotevilla: Hopi Shrine of the Covenant* (New York: Marlowe & Company, 1995), 564.

11. Boissiere, *Meditations With the Hopi,* 117.

12. John Davidson, *The Secret of the Creative Vacuum* (The C.W. Daniel Company Limited, 1989).

13. Michael Drosnin, *The Bible Code* (New York: Simon & Schuster, 1997), 173.

## CHAPTER 5. THE ISAIAH EFFECT

1. *The New American Bible, Saint Joseph Edition,* "The Book of Isaiah," chapter 24, verse 5 (New York: Catholic Book Publishing Co., 1970), 847.

2. Ibid., chapter 24, verse 23, 847.

3. Ibid., chapter 65, verses 17–20, 890.

4. John F. Walvoord, *Every Prophecy of the Bible* (Colorado Springs: Chariot Victor Publishing, 1999), 279.

5. Information regarding ongoing prayers of peace, such as the vigil coordinated on November 13, 1998, is available on the Internet at http://www.worldpuja.org.

6. *New American Bible,* "The Book of Isaiah," chapter 29, verse 11, 853.

7. Ibid., chapter 25, verses 6–7, 848.

8. Ibid., chapter 25, verse 4, 848.

9. Ibid., chapter 25, verse 6, 848n.

10. Ibid., "Bible Dictionary," 335.

## CHAPTER 7. THE LANGUAGE OF GOD

1. Edmond Bordeaux Szekely, ed. and trans., *The Essene Gospel of Peace,* Book Two (Matsqui, B.C., Canada: I.B.S. International, 1937), 32.

2. Szekely, *The Essene Gospel of Peace,* Book Four, 30.

3. Ibid., 30–31.

4. Neville, *The Power of Awareness* (Marina del Rey, Calif.: DeVorss Publications, 1961), 10.

5. Neville, *The Law and the Promise* (Marina del Rey, Calif.: DeVorss Publications, 1961), 14.

6. Holy Bible, Authorized King James Version, New Testament, "John" chapter 16, verses 23–24 (Grand Rapids, Mich.: World Publishing, 1989), 80.

7. Neil Douglas-Klotz, *Prayers of the Cosmos: Meditations on the Aramaic Words of Jesus* (New York: HarperSanFrancisco, 1994), 86–87.

## CHAPTER 8. THE SCIENCE OF MAN

1. Fred Alan Wolf, *Parallel Universes: The Search for Other Worlds* (New York: Simon & Schuster, 1990), 48.

2. Glen Rein, Ph.D., Mike Atkinson, and Rollin McCraty, M.A., "The Physiological and Psychological Effects of Compassion and Anger," *Journal of Advancement in Medicine* 8, no. 2 (Summer 1995), 87–103.

3. Ibid.

4. Edmond Bordeaux Szekely, ed. and trans., *The Essene Gospel of Peace,* Book Two (Matsqui, B.C., Canada: I.B.S. Internacional, 1937), 64–65.

5. Ibid., 61.

6. Holy Bible, Authorized King James Version, New Testament, "Mark," chapter 11, verse 23 (Grand Rapids, Mich.: World Publishing, 1989), 34.

7. Hans Jenny, *Cymatics: Bringing Matter to Life with Sound,* videotape (Brookline, Mass.: MACROmedia, 1986).

8. Neville, *The Law and the Promise* (Marina del Rey, Calif.: DeVorss Publications, 1961), 13.

9. Szekely, *The Essene Gospel of Peace,* Book Four, 30.

10. Ibid., 30–33.

11. Ibid., 15.

12. Szekely, *The Essene Gospel of Peace,* Book Three, 71.

13. Szekely, *The Essene Gospel of Peace,* Book Two, 66–68.

14. Glen Rein, Ph.D., and Rollin McCraty, M.A., "Modulation of DNA by Coherent Heart Frequencies," proceedings of the Third Annual Conference of the International Society for the Study of Subtle Energies and Energy Medicine, Monterey, Calif., June 1993.

15. Vladimir Poponin, "The DNA Phantom Effect: Direct Measurement of a New Field in the Vacuum Substructure," unpublished report, Institute of HeartMath, Research Division, Boulder Creek, Calif.

16. Szekely, *The Essene Gospel of Peace,* Book Two, 31.

17. Poponin, "The DNA Phantom Effect."

## CHAPTER 9. HEALING HEARTS, HEALING NATIONS

1. Edmond Bordeaux Szekely, ed. and trans. *The Essene Gospel of Peace,* Book Two (Matsqui, B.C., Canada: I.B.S. Internacional, 1937), 32.

2. Glen Rein, Ph.D., and Rollin McCraty, M.A., "Modulation of DNA by Coherent Heart Frequencies," proceedings of the Third Annual Conference of The International Society for the Study of Subtle Energies and Energy Medicine, Monterey, Calif., June 1993, 2.

3. *The Gospel of the Nazirenes,* edited and restored with historical documentation by Alan Wauters and Rick VanWyhe, "Prologue: The Historical Context" (Arizona: Essene Vision Books, 1997), xxviii–xxix.

4. Szekely, *The Essene Gospel of Peace,* Book Two, 71.

5. Szekely, *The Essene Gospel of Peace,* Book Two, 47.

6. "When to Jump In: The World's Other Wars," *Time,* 19 April 1999, 30.

7. Matthew Bunson, *Prophecies: 2000: Predictions, Revelations and Visions for the New Millennium* (New York: Simon & Schuster, 1999), 31.

8. Ibid., 30.

9. Ibid.

10. Bunson, *Prophecies: 2000,* 31.

11. Ibid., 35.

12. Ibid., 38.

13. Richard Laurence, tr., *The Book of Enoch the Prophet,* chapter LI, verse 5 (San Diego: Wizards Bookshelf Secret Doctrine Reference Series, 1983), 58.

14. Robert Boissiere, *Meditations With the Hopi* (Santa Fe: Bear and Company, 1986), 113.

15. David W. Orme-Johnson, Charles N. Alexander, John L. Davies, Howard M. Chandler, Wallace E. Larimore, "International Peace Project in the Middle East," *The Journal of Conflict Resolution* 32, no. 4 (December 1988), 778.

16. Michael C. Dillbeck, Kenneth L. Cavanaugh, Thomas Glenn, David W. Orme-Johnson, Vicki Mittlefehldt, "Consci-

ousness as a Field: The Transcendental Meditation and TM-Sidhi Program and Changes in Social Indicators," *The Journal of Mind and Behavior* 8, no. 1 (Winter 1987), 67–104.

17. Orme-Johnson, et al., "International Peace Project in the Middle East," 781.

18. Ibid., 782.

19. "Maharishi Effect: Increased Orderliness, Decreased Urban Crime," *Scientific Research on the Maharishi Transcendental Meditation and TM-Sidhi Programs: A Brief Study of 500 Studies,* Maharishi University of Management Press (Fairfield, Conn.: 1996), 21.

20. Orme-Johnson, et al., 782.

21. Burton L. Mack, *The Lost Gospel: The Book of Q and Christian Origins* (New York: HarperSanFrancisco, 1994), 87.

22. Szekely, *The Essene Gospel of Peace,* Book Two, 31.

# Acknowledgments

Our time in this world is a journey of service both to ourselves and to one another. Sometimes we are fortunate enough to be given the opportunity to acknowledge the efforts of others. This book represents the cooperative skills, focused efforts, and shared vision of many talented individuals. While it is impossible to mention by name each person whose work is reflected in *The Isaiah Effect,* I take this opportunity to express my deepest gratitude and heartfelt thanks to the following:

My dear friend John Sammo, though the opportunity to share our thoughts slipped past us both, my sense is that we were on the same path in the same moment. I miss you in this world and felt your presence often in the final stages of this book. Thank you for our time together.

The many people at Harmony Books from the editorial, art and design, foreign rights, marketing, and publicity departments—especially Brian Belfiglio, Tina Constable, Alison Gross, Debbie

Koenig, Kim Robles, Karin Schulze, Kristen Wolfe, and Kieran O'Brien. Your skills, expertise, and willingness to co-create have produced a work that we can be proud of. A very special thanks to my editor, Patricia Gift, for listening, understanding, after-hours phone calls, late-night counseling, and patience. Most importantly, thank you for the blessing of your friendship in our lives.

Stephanie Gunning, your expertise honed the flow of my words while honoring the integrity of my message during our first-pass edits. Many thanks for your patience, clarity, and for being open to the possibilities.

To my agent, Ned Leavitt, you are everything that I ever imagined a great agent would be. Thank you for your guidance on our sacred journey through the world of corporate publishing. Many blessings to you and your ability to lead others to the fulfillment of their dreams.

To my publicist, Arielle Ford, and her staff at Dharma Dreams, it is your expertise and dedication that is helping *The Isaiah Effect* reach new audiences, opening the door to possibilities of personal healing and planetary peace that were only imagined in the past.

Lauri Willmot, the angel who holds our office together, providing me the freedom to focus and be present for those who participate in our programs. My sincerest thanks for your long hours, short weekends, and being there when it counts. Robin and Jerry Miner, our seminar coordinators and support staff, my gratitude and heartfelt thanks for trusting in the process even when the path has been difficult. Together we have found new ways to marry the reality of business to a message of personal healing and global peace. To each of your families, my deepest gratitude for sharing you with us.

To all the venues and production companies that have invited us into their communities, often without seeing our program in advance. I recognize such demonstrations of trust and consider it an honor to be part of your family. Among those are Patty Porter of

# Acknowledgments

The Cornerstone Foundation; Debra Evans, Greg Roberts, Keilisi Freeman, Justin Hilton, Georgia Malki, and all the great staff of the Whole Life Expo; Robert Maddox and the staff of the Kripalu Yoga Center; Charlotte McGinnis and the Palm Beach Center for Living; all of the wonderful Unity Churches that have hosted us; Suzanne Sullivan of Insight Seminars for her vision; Robin and Cody Johnson of Axiom for your excellence; Linda Rachel, Carolyn Craft, and the dedicated staff of The Wisdom Network; Laura Lee of *The Laura Lee Show;* Paul Roberts of The Radio Bookstore; Art Bell and Hilly Rose of Art Bell Radio Programs; Tippy McKinsey and Patricia DiOrio of the *Paradigm Shift* television program; and Howard and Gayle Mandell for your friendship and the support of Transitions Bookstore.

A very special thanks to the production, art, and sales staff at Sounds True. Tami Simon, your ability to lead, and draw from others their greatest strengths, has created a rare standard of excellence in corporate integrity that I am proud to be associated with. Michael Taft, I especially value your creative genius and willingness to rewire Sounds True's studio to accommodate our unique requirements. Liz Williams, your guidance, honesty, and friendship have been a tremendous blessing in our lives.

To all of the brilliant minds and warm, wonderful hearts of our extended family at Conscious Wave, including Greg Glazier, Ellen Feeney, Rebecca Stetson, and Russell Wright, you have made our journey through filming and production a joy as well as a success. Lynn Powers and Jirka Rysavy, my deepest gratitude for your patience, flexibility, vision, and belief in the message of my work. Jay Weidner, our friendship began nearly a decade ago, under very different conditions. Thank you for remembering my work and recognizing the power of compassion. A very special thanks to Rick Hassen for your attention to detail and the sensitivity with which you have honored our work. Our days of filming with a full crew in the mountains of northern New Mexico conjure up memories of dedication, patience, and the joy that comes from working toward a goal that we each believe in. You forever hold a very special place in our hearts.

My gratitude to the many scientists, researchers, and authors whose work has become the bridge between science, spirit, and consciousness. Among such researchers, many thanks and deepest respect to Robert Tennyson Stevens for your commitment to "upgrade" the way that we communicate through the science of conscious languaging. Many of you have conducted studies regarding concepts that were shunned only a few years earlier. Each of your findings reminds us of our relationship to the cosmos, one another, and the world around us. I am greatly indebted to your relentless pursuit to understand, and I accept full responsibility for the manner in which I have applied your findings and extrapolated your results. Please accept my apologies if I have, in any way, misinterpreted, misrepresented, or prematurely presented unpublished work. My intent has been only to empower those that we love.

To each person who has journeyed with us through seminars, workshops, travels, recording, filming, and production, my deepest gratitude and thanks. You are redefining work, family, and partnerships and we consider you among the great blessings in our lives.

Vivian Glyck, in some ways it seems as though our partnership began a long time ago, although our time together is just beginning to bear fruit. Many thanks of my deepest gratitude for your guidance, patience, expertise, and the clarity that you have brought into our lives.

To Toby and Theresa Weiss, founders of Power Places Tours, your willingness to create new adventures and your commitment to take such good care of us we consider among the great blessings in our lives. You have made it possible for us to open up some of the

Acknowledgments

world's most sacred sites to the eyes and hearts of many of those who trust us to guide them there. I consider your support staff the finest in the industry, with a very special thanks to Mohamed Nazmy, Emil Shaker, Medhat Yehia, Maria Antoinette Nunez, Walter Saenz, Harry and Ruth Hover, and Laurie Krantz, each of whom we consider our brothers, sisters, and among the dearest of friends.

To Gary Wintz, we are forever grateful to your wisdom and expertise in guiding us through the most challenging and rewarding journey of our lives—our pilgrimage into Asia. Thank you for your love of the land as well as the people, and for your willingness to share Tibet's magnificence through your eyes. You represent a rare standard of dedication that remains a constant inspiration and powerful force in my life.

To James Twyman, Liz Story, and Doreen Virtue, it has been an honor to share many stages with you, bringing to life our prayers of peace. Liz, a special thanks for keeping the memory of Michael alive in our hearts and for reminding me of the "Unaccountable Effect." Doreen, thank you for your ability to instill confidence in others by reminding them of their divinity, the sign of a true teacher. Jimmy, my dear friend and partner in peace, my gratitude and respect for your unwavering trust in God and deep reverence for all life, a quality of our friendship that I treasure. To each of you, your courage, conviction, and vision of great possibilities has forged a friendship that feels wonderfully ancient.

Tom Park and Park Productions, it is with tremendous gratitude that I say thank you for believing in my work and trusting the process. Together we have pushed the envelope, offering a new standard of presentations in a world where few models exist. A very special thanks for sharing your extended spiritual family, those who studied with you in the ashrams of India. Their honoring of life has made each of our days away from home feel like homes unto themselves.

# Acknowledgments

To my mother, Sylvia Braden, thank you for believing in me, even when you did not understand me. Through a lifetime of dramatic and sometimes painful change, your friendship has remained a constant, your love an unfailing source of strength.

My beautiful Melissa, thank you for sharing your life with me. From the endless hours of travel, nonstop telephone calls, and late-night hotel arrivals, you are always there. Together we have journeyed into some of the most magnificent, remote, and mystical places remaining in this world. My deepest thanks for your tireless support, unfailing friendship, and the strength that you bring to each of our days.

# Index

# Index

Bible Code, 75–80, 106
Biological unified theory, 220
Birth:
    as metaphor, 15
    miracle of, 10–13, 14–15
    of new world, 15
Blue star, 66–67
Body:
    connected to earth, 22, 44–45, 66, 217–18
    heart, and mind, union of, 187, 195, 207–8
    as a temple, 218–20
Bohr, Niels, 177–78
Bose-Einstein condensate, 98
Brain, unused portion of, 99
Breath, parameter of, 203
Buddha, and passive change, 27
Butterfly effect, 103–6
Bystanders, participation and, 177–78, 186

# C

Carmelites of Mount Carmel, 220
Catastrophes:
    avoiding, 81, 94, 106, 234
    as mirrors of human change, 22
    preparation for, 94
    prophecies of, 2, 3, 23, 56–57, 58–59, 61, 63, 79, 80–81, 85, 113, 114, 233, 238
    radio interview on, 20
    wars, 230–33
    Web reports of, 15–16, 17–19
Cayce, Edgar, 57, 62–65, 68, 80, 114
Centuries, The (Nostradamus), 60
Chance, miracles translated as, 5
Change:
    becoming and, 148
    created by prayer, 25–26
    of focus, 27, 115, 151, 155, 233–34
    language of, 16–19

mirrors of, 22
optimum number for, 237
outcomes and, 105, 106
passive, 27
Chaos theory, 14
Chemistry, 178–79, 207
Ch'i (life force), 89
Chinese clinic, miracles in, 89–92
Choice points, 100–101, 106
Climate, changes in, 17–18
Codes:
    decryption of, 77, 117, 120
    encryption of, 75–80
Coexistence, 26
Collective consent, 239
Colloquial prayer, 158
Comet Shoemaker-Levy, 66–67
Communion, 132, 135
Competition, 239
Consciousness:
    field effect of, 234–35
    mystery of, 216
    prayer as, 170, 216–17
    zone of, 234
Constantine, Holy Roman emperor, 35
Copenhagen View (Bohr), 177–78
Cracking the Bible Code (Satinover), 26
Creation:
    accessing, 221
    faith as force in, 173
    gaps in events leading back to, 98–99
    language of, 187, 192
    possibilities of, 157, 167, 188
    soup of, 155–58, 188
    unified view of, 21, 218
    use of term, 96
Creator:
    our relationship with, 199
    our souls as expression of, 201
Crime, reduction in, 25, 236
Crop circles, 66

# Index

## D

Daniel, Book of, 69–70, 115
David (rain prayer), 160–65, 166, 171–72
Davis, Gladys, 62
Dead Sea Scrolls, 41–43
  angels of, 243
  Bible and, 43, 199
  on the body as a temple, 218–20
  crossover passages of, 199
  Essenes and, 21–23, 41, 43–45, 123–24, 126, 135, 199, 217
  Isaiah Scroll in, 113
  on peace, 148
  redefining outcomes of, 106
  translation of, 2
Desire, emotion and, 149
Destruction, *see* Catastrophes
Determinism, 95–96
Dimensionality, 99
Disease:
  emotion and, 179
  healing and, *see* Healing
  sources of, 201
Disturbances, 235
DNA:
  feeling and, 207–8, 219
  phantom effect of, 209–10
Drosnin, Michael, 76, 77, 78

## E

Earth, our bodies connected to, 22, 44–45, 66, 217–18
Ebionites, 40, 220, 221
Egypt:
  Gnostic libraries of, 2
  group choice in, 86–89, 92, 98
Einstein, Albert, 95
El Niño, 18, 222–27
Emotion:
  alignment of, 188–92, 194–95
  changing, 151

chemistry of, 178–79, 207
  defined, 147
  disease and, 179
  parameter of, 203
  as prayer, 186
  quality of, 149
  as source of power, 149, 153–54, 156, 187
  as vibration, 188
  *see also* Feeling
Encryption, 75–80
"Energy follows attention," 151, 153, 157
Enoch, Book of, 47, 55, 67–69
Essenes, 40–41
  angels of, 49, 132, 242
  and Bible Code, 79
  Carmelites of Mount Carmel, 220
  and Dead Sea Scrolls, 21–23, 41, 43–45, 123–24, 126, 135, 199, 217
  on the dwellings of the Son of Man, 148
  Gospel of Peace of, 101, 135, 194–96, 198, 200
  on healing, 151, 200–208, 242
  heaven on earth, 221
  on interconnectedness, 177, 178, 179, 199, 218
  Jesus and, 49
  and Nazirenes, 124
  on prayer, 40, 132, 147, 178, 185–87, 194–95, 200–208
  in Tibet, 126–27, 130, 132
Everett, Hugh III, 100
Ezekiel, Book of, 69–70

## F

Faith, defined, 172–73
Fear, 149, 150–51, 154, 157
Feeling:
  alignment of, 188–92, 194–95
  chemistry of, 178, 207

# Index

## P

Parallel universes, 100, 105–6
Parameters, choice of, 203
Paul, Apocalypse of, 46
Peace:
  abbot's focus on, 135
  ancient code of, 195
  angels of, 195–96, 242
  becoming, 148, 239
  equation of, 191–92
  Essene Gospel of, 101, 135,
    194–96, 198, 200
  forgotten key of, 192–97, 198
  global, 235
  of knowledge and wisdom, 198
  love and, 199–200
  meanings of, 148
  overlay of, 27
  philosophy of, 191
  power of, 196
  prayer of, 168–69
Perception, threshold of, 234
Peru:
  author's journey to, 16, 223
  Macchu Picchu in, 222–24
  miracle in, 222–27
Petitionary prayer, 159, 172, 188,
    203
Phantom effect, 209–12
Physics:
  classical, 94–95
  quantum, *see* Quantum physics
Planck, Max, 109–10, 210
Politics, global, 239, 242
Poponin, Vladimir, 208, 209–10
Population, 237
Possibility:
  affected by present choices, 4, 23,
    24–28, 81, 109–10, 120,
    185–86, 190, 206
  already in place, 77, 79–80, 97–98,
    160, 188
  of ending all suffering, 211–12

honor to, 167
overlays of, 26
prayer and, 172, 185, 195, 211
predictions and, 2, 25, 27–28, 73,
    77–78, 81, 119
quantum, 24–27, 97, 115
soup of creation as, 157–58, 188
technology of, 202–3
Prayer:
  active, 187, 192, 241–42
  beauty of, 192
  as bridge of science and spirit, 190
  chant of, 136–37
  ch'i and, 89
  of childhood, 182–85
  colloquial, 158
  effects already in place before, 160,
    188, 190, 203
  elements aligned in, 189–92,
    194–95
  empowerment from, 25, 184–85
  Essene view of, 40, 132, 147, 178,
    185–87, 194–95, 200–208
  feeling and, 132, 134–35, 138,
    146–48, 153, 170–71, 184, 186,
    187, 188–92, 203
  focused, 5–6, 25–26, 132, 185,
    192, 199, 216–17, 234
  and healing, 200–208
  intent of, 145
  language of, 28, 132, 145–73, 186,
    187, 190–92, 196, 203, 208, 225
  lost mode of, 6, 50, 160, 167–72,
    190, 203
  mass, *see* Mass prayer
  meditative, 159
  methods of, 158–59
  of peace, 168–69
  petitionary, 159, 172, 188, 203
  philosophy of, 190, 211
  and possibility, 172, 185, 195, 211
  power of, 145–48, 187–88, 198,
    199, 208, 210–11, 225–26, 234,
    240–41

Index

Prayer (*cont.*):
  purpose of, 180–82
  rain, 163–65, 166, 171–72, 224
  ritualistic, 159
  secret of, 145, 166
  as support system, 225
  technology of, 1, 25, 50, 125, 131,
    155, 158, 196, 207–8, 224, 242
  of thanks, 166–67, 173, 182
  in Tibetan monastery, 130–34
  unanswered, 152–55, 183–4
Princip, Gavrilo, 105
Prophecy, 53–81
  contradictions in, 85, 114
  flexible, 123
  of healing, 2, 3, 113, 242
  lost, 71–74, 78
  outcomes and, 104–6
  patterns of, 2–3, 68
  of possibilities, 2, 25, 78, 81
  quantum, 24–27
  science of, 1, 50, 65, 120, 242
  twentieth-century, 57–59
  use of word, 59
  value of, 65
  of war, 230–33
  of Warsaw, 232
Prophet, use of word, 57

Q

"Q" texts, 49, 151, 238
Quanta, defined, 96, 99
Quantum, defined, 96
Quantum physics, 96–99
  Bose-Einstein condensate in, 98
  butterfly effect in, 103–6
  changing focus and, 27, 115,
    233–34
  vs. classical physics, 94–95
  free will in, 96, 239
  group choice in, 6
  Isaiah Scroll and, 117–19
  language of, 26, 117, 120
  parallel universes in, 100

prophecy and, 24–27
  time in, 4, 95, 97, 101–4
  uncertainty principle in, 77–78
Qumran communities:
  ancient traditions of, 21
  and Dead Sea Scrolls, 41–43, 44,
    123–24, 243
  on the potential of prayer, 198

R

Rabin, Yitzhak, 75
Radio:
  interviews via, 19–21, 239–40
  late-night talk shows of, 58
Rain prayers, 163–65, 166, 171–72,
  224
Reality, creation of, 26, 242
Rein, Glen, 178–79
Resonance, 205–7
Revelation, Book of, 68, 72–74
Rips, Eliyahu, 75, 77
Ritualistic prayer, 159

S

Sadat, Anwar, 88
Salivary immunoglobulin A (S-IgA),
  179
Same moment, peace and crime
  coexisting in, 26
Same space, two outcomes in, 98
Satinover, Jeffrey, 26, 98
Scale, differences of, 26
Science, 177–212
  bridge of spirit and, 190
  chemistry, 178–79, 207
  conflicts in, 94–96
  inner and outer, 242
  language and, 178
  lost, 1–3, 211
  mathematical proofs in, 191–92
  of prophecy, 1, 50, 65, 120, 242
  quantum, *see* Quantum physics
  technology and, 95, 242

274

# Index

# About the Author

Author, lecturer, and guide to sacred sites around the world, GREGG BRADEN has been featured on television and radio programs nationwide. He lives in the mountains of New Mexico and in Florida.

# In His Own Words:
## Audios and Video by Gregg Braden, from Sounds True

Join the author of *The Isaiah Effect*
in further explorations on the relevance
of ancient wisdom in modern life.

## Audio:

- *The Lost Mode of Prayer*   Is there a forgotten science that offers each one of us the inner tools we need to heal ourselves, our relationships with others, and even our enduring planet? Through newly translated texts of the Essene Desert Fathers, Braden reveals the inner workings of this powerful spiritual tool—"the Fifth Mode of Prayer"—and shows how we can use it to create profound changes in this crucial point in the history of humanity. 3 hours / 2 audiocassettes / $18.95 / Order #AW00408

- *Beyond Zero Point*   Braden shares new scientific research essential to understanding the prophecies of the Essenes, Hopis, Mayans, Egyptians, and others. Hidden within these ancient teachings, asserts Braden, is a universal set of "sacred technologies" meant specifically for use now, at this critical juncture in our existence. Listeners will learn how to actively participate in the great challenges that lie ahead. Are these the lost keys that will open the door to the next phase of human evolution? Listen to the facts and decide for yourself. 3 hours / 2 audiocassettes / $18.95 / Order #W407

## Video:

• *Walking Between the Worlds: Understanding the Inner Technology of Emotion*   A visual odyssey into ancient prophecy. The recovery of lost texts and their message allows us to make sense of modern chaos and move forward. Viewers see and hear fascinating evidence for a revolutionary shift in human consciousness that will accelerate the evolution of human biology, emotions, and consciousness—and show how we can participate in it ourselves. 4 hours/2 video-cassettes / $39.95 / Order #Y002

*These titles are available from Sounds True.*
*Call 800-333-9185 to order.*
*Or visit the Sounds True Web site: www.soundstrue.com*